GE and EMD LOCOMOTIVES

The Illustrated History by Brian Solomon

Voyageur
Press

First published in 2014 by Voyageur Press, an imprint of Quarto Publishing Group USA Inc., 400 First Avenue North, Suite 400, Minneapolis, MN 55401 USA

Voyageur Press titles are also available at discounts in bulk quantity for industrial or sales-promotional use. For details write to Special Sales Manager at Quarto Publishing Group USA Inc., 400 First Avenue North, Suite 400, Minneapolis, MN 55401 USA.

To find out more about our books, visit us online at www.voyageurpress.com.

ISBN-13: 978-0-7603-4612-9

Library of Congress Cataloging-in-Publication Data available upon request.

Editors: Dennis Pernu, Leah Noel
Design Manager: Cindy Samargia Laun
Cover Designer: Simon Larkin
Design and Layout: Chris Fayers, LeAnn Kuhlmann

Printed in China

10 9 8 7 6 5 4 3 2

Front cover: In July 2012, specially painted Norfolk Southern locomotives were gathered for photographers at the North Carolina Transportation Museum at Spencer Shops in Salisbury, North Carolina. *Patrick Yough*

Frontis: NS-painted SD70ACe No. 2012 sits on the Spencer turntable at the North Carolina Transportation Museum in July 2012. *Patrick Yough*

Title pages, 2–3: On February 19, 1995, in a scene symbolic of the competitive North American locomotive market, GECX lease-fleet B39-8 No. 8000, dressed in GE colors, leads a Burlington Northern intermodal train eastward through Rochelle, Illinois, while an EMD BL20 demonstrator stands by on a siding. *Brian Solomon*

Title pages, 6–7: Toward the end of DASH8 production, Union Pacific received DASH8-41CW models rated at 4,135 horsepower. In this sunrise view, UP DASH8-41CW No. 9486 leads a westward freight on the former Chicago & North Western main line near Colo, Iowa, on October 22, 1995. UP had only recently acquired C&NW, but it had a long history of running through locomotives on the line. *Brian Solomon*

Title pages, 176–177: A quartet of Lehigh Valley GPs, led by GP9 No. 300, works a westward freight near Geneva and Kendaia, New York, on February 3, 1976. In less than two months, Lehigh Valley would become part of the government-sponsored Conrail bailout, and this section of track west of Van Etten Junction would be largely abandoned. *Bill Dechau, Doug Eisele collection*

Back cover: Kansas City Southern has adapted its 1930s *Southern Belle* livery for its modern freight locomotives. On April 29, 2008, freshly painted KCS SD70ACe No. 4108 and a General Electric ES44AC lead a unit grain train of matching KCS hoppers at DeQuincy, Louisiana. *Chris Guss*

CONTENTS

GE
LOCOMOTIVES

ELECTRIC LOCOMOTIVES

The emergence of commercial electric enterprise in the 1870s and 1880s made possible a whole new form of railway motive power. The prospects of developing and selling electric railway propulsion intrigued electrical pioneers. Railways were among the biggest businesses at the time, and railway applications were one of the first large markets for electrical technology.

In the decades before the development of commercial electrical power grids, electric railways provided a base for experimentation and demonstration. Experiments in electric railway propulsion had been undertaken as early as the 1830s, using battery-powered miniature locomotives. In 1879, Werner Von Siemens exhibited a small electric railway in Berlin, marking the first practical public demonstration of an electric locomotive powered by a generator, or—as they called it then—a dynamo. Inspired by this, General Electric's founder, Thomas A. Edison, began experimenting with electric railway propulsion in 1880. Following initial testing on a very short segment, Edison conducted more extensive experiments at the behest of Northern Pacific's Henry Villiard, using a test track 2-1/4 miles long. This track, like the first, was located in Menlo Park, New Jersey. According to *Railway Wonders of the World*, published around 1914, Edison built a small standard gauge electric locomotive sufficiently powerful to haul three cars.

Opposite: The New Haven Railroad pioneered mainline electrification. Its first electrified route from New York to Cos Cob, Connecticut, began regular service in June 1907. On June 28, 1958, an unusually painted New Haven EP-3 electric leads train No. 145 westbound at Stamford, Connecticut. General Electric built the New Haven's 10 EP-3s in 1931. They used a 2-C+C-2 wheel arrangement and inspired the Pennsylvania Railroad's GG1 electric design of 1934. *Richard Jay Solomon*

General Electric's first double-truck electric locomotive (and its second locomotive) was built in 1894 for the Cayadutta Railway and spent most of its working life at a cotton mill in Taftville, Connecticut. GE classified the locomotive as Type 404-E70-4 LWP 20-500 volts. Significantly, it used nose-suspended traction motors, the arrangement that became standard on nearly all diesel-electric locomotives.
Duke-Middleton collection, photographer unknown

By the early 1890s, American engineers, including Leo Daft, Stephen Field, and Frank J. Sprague, were among the world leaders in the development of electric railway technology. Sprague, a onetime employee of Edison, was an inventor responsible for many important innovations in electric railway technology, including the first large-scale applications of electric propulsion, on the Richmond Union Passenger Railway in Virginia in 1888. Sprague's company became part of Edison-GE in 1890. Following this success, numerous horse-drawn street railway lines in the United States and other parts of the world were electrified. The electrically powered trolley car became a symbol of progress. More than 850 electric street railway systems were operational by 1898, and just about every self-respecting city or town had invested in electric trolleys.

A spinoff of the electric street railway was the electric interurban line, which connected cities and towns and by the first decade of the twentieth century in almost every region in the United States. In general, these electric lines, including their track and roadbeds, were built to much lower standards than conventional steam-powered railways. Their cars were also smaller and lighter than were those on steam trains. Interurbans competed directly with the steam railways for passenger traffic and, in some cases, freight. General Electric was a primary supplier of electrical gear used on street and interurban railways, and supported electrical infrastructure, such as the power stations and substations needed to generate and transmit electricity.

General Electric was also a pioneer in the construction of electric locomotives. In 1893 at its Lynn, Massachusetts, facility, GE built its first commercial electric locomotive for steam railway service. In his book, *When the Steam Railroads Electrified*, William D. Middleton describes it as a 30-ton, four-wheel machine, capable of 30 miles per hour. GE built a second, larger locomotive in 1894. Middleton indicates that this steeple cab was 24 feet long, weighed 35 tons, and rode on a pair of twin-axle trucks powered by nose-suspended traction motors of a type developed by Sprague. This locomotive is of interest today because its double-truck design set an important precedent, and its nose-suspended traction motors were the prototypes for those used by GE's later electrics and nearly all modern diesel-electric locomotives. (A nose-suspended motor is supported on one end by the axle and on other end by the truck frame. It typically uses single-reduction gearing to power the axle.) This original steeple cab had an extraordinarily long career working a cotton mill in Taftville, Connecticut. It was retired in 1964 and today is displayed at the Connecticut Trolley Museum at Warehouse Point, Connecticut. Steeple-cab electrics of a similar design became a standard type built by General Electric and were used by electric railways for many years.

The Pros and Cons of Electrification

Heavy railway electrification was a logical outgrowth of street railway and interurban electrification, although railroads were slow to explore its potential. The earliest electric

This photograph, made July 22, 1894, shows one of the Cayadutta Railway locomotive trucks that featured nose-suspended traction motors, a standard arrangement on electric trolley cars of the period. General Electric's early nose-suspended motors were the technological predecessors to the successful DC motors used by most diesel-electric manufacturers. *Duke-Middleton collection, photographer unknown*

General Electric pioneered heavy railroad electrification when it contracted to electrify Baltimore & Ohio's new Howard Street Tunnel in 1892. Electric service began in 1895. In this period photo, B&O electric No. 1 poses beyond the south portal of the tunnel, near the railroad's Camden Station in Baltimore. In the first few years, B&O electric locomotives took power from a rigid overhead system, seen here above the locomotive. After 1900, a more conventional outside third-rail replaced the overhead system. *Industrial Photo Service, William D. Middleton collection*

propulsion systems were not powerful enough to power mainline trains, although in the mid-1890s the New Haven and Pennsylvania railroads experimented with short electrified sections akin to trolley lines.

The prospects of major steam railway electrification generated considerable controversy during the last decade of the nineteenth century and the first decades of the twentieth. Proponents of electrification claimed numerous potential advantages. Electrification was a more efficient use of energy and could lower fuel and maintenance costs. Electric motors also provided greater starting power than steam power. Electrified operations could lower labor costs and simplify operations by using double-ended equipment and eliminating fuel and water stops required by steam

engines. However, the most conspicuous advantages of electrification from the public viewpoint were significantly cleaner and quieter trains. Coal-burning steam locomotives are dirty machines that belch smoke, leaving a layer of soot on everything they pass. These latter considerations, as much as operational efficiency, encouraged the installation of America's first heavy-duty electrification.

Despite the many prospective advantages of electrification, railroads observed the developing technology cautiously. In the 1890s, a lack of suitable technology for heavy railroad operations precluded serious investment. The high initial costs of electrification were difficult for railroads to justify, despite the allure of lower operating costs. In addition to the great expense of electrical supply equipment and

Between 1903 and 1906, General Electric built five boxcab electrics for Baltimore & Ohio's Howard Street Tunnel electrification. These B&O boxcabs, Nos. 7, 6, and 9, lead a freight in about 1915. Electrics would haul trains, complete with steam locomotive, through the tunnel to avoid smoke problems. Notice the brakemen riding on the freight cars. *Smithsonian Institution Neg. No. 49870, courtesy of William D. Middleton*

New York Central & Hudson River Railroad's pioneer electric locomotive, No. 6000, operates with a five-car train on the Schenectady test track near Wyatts Crossing, New York, on November 12, 1904. Experiments with this locomotive demonstrated the capabilities of electric motive power. *Industrial Photo Service, William D. Middleton collection*

specialized locomotives, electrification required separate shops and specially trained mechanics to maintain the equipment. Other costs included expensive signaling equipment that was shielded from interference with its electrical transmissions. Safety concerns due to hazards posed by high-voltage lines also fueled electrification opponents. The specialized and somewhat inflexible equipment imposed operational constraints.

First Mainline Electrification

By the 1880s, America's first public railway, the Baltimore & Ohio, was moving a vast quantity of freight and passengers through its namesake port. It was also looking to improve its route through Baltimore to better compete with the Pennsylvania Railroad, which had just completed its through line across that city. Saddled with complex terminal arrangements that made the operation of through trains slow and difficult, B&O planned a new "Belt Line" through Baltimore that included a long tunnel beneath a residential area of downtown. The railroad faced serious public opposition to its plan, as residents were appalled at the thought of

steam trains spreading foul smoke and soot as they passed under vents near their homes. To overcome an impasse over the proposed tunnel, B&O made the unprecedented decision to electrify.

The railroad turned to General Electric for equipment and locomotives to electrify the Belt Line, which included the new 1-1/4-mile Howard Street Tunnel and a new passenger station and shed at Mt. Royal. Today, this may seem like a logical solution to a difficult problem, but at the time it was a bold step. Despite the growing number of lightweight electric street railways and a few branchline experiments, up until then no railway in the world had attempted to electrify a full-scale mainline operation.

The first electric operations began at the end of June 1895, and regular operations began in July. The electrified section was very short, a little more than 3 miles of mainline. The system of electrification was derived from the 600-volt direct current systems employed by most contemporary street railways, but required a substantially heavier delivery mechanism than provided by lightweight overhead trolley wire. The voltage was 675 volts (some sources indicate 650 volts); instead of wire, General Electric devised a peculiar rigid overhead electrical supply system. Locomotives drew power from the overhead rail using an angled, flexible pantograph fixed to the locomotive on its bottom and gripping the rail with a brass fitting. Initially, the B&O used three steeple-cab locomotives built by GE at Schenectady, New York. Each locomotive weighed about 192,000 pounds, making them much heavier than typical steam locomotives of the period. Brian Hollingsworth points out in *The Illustrated Encyclopedia of North American Locomotives* that the first B&O electrics were nine times heavier than any other electrics operating at that time. Each was designed to haul a train weighing up to 1,870 tons up the 0.8 percent grade in the Howard Street Tunnel. Propulsion was provided by four gearless, 360-horsepower direct current electric motors. Motor armatures engaged hollow quills that surrounded the driving axles, and the quills connected to 62-inch spoked driving wheels using rubber blocks. The blocks provided a flexible connection that cushioned shocks to the motors.

Electric locomotives hauled trains, steam locomotives and all, through the tunnel. (Leaving the regular road locomotive on its train reduced transit delays.) Since the steam locomotive did not have to work in the tunnel, smoke emissions were minimal. When the train reached the end of the electrified section, the electric locomotive would be cut off and switched out of the way, and the steam locomotive would take over again.

The electrics proved a practical motive power solution, though the electrical distribution was awkward. After 1900, B&O replaced the fixed overhead system with a more suitable ground-level, overrunning third-rail, similar to that used on the newly electrified New York City elevated rapid transit lines. Baltimore & Ohio's pioneering electrification, America's only significant mainline electric operation for the better part of a decade, set important precedents for later electric operations.

Baltimore & Ohio bought additional electric locomotives from General Electric between 1909 and 1912. These more modern machines, Classes OE-1 and OE-2, were of a boxcab design and allowed B&O to retire its pioneer steeple cabs. Between 1923 and 1927, B&O added more GE locomotives, Classes OE-3 and OE-4. These brought back the center-cab design, with a B-B wheel arrangement.

The OE-4 employed four GE 209C traction motors that developed 1,100 horsepower. The locomotive was 41 feet, 4 inches long and 14 feet, 3-1/2 inches tall (including headlamps). It weighed 242,000 pounds and could deliver 60,500 pounds starting tractive effort. The advent of modern diesel-electrics negated the need for the Baltimore Belt Line electrification, and Baltimore & Ohio discontinued electric operations in the early 1950s.

New York's Grand Central Quandary

At the end of the nineteenth century, New York City was the largest city in the United States and its population was growing rapidly. Suburban railways that fed Manhattan allowed

GE built New York Central's Class R-2 electrics for the railroad's West Side electrification in Manhattan. General Electric designated these locomotives C+C-270/270-6GE286. Although the C-C wheel arrangement was unusual in 1930 and 1931 when they were built, it has since become the standard wheel arrangement used by American diesel-electrics in freight service. *General Electric photo, William D. Middleton collection*

General Electric sold electrification systems, including power-generating systems, substations, and locomotives. This GE rotary converter located in a substation at East Troy, Wisconsin, was used to convert high-voltage AC power into low-voltage DC for The Milwaukee Electric Railway & Light Company. *Brian Solomon*

workers to live much farther from the city than was possible in earlier times. While numerous railway lines served the New York area, most reached Manhattan by way of ferry connections. The only direct passenger route was New York Central's Park Avenue Tunnel to Grand Central Depot, a station that it shared with the New York, New Haven & Hartford Railroad. The latter utilized trackage rights over New York Central between Woodlawn Junction in The Bronx and Grand Central. Between the two railroads, some 500 daily trains served Grand Central, making it among the busiest stations in the world.

New York Central enlarged Grand Central in 1898 to accommodate the growing tide of passenger traffic, but even as the enlargement was being completed, it recognized the inadequacies of the new station and started investigating the construction of an entirely new terminal on the site. Capacity was a primary concern. Even in the 1890s, Manhattan real estate was expensive, putting serious space constraints on the terminal and making expansion difficult. As a result, the railroad needed to make the maximum use of the space. According to William D. Middleton in his

book, *Grand Central: The World's Greatest Railway Terminal*, in 1899, William J. Wilgus, New York Central vice president and chief engineer, envisioned a two-level underground terminal station. However, this novel solution was not possible with conventional steam power because of smoke. As it was, the existing station suffered badly from smoke, and locomotives were kept outside the station shed until they were needed to move trains. Wilgus' concept would be practical only if the new station was electrified. And so, envisioning an electrified suburban railway system for New York, Wilgus met with electric traction pioneer Frank J. Sprague to discuss the possibilities of electrifying Grand Central. Nothing like this had ever been accomplished on such a grand scale. While Wilgus was pondering the potentials of electrification, a horrible disaster propelled the railroad to the forefront of electric railway technology.

Trains to Grand Central traversed deep cuts and a long tunnel below Park Avenue. At times of peak traffic, smoke made it difficult for locomotive engineers to see line-side signals that governed train movements. On the morning of January 8, 1902, an inbound New York Central

passenger train approaching Grand Central overran a stop signal obscured by smoke and collided at speed with a standing New Haven suburban train waiting for permission to enter the station. The collision splintered fragile wooden passenger cars and when the smoke cleared, 15 people were dead and many others seriously injured. While rear-end collisions were a common accident in those days, because this disaster occurred in Manhattan, it was sensationalized by the media, resulting in a tide of public outrage. The fury fueled legislation that effectively banned steam locomotive operation in Manhattan. In effect, these laws precipitated some of the most significant motive power developments in American railroad history, as New York City's railroads were forced to develop a whole new magnitude of electric railway technology.

To meet the challenge set by state lawmakers, the Central established the Electric Traction Commission (ETC)—a think tank of the nation's foremost experts on electrical engineering, including Wilgus, Sprague, and George Gibbs. By studying previous applications of electric railway traction on street railways—namely the Baltimore & Ohio's 1895 electrification and recent third-rail electrifications on elevated rapid transit lines in Manhattan, Brooklyn, and Chicago—the ETC concluded that a 660-volt, direct current system delivered by outside third-rail was the most appropriate for the railroad's needs.

In the 1890s, there had been great discussion about the virtues and disadvantages of direct current (DC) and alternating current (AC) electrification schemes, not just for railway traction, but for general power distribution. The advantages of DC were its overall simplicity and ease of motor control. Disadvantages were inefficiency of long-distance transmission, requiring frequent and expensive electrical substations to provided adequate power. Direct current

worked well on electric street railways, where short distances and light vehicle weights were predominant. General Electric had promoted DC electrification, while Westinghouse favored AC schemes, but in 1896 the two companies agreed on a patent exchange that facilitated the manufacture of either technology by either company. Despite this exchange, GE continued to promote DC, while Westinghouse went on to pioneer early high-voltage AC transmission. New York Central selected a DC system, which was the best developed for railway applications at the time. Logically, the Schenectady, New York–based General Electric was chosen as its main supplier.

In 1895, GE's competitor, Westinghouse, had teamed up with Baldwin to build electric locomotives. (Both Westinghouse and Baldwin were Pennsylvania-based companies.) Baldwin manufactured mechanical components and Westinghouse supplied electrical gear. In response, GE teamed up with Alco in the construction of electric locomotives. Conveniently, GE and Alco both had primary manufacturing facilities at Schenectady. Later, GE and

Alco became closely involved in the manufacture of diesels. Baldwin and Westinghouse were similarly linked, and in 1948 Westinghouse took control of its longtime locomotive-building partner.

New York Central's First Electric

A formal arrangement between GE and Alco was still a couple of years away when New York Central contracted with GE for a prototype locomotive in anticipation of its Grand Central electrification. Working with New York Central's Electric Traction Commission in 1904, GE designed and built No. 6000, a double-ended machine with a 1-D-1 wheel arrangement. (Powered axles are counted in groups represented by a letter: A for one axle, B for two, C for three, etc. Numbers indicate unpowered axles. Hence, No. 6000 had four powered axles between two unpowered axles.) It employed a center-cab configuration, a common arrangement on many early electrics. As the 6000 was intended to haul New York Central's fast express trains, it needed the same capabilities as Central's state-of-the-art passenger

steam locomotives. Four 550-horsepower bi-polar (two pole) traction motors produced a total continuous output of 2,200 horsepower and were capable of a short-term output of up to 3,000 horsepower. It used a gearless traction motor design, in which motor poles were mounted on the locomotive frame and armatures directly on the axles. Both poles and armatures were spring-loaded to maintain flexibility. According to Brian Hollingsworth in *The Illustrated Encyclopedia of North American Locomotives*, the total locomotive weight was 200,500 pounds, with approximately 142,000 pounds on driving wheels, giving the machine a maximum axle load of about 35,500 pounds. The locomotive was designed to haul a standard 450-ton passenger train and was capable of hauling trains weighing almost twice that amount.

The 6000 set many precedents that were copied and improved upon in later locomotives. Its design was largely the work of GE's Asa Batchelelder, but it also incorporated important innovations designed by Sprague. Perhaps most significant was the first use of Sprague's electro-pneumatic multiple-unit (MU) control system on a locomotive. Sprague's MU control was developed in 1897 to allow two or more electric units (railcars or, in this case, locomotives) to be operated synchronously under the control of a single engineer (operator). This pioneering use of MU control has significant historical precedent. Nearly all diesel-electric locomotives today are built with MU controls and it is standard practice to operate locomotives in multiple. The ability to operate multiple electric, and subsequently diesel-electric,

Continued on page 24

One of the most ambitious American mainline electrification schemes was the wiring of Milwaukee Road's Pacific Extension. One of Milwaukee's massive EP-2 "Bi-Polar" electrics is seen with train No. 17, the westbound *Columbian*. This July 11, 1925, photo features the railroad's Washington State electrification west of Rockdale Yard on Snoqualmie Pass. *Asamel Curtis, Washington State Historical Society, courtesy of William D. Middleton*

Above: Three-phase AC-traction diesel-electrics are commonplace today, but GE was building them long before modern diesels. In 1911, GE electrified Great Northern's Cascade crossing at Stevens Pass using a 6,600-volt, three-phase overhead system that required two sets of delivery wires. The electric locomotives, such as these seen at Tye, Washington, in May 1915, used four GE-1506 induction traction motors to produce a total of 1,500 horsepower. In the 1920s, Great Northern relocated its Cascade crossing and re-electrified it, using a more conventional 11,000-volt, single-phase AC system. *Asamel Curtis, Washington State Historical Society, courtesy of William D. Middleton*

Opposite: In 1947, General Electric built two massive streamlined motor-generator electrics for Great Northern. Rated at 5,000 horsepower, they were the largest electrics in the world at that time. Here, GN No. 4933 leads a freight train through the Cascades near Leavenworth, Washington. *Great Northern Railway photo, William D. Middleton collection*

Opposite, inset: The running gear for one of Great Northern's 360-ton electrics is seen on the shop floor at Erie, Pennsylvania, on January 28, 1947. GE classified these monster electrics as B-D+D-B-720/720-12GE745. All axles on this machine were powered by GE-745 traction motors. *Great Northern Railway photo, William D. Middleton collection*

Continued from page 21

locomotives was one of the great advantages of electric motive power over steam, dramatically increasing the amount of work one person could do.

Initially, NYC No. 6000 was listed as Class L, but was soon changed to Class T. Following later modifications, it was again changed to Class S. Locomotive 6000, later renumbered 100, was the railroad's sole S-1 electric. In 1905, it was used in extensive experiments on a 6-mile electrified test track parallel to New York Central's Water Level Route mainline in the shadow of GE's plant at Schenectady. To determine its full capabilities and to demonstrate the potential of electric traction, No. 6000 hauled trains of various weights back and forth on the test track. Although fairly level, portions of the line climbed a nominal grade of 0.36 percent. With a heavily loaded train, the locomotive accelerated to a speed of 65 miles per hour; in one test, 6000 is reported to have hauled a single coach at a speed of 79 miles per hour. Running light, it was capable of speeds of over 80 miles per hour, and is reported to have briefly attained 85 miles per hour.

No. 6000 was built during a period when publicity stunts were popular in America, and New York Central's George Daniels, the railroad's "general passenger agent," made the railroad's trains famous by staging widely publicized high-speed runs. The best remembered of these took place on May 10, 1893, when Daniels caught the world's eye with the record run of the *Empire State Express* behind 4-4-0 No. 999, a locomotive specially equipped with 7-foot-tall driving wheels for fast running. On that day, 999 is reported to have attained the improbable high speed of 112-1/2 miles per hour west of Batavia, New York.

As part of the 1905 experiments, New York Central staged races between its best steam power and its experimental electric, the results of which were published in *Railway Wonders of the World* (1914). At the time of the tests, one of New York Central's fastest and most modern passenger locomotives was the Pacific-type 4-6-2 No. 2799, built by Alco-Schenectady in 1903. According to Al Staufer in *New York Central's Later Power*, this locomotive featured 22x26-inch cylinders and 75-inch driving wheels, placed 140,000 pounds on drivers, and could deliver

28,500 pounds tractive effort. No. 2799 and No. 6000 were assigned to comparable passenger trains, taking into account the minor differences in locomotive weight, and raced against one another along the test track section of Central's mainline.

In the early tests it was found that the steam locomotive accelerated faster because initial voltage drops affected the electric's ability to gain speed. Once the electric got moving, however, it quickly overtook the Pacific, thus proving to ob-

servers the viability and superiority of electric motive power. In one test, it took No. 6000 just 127 seconds to accelerate its train to 50 miles per hour, which was 76 seconds faster than the Pacific. New York Central also ran the electric in deep snow to demonstrate that it was an all-weather machine. Satisfied with the capabilities of the electric, New York Central ordered a fleet of 34 similar electrics from GE for its express and long-distance passenger service to Grand Central. These were originally classed as T-2, but were soon

On February 3, 1959, New Haven EP-4 No. 360 leads a train toward Penn Station through Sunnyside Yard in Queens, New York. In 1938, General Electric built 10 EP-4 electrics for New Haven Railroad based on the earlier EP-3 boxcab. *Richard Jay Solomon*

reclassified as S-2. The majority of Central's suburban services were handled by electric multiple units (self-propelled passenger cars) instead of locomotive-hauled trains.

Although New York Central was undertaking ambitious plans for an all-new Grand Central Terminal, it had to comply with a ban on steam power that went into effect July 1, 1908. As a result, the old Grand Central was electrified as an interim operation while the new terminal was built around it. The first electric services began on September 20, 1906, and by 1907 the station was mostly electrified. Initially, electric services only extended a few miles beyond Manhattan, but Central gradually extended the electrification to take better advantage of electric power and minimize the need for engine changes. By the mid-1920s, the third-rail extended 33 miles north of Grand Central to Croton-on-Hudson (now known as Croton-Harmon) on its famous Hudson Division, to North White Plains on its Harlem Division, and on the Getty Square Branch of its Putnam Division. In the 1930s, Central electrified its West Side freight line in Manhattan.

Shortly after the initiation of electric service, a second disastrous accident occurred when a train derailed at speed, killing 23 people. The tragic irony of the accident was that it demonstrated the fallibility of the new electric service that

had been introduced in specific response to the 1902 crash. The second disaster, like the first, had serious repercussions. Wilgus resigned, and New York Central was forced to re-evaluate the design of its electric locomotives. Sensational press reports propelled technical details of railway operation into public consciousness and resulted in a greater demand for safety. New York Central took action by rebuilding all of its electrics with leading bogie trucks in place of pony trucks, resulting in a 2-D-2 wheel arrangement and the electrics' reclassifications as S-motors.

In 1908 and 1909, New York Central ordered an additional 12 electrics, which were classed S-3, from General Electric.

Some of Central's S-motors served the Grand Central electrification until the early 1980s, outlasting the New York Central and its successor, Penn-Central. Several S-motors, including the pioneer, have been preserved, yet as of this writing in 2002 none have been properly restored for public display.

New York Central's Later Electrics

Between 1913 and 1926, General Electric built more advanced electric locomotives for New York Central. Classified as T-motors, they should not be confused with the

original T description. The Central listed 36 Class Ts in five subclasses that reflected slight variations on the design. All T-motors used an end-cab articulated design with an articulated B-B+B-B wheel arrangement, in which all wheels were powered. This allowed for a significantly more powerful locomotive with the full weight of the machine placed on the driving wheels, yet a lighter axle load as the weight was distributed more equally. According to *Jane's World Railways*, the T-2a motors weighed 280,500 pounds, all of which was available for traction, and produced 69,775 pounds starting tractive effort with a continuous tractive effort rating of 12,500 pounds at 57 miles per hour. Eight 330-horsepower gearless traction motors, one on each axle, produced 2,640 horsepower at 48 miles per hour, according to Hollingsworth. By comparison, New York Central information indicates that S-3 motors weighed 249,800 pounds, with 152,300 pounds available for adhesion. The S-3s produced just 38,075 pounds starting tractive effort and 4,870 pounds continuous tractive effort at 61 miles per hour. (Sources vary on the weight and tractive effort produced by these electrics, making accurate comparisons difficult.)

The articulated arrangement and smaller, lighter traction motors meant that the T-motors were much less damaging to tracks, and their superior performance earned them

25

the majority of road passenger assignments and relegated the S-motors to secondary services.

New York Central later gave GE an order for seven Class Q motors that used steeple-cab design with a B-B wheel arrangement. Another type of B-B locomotive was the end-cab Class R. Central also ordered a fleet of R-1 electrics for its Detroit River Tunnel electrification that was undertaken following the success of Grand Central's electric operations. Like the New York electrification, this operation used a direct current (DC) underrunning third-rail. The R-1s were built in three subclasses, some of which were manufactured jointly by General Electric and Alco, while GE, in a pattern that seems to have been common for many years, solely built others.

Significant to the study of modern locomotives were big electrics using a 2-C+C-2 wheel arrangement built by GE in 1928 for the Central's Cleveland Union Terminal electrification, and 42 six-motor R-2s built in 1930 for Central's West Side operations. Both types used state-of-art, nose-suspended traction motors made possible by recent advances in motor technology. These powerful motors had made most earlier methods of DC motor-transmission designs obsolete. Although nose-suspended motors had been used since the 1890s on lightweight electric streetcars and small locomotives, until the 1920s these motors were not sufficiently pow-

erful for heavy traction applications. The power-to-weight ratio of a nose-suspended motor using older technology would have resulted in a motor too large and heavy for practical application, as the weight of such motors would have raised axle weights above acceptable limits. Other types of motors used more complicated types of motor transmission, such as the quill drives used on early electrics like the S-motors. Today, nose-suspended motors are standard equipment on diesel-electrics.

New York Central's R-2 electrics are of special interest to modern locomotive study not just because of their nose-suspended motors, but because they employed a C-C wheel arrangement (a pair of three-axle, three-motor, powered trucks). This same wheel and motor arrangement has subsequently become predominant on American road diesels today. The Central's pioneering use of the C-C arrangement predated its regular use on American lines by nearly three decades. In actual service, the Central's R-2 electrics were relatively obscure types primarily used on freight services on the route on the West Side of Manhattan, and thus were often relegated to nocturnal operation. In later years, a few R-2s were assigned to the Central's Detroit River Tunnel

electrified line, and in the late 1950s, the Chicago-area interurban Chicago, South Shore & South Bend acquired some former R-2s for freight services on its 1,500-volt DC overhead electric lines. The Cleveland Union Terminal electrics were originally designated P-1a. After the Cleveland Union Terminal overhead electrification was discontinued in favor of dieselization, the P-motors were rebuilt (receiving new subclasses P-2a and P2b) for third-rail operation on the Grand Central electrified lines.

More Electrification and More Electrics

In the first decades of the twentieth century considerable interest developed in electric operations, yet there was still disagreement as to what forms electric operations should take. The primary types of electrical systems were direct current, single-phase alternating current (AC), and three-phase AC. Several different electrification schemes developed, based on these basic types, and there were few established standards even among common types of electrification. The basic electrification configurations that emerged were low-voltage DC, transmitted via third-rail (as with the New York Central) or by overhead trolley wire (as used by street

Pennsylvania Railroad GG1 No. 4802 electric sits under wire at Ivy City Engine Terminal at Washington, D.C. This was one of 14 GG1s built for PRR by General Electric at Erie, Pennsylvania. In addition to these, GE supplied electrical components for many other GG1s. Although largely a PRR design, several firms undertook the construction of the 139-unit GG1 fleet. *Jim Shaughnessy*

Pennsylvania Railroad GG1 No. 4924 leads a westbound train on the High Line in the New Jersey Meadows near the west portal of the Penn Tunnels below the Hudson River. This GG1 was built by the railroad at its Altoona, Pennsylvania, shops using GE electrical components. *Richard Jay Solomon*

DC third-rail. Pennsylvania Railroad also electrified its New York terminal operations, which included newly bored long tunnels under New York's Hudson and East Rivers. The Pennsy also electrified its extensive suburban operations on its Long Island Rail Road subsidiary, using a third-rail system similar to the New York Central's. The Pennsy chose Westinghouse as its supplier, and used an overrunning third-rail instead of the underrunning variety employed by New York Central. The greater efficiency of high-voltage AC transmission over long distances made this system more attractive for large-scale mainline electrification. Although the Pennsylvania had committed to DC third-rail for its New York terminal operations, it later adopted a high-voltage overhead system similar to the New Haven's for its Philadelphia suburban services. In the 1920s and 1930s, PRR expanded its overhead system for its Northeast Corridor electrification project between New York, Philadelphia, and Washington, D.C., and eventually to Harrisburg.

High-voltage AC projects were largely the domain of Westinghouse. By contrast, General Electric continued to develop and promote its own systems through the 1920s. While GE primarily built DC systems ranging from 600-volt electric trolley networks to extensive 3,000-volt systems, one of the most unusual projects the company undertook was the electrification of the Great Northern's Cascade Tunnel in 1911, using a three-phase AC system. Three-phase AC motors offer superior traction characteristics to DC motors, making them especially desirable for use on heavily graded lines. The difficulty in controlling three-phase AC motors, however, precluded wide-scale adoption of the system. Great Northern's electrics worked at 6,600 volts and required two separate sets of delivery wires. To haul GN trains, General Electric built a small fleet of boxcab electrics, each of which was rated at 1,500 horsepower, using four induction motors. The locomotives drew current using a pair of trolley poles, one pole for each set of wires. Great Northern's novel electrification was converted to a more conventional single-phase 11,000-volt AC system in the late 1920s, when the railroad relocated its Cascade crossing, which included a new and much longer Cascade Tunnel of 9.1 miles in length.

General Electric introduced higher-voltage DC electrification on interurban and suburban railway systems, such as Southern Pacific's Oakland, California, electrification. The

railways); moderate-voltage DC (usually between 1,500 and 3,000 volts), transmitted by overhead wire; high-voltage, single-phase AC (typically 11,000 volts in the United States); and three-phase AC (discussed in greater detail later).

As the New York Central was undertaking its third-rail DC electrification of Grand Central, New Haven Railroad worked with Westinghouse to pioneer high-voltage AC overhead for its suburban New York City lines. Since New Haven's trains accessed Grand Central via the New York Central, they also had to be able to operate off the Central's

There should be little doubt as to the manufacturer of New York Central P-2b No. 235, seen here on April 13, 1957, with the *Empire State Express* at Grand Central Terminal in New York. General Electric rebuilt this former Cleveland Union Station electric in 1955 for New York third-rail service. In its modified form, it weighed 388,000 pounds and used six GE-755A traction motors.
Jim Shaughnessy

New Haven EP-5 No. 375 (left) and an EMD-built FL9 diesel-electric/electric are seen at the New Haven, Connecticut, engine terminal. The EP-5s were the first locomotives to wear New Haven's new "McGinnis" livery. Drawings of the EP-5 when the model was ordered show the type wearing the older green-and-gold scheme, such as that used on New Haven EP-4s.
Jim Shaughnessy

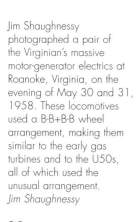

Milwaukee Road displayed one of its freshly shopped Bi-Polar electrics in Milwaukee, Wisconsin. One of these locomotives is now preserved in St. Louis, Missouri. *Richard Jay Solomon collection, photographer unknown*

success with a 2,400-volt DC electrification on Montana's Butte, Anaconda & Pacific Railroad, the Milwaukee Road was keen to take advantage of cost savings afforded by electrified operations, and the railroad contracted with GE to supply it with 3,000-volt DC overhead electrification.

The Milwaukee's Rocky Mountain electrification stretched 440 miles from Harlowton, Montana, to Avery, Idaho, a small, isolated village located deep in the Bitterroot Mountains. Milwaukee's Cascade Mountain electrification ran from Othello, Washington, over the mountains to Tacoma and eventually on to Seattle.

Milwaukee's electrification, which began in 1915 and reached its fullest extent by 1927, was developed to satisfy different criteria than early eastern electrification programs. The Milwaukee Road used electrification to lower mainline operating costs on the Pacific Extension, where the railroad faced an unusual combination of circumstances. As one of the last transcontinental mainlines, the Milwaukee Road's route was completed in 1909, 40 years after the first transcontinental railroad. Operations were very difficult and faced steep and prolonged grades in the Rockies, Bitterroots, and Cascades of Montana, Idaho, and Washington. Where other western lines had supplies of coal or used oil-burning steam locomotives, Milwaukee's remote operations were

foremost example of GE's high-voltage DC system, however, was the electrification of the Milwaukee Road's fabled Pacific Extension, a route that ultimately consisted of more than 660 route miles of electric operation and involved two long but noncontiguous sections of electrification. Inspired by GE's

Jim Shaughnessy photographed a pair of the Virginian's massive motor-generator electrics at Roanoke, Virginia, on the evening of May 30 and 31, 1958. These locomotives used a B-B+B-B wheel arrangement, making them similar to the early gas turbines and to the U50s, all of which used the unusual arrangement. *Jim Shaughnessy*

hampered by a lack of available fuel, and it needed to haul coal for hundreds of miles to supply its steam locomotives. Electric operations solved Milwaukee's fuel problems, as it harnessed hydroelectric power to provide electricity and more efficient propulsion. Another benefit was the ability of electric motors to develop very high starting tractive effort, useful in ascending the railroad's grades, some of which reached 2.2 percent. Through electrification, the Milwaukee Road minimized the use of helpers and operated longer, heavier freight trains over the mountains. Another cost saving was the pioneering use of regenerative braking, a feature that turned traction motors into electric generators that fed current back into the system when descending grades. This saved electricity costs and reduced brake-shoe wear.

Milwaukee's Bi-Polar Electrics

GE and Alco jointly built two varieties of locomotives for Milwaukee's electric operations that appeared quite different externally. The freight locomotives were semi-permanently coupled pairs of Class EF-1 boxcabs built in 1915. These used a 2-B-B+B-B-2 arrangement, measured 112 feet long, and weighed 576,000 pounds, placing 451,000 pounds on the driving wheels. Using eight GE motors, one powering each driving axle, the boxcabs could produce 112,750 pounds tractive effort. (In his book, *The History of the Electric Locomotive*, F.J.G. Haut indicates a higher figure of 135,000 pounds of starting tractive effort and continuous output rated at 3,000 horsepower with a one-hour output at 3,440 horsepower.) These boxcabs were used on both electrified sections. Similar machines, designated EP-1, were

The year is 1938, and GE's Building 10 at Erie, Pennsylvania, is filled with New Haven EP-4 streamlined passenger electrics under construction. Over the decades, GE has built thousands of locomotives in this very same building, from GG1s and gas turbines to the latest AC6000CWs. *Smithsonian Institution Neg. No. 34206, William D. Middleton collection*

initially used for passenger services on the Rocky Mountain electrified section.

In 1919, GE and Alco built five massive, three-piece articulated EP-2 electrics that used an unusual 1-B-D+D-B-1 arrangement, indicating the machines rode on 28 wheels, of which 24 were powered. They used a peculiar-looking center-cab configuration with elongated wagon-top hood-end sections that were slightly lower than the cab section. The entire machine was articulated, with the cab split in three sections. Enormous headlights rode on the top of the end hoods, and a General Electric Type 100 gearless bi-polar motor powered each of the 12 driving axles. As a result, the EP-2s were commonly known as the *Bi-Polars*. Maximum tractive effort figures vary, with some sources indicating 114,450 pounds. Haut indicates a higher figure of 137,340 pounds. Drawing 888 amps, the Bi-Polars could deliver 42,000 pounds of continuous tractive effort at 28.4 miles per hour and produce 3,200 horsepower for traction. (One hour of output was about 10 percent higher.) Today we might not be impressed by a single locomotive with a 3,200-horsepower output—GE's most powerful modern diesels can produce nearly double that figure—but in 1919, the Bi-Polars were real monsters. To demonstrate their

great power, Milwaukee staged a well-publicized tug of war in the Cascades between a single Bi-Polar electric and two steam locomotives, a 2-6-6-2 Mallet compound and a conventional 2-8-0 Consolidation. In a show of brute force, the electric dragged the working steam locomotives across the bridge. In daily service, the Bi-Polars were intended to lift a 1,000-ton transcontinental passenger train up a 2 percent grade at a steady 25 miles per hour.

At the time, the Milwaukee Road's great mountain electrification was viewed as a triumph for modern technology. Proponents of electrification hoped that the Milwaukee's electrification would set an example that other lines would follow. It even inspired a work of fiction, *Tom Swift and His Electric Locomotive*. But while Milwaukee's electrification offered operational benefits, it remained an anomaly in American operating practice and was not repeated on such a scale; high-voltage AC ultimately prevailed over GE's DC system for use on heavy overhead electrification. However, electrification, which seemed to be the power of the future in 1920, never caught on in America. While more lines were electrified, the percentage of electrified mainline remained very small. The situation was different overseas, where a different economy prevailed. In Europe, not only did electrification become the dominant form of railway power, several countries adopted the 3,000-volt DC standard, including Belgium, Italy, and Poland. Perhaps the most extensive use of DC electric traction is in the former Soviet Union.

Oddly enough, Russian railways influenced Milwaukee's last electric motive power acquisition. In 1947 and 1948, General Electric was building a fleet of 20 massive double-ended streamlined 2-D+D-2 electrics for the Soviet electrified railways when Cold War politics intervened to prevent their delivery. With American-Soviet relations tenuous at best, GE sought other buyers for the orphaned machines. With its extensive 3,000-volt electrification, the Milwaukee Road was an obvious sales candidate, so GE lent the railroad a locomotive for testing. Because the locomotives were designed for Russian gauge—which, thanks to American engineer George Washington Whistler, had been established 100 years earlier as 5 feet instead of the 4 feet, 8-1/2 inches used in the United States—the big machine needed to be re-gauged for operation on the Milwaukee. The locomotives earned the nickname "Little Joes" after Soviet dictator Joseph Stalin. The

Milwaukee Road bought 12 Little Joes in 1950 for its Rocky Mountain lines, while Indiana interurban South Shore picked up three. The remaining five were sold to the Paulista Railway in Brazil.

More AC Electrics

By 1930, high-voltage, single-phase AC transmission systems had become the predominant choice for electrification. The New Haven, Pennsylvania, Boston & Maine, Virginian, and Norfolk & Western railroads, among others, all adopted 11,000-volt AC systems. General Electric built a variety of single-phase AC machines for various lines. In the 1930s and early 1940s, it built several classes of electrics for the New Haven, including 10 EP-3 articulated boxcabs in 1931. These were designed for 70-mile-per-hour passenger service; they used the 2-C+C-2 wheel arrangement developed a

few years earlier for the Cleveland Union Terminal electrics. New Haven's EP-3s were 77 feet long with a 66-foot wheelbase. They used six twin-arm, 12-pole motors, one for each powered axle, using a quill-and-cup drive, providing a continuous 2,740 horsepower with a 3,440-horsepower one-hour rating (in AC territory). When operating on DC third-rail trackage to reach Grand Central Terminal, motor output was slightly lower. The type delivered 68,400 pounds of starting tractive effort. The EP-3's high output and excellent tracking qualities at higher speeds led the Pennsylvania Railroad to borrow one for testing in 1934 when it was trying to develop a better electric for its Northeast Corridor operations. Experiments with the EP-3 led the PRR to adopt the 2-C+C-2 wheel arrangement for its very successful high-output, high-speed streamlined GG1 electric. Several manufacturers, including GE, over a nine-year period beginning in 1934, built the Pennsy's GG1 fleet. General Electric also provided electrical equipment for

GG1s built by PRR at Altoona, as well as by Baldwin. The railroad divided the supply of electric gear for its electric fleet between GE and Westinghouse.

In 1938, the New Haven placed a repeat order with GE for six EP-4 electrics based on the EP-3 design. The EP-4s were similar to the EP-3s in most respects but featured a handsome double-ended streamlined carbody and were slightly more powerful. They were given a 3,600-horsepower continuous output rating and designed to operate up to 93 miles per hour. In 1943, Alco-GE and Baldwin-Westinghouse evenly split an order for 10 similar streamlined EF-3 electrics designed for freight service. These were numbered in the 0150 series and strictly intended for AC overhead operation. As a result, they were not equipped with third-rail shoes and could not run into Grand Central. The EF-3s used a lower gearing and developed 90,000 pounds starting tractive effort while producing 4,860 horsepower at their maximum speed of 65 miles per hour.

慶祝鐵路電化一期工程竣工通車

Although the American market for electric locomotives has not amounted to much since the end of World War II, General Electric has sold numerous electrics for export. On February 24, 1978, the Taiwan Railway Administration opened its electrification with GE electric E42 No. 201 and a 15-car special train. *William D. Middleton*

On February 21, 1976, five weeks before bankrupt Penn-Central would become the primary component of Conrail, a pair of former Pennsylvania Railroad E44s leads a freight at Harrisburg, Pennsylvania. Electrified freight railroading did not fit into Conrail's operating scheme, and a few years after this photo was made, Conrail's electric operations were discontinued.
Doug Eisele

AC-DC Converter Locomotives

In the early years, AC-electrified lines employed motor-generator locomotives that reduced line current to a lower voltage for use by single-phase AC-traction motors. By the mid-1920s, advances in technology resulted in the construction of hybrid locomotives that converted single-phase AC power to DC power, which allowed high-voltage AC locomotives to use DC-traction motors that were better suited for railway traction. Between 1926 and 1930, both Baldwin-Westinghouse and Alco-GE built several classes of AC-DC motor-generator locomotives for the Great Northern Railway. The most impressive GN electrics were

two massive streamliners constructed by Alco-GE in 1946 that measured 101 feet long and weighed 735,000 pounds. They employed a B-D+D-B wheel arrangement in which all axles were powered. Transformers converted line voltage from 11,000 volts AC to 1,350 volts AC. This current was used to turn a pair of DC generators, which, in turn, fed power to 12 General Electric 746 nose-suspended traction motors, one powering each axle. Using a 17:70 gear ratio, these electrics developed 183,750 pounds starting tractive effort and 119,000 pounds continuous tractive effort at just over 15 miles per hour; they were rated at 5,000 horsepower. The Great Northern's electrics were followed two years later by two pairs of streamlined AC-DC motor-generator electrics for the Virginian; each pair used a B-B-B-B+B-B-B-B wheel arrangement with GE 752 traction motors.

By the 1950s, advances in mercury-arc technology made for the development of high-voltage AC-DC rectifiers that superseded motor-generator technology. New Haven was among the first lines to use rectifier electric locomotives. After first employing the technology in a fleet of passenger electric multiple-unit cars, New Haven ordered 10 EP-5 streamlined passenger electric locomotives from GE that used Ignitron rectifier tubes. These machines rode on C-C swing-bolster trucks and nose-suspended traction motors similar to those used by modern diesel-electrics. The EP-5s were 68 feet long, weighed 348,000 pounds, and produced 87,000 pounds maximum tractive effort. They featured the modern, new McGinnis livery using swatches of white, black, and orange, replacing New Haven's more traditional dark green–and-gold scheme.

Virginian ordered one dozen Ignitron rectifiers from GE in 1955 for coal service. Delivered over the next two years, they were among the first electrics to use a road-switcher configuration. They rode on C-C trucks and produced 3,300 horsepower. The Virginian's electrification was discontinued after the company was bought by Norfolk & Western in 1960. New Haven bought the 12 Ignitron electrics in 1963, repainted them, and reclassified them as EF-4s for freight service between New York City and New Haven, Connecticut.

The Pennsylvania Railroad followed Virginian's example and ordered a fleet of Ignitron rectifier electrics using the C-C road switcher configuration. Designated E44 (electric, 4,400 horsepower), they were intended to replace the PRR's aging fleet of 1930s-era boxcabs in freight service. While the E44 was in production, advances in silicon diode technology superseded the use of water-cooled Ignitron rectifier tubes. The later E44s were built as silicon-diode rectifiers, while earlier machines were later retrofitted with the updated technology. A total of 66 E44s were built, with the first delivered in 1960.

Diesel-Electric vs. Straight Electric

For decades, American railroads eyed electrification cautiously, carefully weighing the advantages of straight-electric operations against the high costs of electrifying their lines.

In his book, *From Bullets to BART*, William D. Middleton points out that "in 1938, America led the world in railroad electrification." Yet, from that point onward, very little new mainline electrification was undertaken in the United States. Following World War II, American railroads favored large-scale dieselization, and in the two decades from 1940 to 1960, railroads rapidly dispensed with their steam locomotive fleets in favor of new diesels. During this steam-diesel transition period, many railroads that had experimented with electrification discontinued their electric operations. Since many early railroad electrifications were implemented to avoid the negative effects of steam locomotive smoke, the use of diesels had most the advantages of electrification while providing greater operational flexibility. Railroads found little cost incentive to maintain separate fleets of electric locomotives.

Short-term economics was a dominant consideration in switching from steam power to another power source, and American railroads found it difficult to justify the much greater initial expense of electric operations over dieselization. To offset high costs, the Pennsylvania Railroad's 1930s electrification had benefited from government loans.

In Europe, the situation was different. European railways were generally state-run institutions and viewed by their respective governments as strategic national infrastructure. As a result, railways enjoyed the benefits of long-term strategic planning and large subsidies and investment. Following World War II, European countries invested heavily in railway infrastructure, while the U.S. government focused on a nationally subsidized highway infrastructure. European railways embraced large-scale electrification for a variety of reasons: The high costs of electrification were less of a concern there because the cost could be financed by government sources. Also, European railways were not taxed on capital improvements, as were America's private railroads. In addition, most European countries rely more heavily on imported fuels, with significantly higher costs than in the United States. Electrification allowed countries without substantial oil reserves to take advantage of another form of power.

By the early 1980s, remaining mainline electrified operations in the United States were almost exclusively for passenger services. The Milwaukee Road discontinued its last electric operations in 1974, and Conrail, which had

assumed operation of freight services on former Pennsylvania Railroad and New Haven lines, discontinued electric operations by 1981. One example of new electrification occurred in the late 1990s, when Amtrak electrified its Northeast Corridor line from New Haven to Boston in preparation for its new *Acela Express* high-speed passenger services.

Massive investment in the electrification of European railways, meanwhile, spurred greater levels of research and development in European electric locomotive designs and gave companies such as ASEA, Alstom, and Siemens direct access to substantial markets for new electrics. So, advanced electric locomotive designs became the domain of European, as well as Japanese, builders. While General Electric continued to offer electric locomotives through the 1970s and 1980s, the lack of demand and more advanced

European designs resulted in only a handful of GE electrics for domestic services. GE has, however, sold numerous electrics for export to a variety of nations.

Today, the American market for electrics is dominated by European designs that are usually manufactured domestically under contract.

E60 Electrics

In the early 1970s, Amtrak needed new electrics to replace the aging former Pennsylvania Railroad GG1 fleet. Amtrak, of course, had acquired the fleet when the federal government created the national passenger company to relieve ailing freight railroads of revenue-losing passenger services. To meet these requirements, GE built a fleet of 26 double-ended, high-horsepower E60CP/E60CH electrics for

high-speed passenger services. According to *The Contemporary Diesel Spotter's Guide* by Louis Marre and Jerry Pinkepank, the E60CP contained a steam generator to provide heat and lighting for traditional passenger equipment; the E60CHs were equipped with the more modern head-end electric power for heat and electricity.

Amtrak's locomotives were based on a single-ended E60C type built for the Black Mesa & Lake Powell line in Arizona. The E60 types use a cowl design, in which the outer body is not integral to the structure of the locomotive. Amtrak's E60CP/E60CHs were unadorned, flat-fronted machines dressed in its red-blue-and-silver scheme. These Spartan-looking utilitarian machines produced 6,000 horsepower output and delivered 75,000 pounds starting tractive effort. Although intended for 120-mile-per-hour service, Amtrak's E60CP/E60CH locomotives suffered from a

flawed truck design and were later relegated to a maximum speed of 85 miles per hour.

As a result, Amtrak sought a more effective high-speed locomotive and ultimately settled on a derivative of the highly successful Swedish Rc4 type, designated AEM-7, and built under license by EMD. Following the arrival the AEM-7s in the early 1980s, Amtrak sold some of its E60s to New Jersey Transit, a suburban passenger operator, and the Navajo Mine, a mining railway in New Mexico. However, some were retained by Amtrak and remain in regular passenger service. In later years, Amtrak E60s were frequently used on heavy long-distance trains that traverse the Northeast Corridor between New York and Washington, D.C. In the early 1980s, GE built a pair of E60C-2s for the Deseret Western, a 35-mile-long coal railway operating in Colorado and Utah, as well as similar types for export.

General Electric built 26 double-ended, high-horsepower E60CP/E60CH electrics for Amtrak in 1974 and 1975. In later years they were often assigned to heavy trains, such as through New York–Florida runs. Amtrak E60CP No. 607 leads a 16-car *Silver Star* through Newark, Delaware, on Election Day, November 3, 1992. *Brian Solomon*

EARLY DIESELS, ALCO-GE, AND SWITCHERS

Generous Electric was instrumental in the early development of internal-combustion motive power and electrical transmission for railway applications. Perhaps no other company in the world contributed as much basic research and development during the formative era of diesel-electric development. General Electric was one of the first to experiment with gas-electric railcars, internal-combustion locomotives, and the first to experiment with, build, and sell diesel locomotives. Much of GE's early work contributed directly to the development of its later locomotive designs, as well of those of its competitors.

By 1904, General Electric was a leader in electric traction systems. Its work with electric streetcar and electric interurban systems was well established, and it was a preferred supplier for emergent heavy-railroad electrification systems. A logical extension of this business was the development of self-powered electrical railway motive power. GE was not the first to experiment with gas-electrics; William Patton had built a gasoline-electric-powered railcar using a small 10-horsepower Van Duzen engine in 1890, believed to be the first such application of this technology on a railway vehicle. Patton later built more gasoline-electric railcars, but ended production in 1893. He is also credited with building a few gasoline-electric locomotives, but

Opposite: Rapid acceleration made the RS-3s popular suburban passenger locomotives and many railroads, including Boston & Maine, New York Central, Erie, and Rock Island, assigned RS-2s and RS-3s to commuter services. Erie's RS-3s numbered 914 to 933 were built by Alco-GE between 1950 and 1953. Erie No. 921 is seen leading a pair of Stillwell passenger cars in New Jersey-area suburban service. *Richard Jay Solomon*

41

these did not function well and his ideas did not have an immediate effect on the development of more effective technology. A few years later, the self-propelled gas-electric car gained interest in England.

General Electric had followed these developments and in 1904 initiated its own gas-electric experiments. (This was the same year that GE built the New York Central's prototype electric locomotive for the Grand Central Terminal electrification.) GE used a wooden Barney & Smith combine-coach provided by the Delaware & Hudson and a Wolseley gasoline engine from England. Based on these early trials, GE developed its own gasoline engine line and became one of the largest early manufacturers of gas-electric railcars—lightweight, self-propelled passenger cars commonly known as *Doodlebugs*. These cars used bodies manufactured by the Wason Car Manufacturing Company of Springfield, Massachusetts, and were very similar to the types of cars used by electric street railways. GE sold its first gas-electric cars in 1906 and built approximately 89 of them through 1917. Most of GE's cars were built prior to 1914, and only a few were built after that.

The production of gas-electric railcars led to GE's development of internal-combustion locomotives. Although today we may differentiate between *railcars* and *locomotives*, the development of these two types of machines is closely intertwined. In GE's case, both used internal-combustion engines for power with an electric-traction transmission. While this initial effort did not result in a commercial enterprise, it

A vintage General Electric herald. *Brian Solomon*

was part of the process that ultimately led GE into the diesel-electric locomotive business. (The company's earliest work with Rudolf Diesel's engine is described in the sidebar "The First Diesel" by John Gruber.)

General Electric engineers Henry Chatain and Hermann Lemp are credited with pioneering much of the company's early internal-combustion locomotive technology. Interestingly, both men were immigrants from Switzerland. According to Jerry A. Pinkepank in the November 1996 issue of *TRAINS Magazine*, Chatain designed GE's early gas engines, while Lemp was responsible for the development of electrical control systems. It is known that Chatain met with Rudolf Diesel and the men exchanged ideas. According to an article titled "A Brief History of Erie General Electric 1911–1994," published in *The Journal of Erie Studies* in the spring of 1995, GE in 1906 put Chatain in charge of its Gas Engine Department, which was relocated to Erie, Pennsylvania, in 1911. As a result, the Erie facility, rather than the one in Schenectady, developed as GE's primary locomotive works. In 1912 Chatain filed a patent with the U.S. Patent Office detailing improvements in the design of an internal combustion–electric locomotive. In it, Chatain articulated his idea in great detail:

> "In a locomotive, the combination of an engine, projections that extend downwardly from the engine base and form with the base the magnet frame of an electric motor, field coils carried by the projections, a truck, and armature for the motor that is mounted on an axle of the truck and is located between said projections, and a generator driven by the engine which is adapted to supply current to the motor."

While the precise arrangement described by Chatain may seem peculiar, the fundamentals of the modern diesel-electric are clearly outlined.

Dan Patch 100

Among GE's gas-electric railcar customers was the newly formed Minneapolis, St. Paul, Rochester & Dubuque Electric Traction Company, a lightly built interurban railway better known as the Dan Patch Line. While it was similar to many interurban lines operating all over the United

Although not the first diesel-electric locomotive, Central Railroad of New Jersey No. 1000 is generally considered the first successful commercial diesel-electric locomotive. It was built in 1925 by a consortium of General Electric, Alco, and Ingersoll-Rand. Today, old CNJ 1000 is proudly displayed at the Baltimore & Ohio Railroad Museum in Baltimore, Maryland. *Brian Solomon*

States, it differed from most "electric" railways in that it used gas-electric technology instead of overhead trolley wire or a third-rail for propulsion. To meet the needs of the Dan Patch Line, General Electric built a small boxcab gas-electric locomotive using a carbody constructed by the Wason Car Company. GE installed two of its 8x10-inch V-8 engines rated at 175 horsepower each. The locomotive was 36 feet, 4 inches long, weighed 57 tons, and rode on a pair of two-axle trucks giving it a B-B wheel arrangement—typical of interurban electric locomotives of the period. While not the very first gasoline-electric locomotive, Dan Patch No. 100 is generally considered the first commercially successful internal combustion–electric locomotive in the United States. GE built several more similar machines for the Dan Patch Line and other railways.

One of the difficulties with the early gas-electric cars and locomotives was effectively controlling engine output. For an internal combustion–electric engine to operate efficiently, output must match the load drawn by the traction motors—excess engine output wastes energy, and inadequate output can result in the locomotive stalling. In extreme situations, mismatched output and load can damage equipment and delay a train. Between 1916 and 1919, Hermann Lemp devised a control system for optimal performance by matching engine and traction characteristics and placing them under the direction of a single throttle handle. This pioneering work became the basis of most practical diesel locomotive control systems used by American manufacturers.

Commercial Diesel Development

In 1917, General Electric pioneered another technological development with the construction of an experimental diesel-electric locomotive based on its earlier gas-electric designs. The new locomotive used a GM50 engine, a V-8 designed by Chatain and similar to GE's gasoline engines. According to John Kirkland in *The Diesel Builders*, it employed concepts adopted from German Junkers engines designed for aircraft applications. It produced 225 horsepower, 50 more than GE's gasoline engine, and weighed almost 7 tons. GE built several diesel-electric locomotives based around this engine for commercial use in 1918. One was delivered to the Jay Street Connecting Railroad, where it

Continued on page 48

THE FIRST DIESEL By John Gruber

General Electric supplied the generator and electric parts for the first diesel-electric locomotive, built for Southern Pacific, in 1904 and 1905, while a GE founder provided the technical expertise for its development.

Dr. Rudolf Diesel, the engine's inventor, had been in the United States in May to promote a stationary engine displayed at the St. Louis World's Fair. St. Louis brewery magnate Augustus Busch, through the Diesel Motor Company of America and later the American Diesel Engine Company, controlled the U.S. patent rights for the engine Diesel had developed in Germany.

Word of the new locomotive appeared in *The New York Times* on October 2, 1904, as Busch returned from a five-month tour of Europe. Busch proclaimed that the oil-burning diesel engine was "the most economical stationary engine, in which capacity it is being used here as well as abroad in generating power for water works, electric lighting plants, and industries generally." He went on to reveal that the engine was presently "being applied to locomotives, a 200-ton internal-combustion locomotive having just been ordered by the Southern Pacific Railroad for a thorough trial."

After the *Manufacturers' Record* of Baltimore, Maryland, confirmed the details in its October 13, 1904, issue, newspapers around the country picked up the story. "New Locomotive Monster Coming," the *San Francisco Chronicle* headline said. "New Type of Locomotive To Do Wonders," added the *Chicago Tribune*.

The International Power Company, which had been making stationary diesel engines, coordinated the production of the new locomotive. Its president, Joseph H. Hoadley, applied for a patent for an "improved system of electric railways," using an internal-combustion engine and generator. Walter H. Knight, the General Electric founder and its first chief engineer, was chief engineer for International Power. The Corliss Works of Providence, Rhode Island, built the diesel engine, and American Locomotive Company of Schenectady, New York, built the trucks and frame.

Kyle Williams Wyatt, now a curator at the California State Railroad Museum in Sacramento, wrote about the SP diesel in *The Railway &*

Locomotive Historical Society Newsletter (Fall 1996), based on a two-page article in the *Marconigram* (December 1904). "The locomotive for which the Southern Pacific has contracted is of revolutionary design, and might be easily characterized as a powerhouse on wheels…. It uses no coal and therefore there are no ashes, sparks or cinders with the customary attendant nuisances," wrote J. Langford King in the New York City magazine. The *Marconigram*, *New York Press*, and *Chronicle* carried an identical illustration of the locomotive in November and December.

Wyatt also cited an item in the *Railway Master Mechanic* (April 1905): "The Southern Pacific company has been making a series of experiments with a motor car which is driven by electric motors at the axles, the current being furnished by dynamos, directly connected to large Diesel oil engines, located in the car."

John P. Hankey, a historian, provided an international context for the development in a talk at the Association of Railroad Museums in 2000. Even a century ago, American railroading was part of a global technological community. "The diesel-electric locomotive is based on a prime mover perfected by an eccentric German engineer (Rudolf Diesel), using the thermodynamic theory of a mid-nineteenth-century French mathematician (Sadi Canot)," Hankey stated. "The electrical gear was based on the dynamo invented by Thomas Edison, who relied on the work of an English physicist named James Clerk Maxwell.

"The control technology was made possible by a Serbian-born electrical engineer named Nicola Tesla, and it all basically started with an Italian named Alessandro Volta, who perfected the pile, or electric storage battery, about 1800. We won't even speak of steel technology perfected by the Germans, French, and English, or about petroleum refining, or the inventors of the machine tools used to make the locomotives."

Magazines, newspapers, and trade publications confirm the 1904 and 1905 dates. What happened during the tests is not known, but they must have been unsuccessful, since the locomotive dropped out of sight. Nevertheless, the story of its planning offers new insights into the development of diesel-electric locomotives in the United States.

Continued from page 46

was designated No. 4 and joined the earlier GE gas-electric, No. 3. Two others were built, one for the city of Baltimore and the other for the U.S. Army. None of the diesels performed well, and all had very brief careers. Shortly after they were built, GE decided to exit the business of designing and manufacturing internal-combustion engines.

For several years, General Electric's diesel-electric work lay mostly dormant. After World War I, the growth of highway-based transport started to seriously affect railroad revenue, as cars, buses, and trucks competed for railroad traffic. In the early 1920s, however, there was a resurgent demand for gas-electric railcars as North American railways sought measures to reduce the costs of operating lightly traveled branchline and rural passenger services. Although GE did

not redevelop its gas-electric railcar business, it became the dominant electrical supplier for the Electro-Motive Corporation, a new company led by Harold Hamilton that dominated the gas-electric railcar market in the 1920s. By mid-decade, General Electric had renewed its interest in diesel-electric technology. (In 1930, EMC was bought by General Motors and eventually developed into the foremost locomotive builder, Electro-Motive Division, or EMD.)

General Electric decided against further design of its own diesel engines and instead worked with established engine producer Ingersoll-Rand (IR). The two companies joined forces in 1923 and constructed an experimental diesel-electric locomotive using GE electrical and mechanical components and IR's successful 10x12-inch, six-cylinder diesel engine. This slow-speed engine operated at

550 rpm, about half the speed of today's 7FDL used in modern GEs, and generated just 300 horsepower. Designated No. 8835 (GE's construction number), this machine first moved under its own power at IR's Phillipsburg, Pennsylvania, plant on December 17, 1923. In June 1924, No. 8835 began a tour of eastern railways and was tested by 13 different companies, including Central Railroad of New Jersey.

Development of GE's diesel prototype coincided with the passing of New York City's Kaufman Act, legislation that expanded on earlier pollution laws and effectively banned the operation of steam locomotives within New York City by 1926. While most passenger operations had been electrified as a result of early laws, freight and switching operations in New York had remained steam powered. The worst offender was New York Central's heavily used West Side freight line in Manhattan. New York's other railroads were not afforded direct land access to the city and instead served New York via car float and barges that reached small isolated yards along the city's rivers and bays. It was not economical to electrify these small yards, and the diesel switcher allowed railroads to comply with the Kaufman Act without electrification. Amendments eventually postponed the Kaufman Act's strict 1926 deadline. Like the legislation that preceded it, however, the act forced railroads to seek alternative power, creating a market for GE's diesel-electric switchers.

The success of No. 8835 encouraged GE, Ingersoll-Rand, and the locomotive builder Alco to enter a business consortium to construct diesel-electric switching locomotives for commercial application. The arrangement was similar to the agreement that GE and Alco had enjoyed for two decades in the construction of straight electrics. Alco built mechanical components—frames, wheels, trucks, etc.; GE provided electrical components; and Ingersoll-Rand supplied the diesel engine and was also responsible for marketing. Between 1925 and 1928, the Alco-GE–Ingersoll-Rand consortium built 33 of the boxcab diesel-electrics, primarily for switching in eastern cities, especially New York City. Two models were offered: a 60-ton, 300-horsepower locomotive similar to demonstrator No. 8835, and a dual-engine, 100-ton locomotive that generated 600 horsepower.

In 1925, the Central Railroad of New Jersey took delivery of the first commercially built locomotive, one of the 300-horsepower boxcab variety that it designated No. 1000. This pioneering locomotive, today regarded as the first successful

During World War II and the immediate postwar dieselization, Alco and General Electric worked together in the production and marketing of diesel-electric locomotives. The new locomotives carried joint builders' plates. *Brian Solomon*

diesel-electric built in the United States, was assigned to CNJ's isolated waterfront terminal in The Bronx. Unlike GE's earlier diesels, No. 1000 enjoyed a long and productive career, running for more than 30 years in the service it was built for. It was retired in 1957 and sent to the Baltimore & Ohio Railroad Museum in Baltimore for public display.

New York Central had the largest and most extensive freight operation in New York City. Although the railroad undertook the elevation and electrification of its West Side line in the late 1920s, it was not practical to electrify all of its branches and spurs. Furthermore, some of its spurs operated directly into warehouses in Manhattan, where even

Among the types built jointly by Alco-GE were the RS-1 and RS-2/RS-3 road switchers. In this June 1961 photo made in Chicago, a Chicago & Western Indiana RS-1 leads a short passenger train, while Rock Island RS-3s (built in 1950 and 1951) idle between assignments. *Richard Jay Solomon*

General Electric's 44-ton model was specifically designed to weigh less than the 90,000 pounds maximum allowed for operations without a fireman under union work rules. The 44-tonner was popular with both shortlines and some Class I railroads for use on lightweight lines. On January 25, 1977, a pair of Aroostook Valley 44-tonners works at Washburn Junction, Maine. Locomotive No. 11 is a 380-horsepower model built in 1945, while No. 12 is a 400-horsepower model built in 1949. *Don Marson*

a diesel engine would produce unacceptable emissions. To solve Central's switching quandary, GE and Alco developed a tri-power locomotive that could operate as a straight third-rail electric, as a battery-powered electric, or as a battery-electric/diesel-electric drawing power from batteries while being charged by the onboard diesel engine. (The diesel engine would charge the batteries, but the third-rail connection could not.) After testing a center-cab tri-power prototype in February 1928, New York Central ordered a fleet of the locomotives using a more typical boxcab configuration. Most tri-power locomotives worked in the New York terminal area, although some were assigned to Chicago, Detroit, and Boston. Another locomotive, built to New York Central's specs, was delivered to the Rock Island for switching at LaSalle Street Station in Chicago. Alco left the consortium in 1928 to pursue its own diesel manufacturing business, while GE and Ingersoll-Rand continued to manufacture diesels together until the mid-1930s.

In 1934, the Electro-Motive Corporation—by this time owned by General Motors—stunned the railroad world with flashy, high-speed diesel streamlined trains. Sleek streamliners were an outgrowth of EMC's railcar business, which combined new automotive manufacturing techniques with recently developed compact, high-horsepower diesel engines.

General Electric had provided EMC with electrical gear during that company's formative years as a diesel-electric producer. Although diesel-electric streamliners captured the public spotlight during the mid-1930s, the largest segment of the diesel locomotive market was actually for new switchers. General Electric continued to focus its own diesel production on freight diesels and left the production and design of streamlined trains to other manufacturers. GE employed a variety of different diesel engines, including those manufactured by Busch-Sulzer, Caterpillar, Cooper-Bessemer, and Cummins. Its locomotives varied from relatively small switchers to the largest and most powerful diesel-electrics constructed up to that time.

In 1936, GE built two heavy six-motor diesels for Illinois Central, powerful machines designed for slow-speed transfer service in the Chicago area. Illinois Central No. 9200 was an 1,800-horsepower machine powered by a pair of Ingersoll-Rand six-cylinder engines, while IC No. 9201 was rated at 2,000 horsepower and powered by a 10-cylinder Busch-Sulzer diesel. According to Louis Marre in *Diesel Locomotives: The First 50 Years*, the latter locomotive was the most powerful single-engine diesel in the United States until the Alco-GE PA passenger locomotive was introduced a decade later.

The Alco–GE PA passenger locomotive owes its distinctive and attractive design to GE design engineer Raymond E. Patten. An Erie Railroad PA is seen with a suburban train at Lackawanna's Hoboken, New Jersey, terminal. Erie moved into Lackawanna's terminal in the late 1950s, prior to the official merger between the two railroads. Lackawanna's suburban passenger services were electrified by General Electric in the late 1920s and early 1930s using a 3,000-volt DC overhead system. Lackawanna's multiple units, such as those seen here, were known as "Edison Electrics." *Richard Jay Solomon*

Alco-GE

In the mid- to late 1930s, the locomotive industry was in flux. Some railroads remained firmly committed to traditional steam power, others considered large-scale electrification, and still others watched the development of new and more powerful diesel-electrics with close interest. (During this time, the Pennsylvania Railroad was enjoying the benefits of having electrified its New York–Washington lines.) The development of new steam types and unusual motive power, such as GE's steam turbine–electric, made uncertain the future of railroad locomotion. General Electric, however, was in a pretty comfortable position in the railroad industry, as the primary supplier of electric traction systems and electric locomotives, and as an established builder of diesel-electric switchers.

By the late 1930s, Electro-Motive had emerged as the leading producer of diesel-electric locomotives. EMC had introduced its E-unit line of passenger locomotives and developed its new and more reliable 567 series two-cycle diesel to replace the troubled Winton 201A engine used in its earliest locomotives. In 1938, EMC began manufacturing its own electrical components, basing its designs largely on GE's. As a result, GE no longer had EMC as a customer. Then in 1939, EMC debuted its four-unit FT road freight diesel, a machine that would convince many railroads that full-scale dieselization was both practical and affordable. While steam manufacturers believed they could hold on to a portion of the market for a few more years, many in the industry realized that the total dieselization of American railroads would soon be under way.

General Electric's 70-ton locomotives were designed to provide a reasonably powerful machine capable of relatively high track speeds on lightly built tracks. An eastbound Claremont & Concord freight rolls along the Sugar River behind GE 70-tonner No. 12 near Newport, New Hampshire, on October 28, 1957. *Jim Shaughnessy*

In 1940, Alco and GE combined forces to counter the diesel-producing power of EMC, soon to be reorganized as EMD, the Electro-Motive Division of General Motors. The two companies entered an agreement for the production and marketing of diesel-electric locomotives and worked together in the design of locomotives. Both manufacturers were listed on builders' plates, promotional literature, and advertising. Although General Electric's most notable contributions remained locomotive electrical systems, it also contributed to the industrial design of some postwar locomotives. (See the sidebar "GE Industrial Design" by John Gruber.)

In the 1930s, Alco had developed a successful line of heavy switchers powered by McIntosh & Seymore 531 series diesels. Alco expanded upon this engine design and by 1940 had upgraded to its 539 engine line, which was used to power its 600- and 1,000-horsepower S-model switchers. Both models used a six-cylinder diesel, but the 1,000-horsepower units used a turbocharged variety to obtain the higher horsepower rating. These switchers, like Alco's earlier models, used an end-cab design.

In 1941, at the request of the Rock Island, Alco expanded its switcher line to include a road-switcher type, the

first of its kind. Rock Island had desired a branchline loco-motive capable of a variety of tasks with the intent of reduc-ing branchline expenses by eliminating steam locomotives. Alco's RS-1 (a designation assigned to the type many years after the first locomotive was actually built) was basically a 1,000-horsepower switcher on a longer frame that allowed for a short hood that could house a boiler for steam heat. Many authorities concur that the RS-1 was the first true diesel-electric road switcher, a locomotive type that became predominant from the late 1950s onward. The RS-1 was de-veloped immediately prior to the United States' involvement in World War II, and the U.S. Army found the new loco-motive especially well suited to military applications. Consequently, it ordered several for work overseas. Many of these locomotives used six-axle trucks rather than the

four-axle trucks applied to civilian locomotives. Alco also built an export model of the RS-1 that used A1A trucks to reduce axle loadings and allow the type to work on lightly built track.

Beginning in 1940, Alco offered a streamlined road diesel designed for either high-speed passenger service or road freight work. These locomotives were known by their specification numbers, DL-103 to DL-110, and featured dis-tinctive styling by noted industrial designer Otto Kuhler. A pair of turbocharged 538 or 539 series diesels powered them, and most were used exclusively in passenger service. The largest fleet comprised 60 DL-109s built for New Haven.

The advent of World War II had profound implications for the development and production of diesel-electric loco-motives. In April 1942, the War Production Board (WPB),

A U.S. Navy Public Works GE center-cab switcher works a Chesapeake & Ohio car float ferry at the Norfolk, Virginia, Naval Base in 1963. General Electric built more than 1,100 switchers for use by the U.S. military and for dock companies. *William D. Middleton*

GE INDUSTRIAL DESIGN By John Gruber

Raymond E. Patten (1897–1948) helped shape the distinctive appearance of Alco and General Electric locomotives. Among his best-known railroad designs were the Alco-GE PA (passenger) and FA (freight) diesel locomotives in 1946. Patten, director of GE's Appearance Design Division of the Appliance and Merchandising Department in Bridgeport, Connecticut, also influenced the designs of electric and industrial locomotives and the ill-fated Union Pacific steam turbine–electric.

Design patents applied for in 1946 and granted in 1949 confirm Patten's role in the PA/FA models. From 1940 to 1953, Alco and GE jointly marketed large road locomotives and distributed a six-page article that Patten prepared. The goal, he said, was "A locomotive so distinctive and so powerful looking that it actually helps the railroads sell their services to passengers and shippers."

From rough pencil sketches of the exterior, executives selected the basic design. The fluted headlight, "devised to obtain product identity and serve as a focal point," had to be changed to meet Interstate Commerce Commission (ICC) regulations. The modifications throughout the design process are reflected in the advertising. Melbourne Brindle's painting for the August 1946 GE calendar and other early illustrations, for example, show the headlight grille before it was moved higher on the nose. *TRAINS Magazine in* September 1946 also featured an early version of the PA.

Patten attended Massachusetts Institute of Technology, started his career with the Hume Body Corporation of Boston, and continued custom body designs with the Dayton Wright Company. He spent five years with the Packard Motor Car Commune of Detroit and joined the Edison GE Company in Chicago in 1928. When he moved to Bridgeport in 1934, he was the only person in the appliance design department. Under his leadership, the department grew to 50 by 1946, broadening its tasks to include packaging and the design of dealer stores.

Patten won a $1,000 award in 1940 for "an electric range as sightly as a grand piano," according to an announcement in *The New York Times*. In the same competition, Henry Dreyfuss, who streamlined the *20th Century Limited*, received an award for "a washing machine elegant enough for a drawing room." Patten's contacts with the GE builders were mostly through the mail and purchase orders. He made airbrush renderings of locomotives for presentation to railroad customers; using engineering drawings, he made preliminary sketches and final renderings. Patten also made styling contributions to GE diesel-electric industrial switchers (a 1937 80-ton model for Ford Motor Company, with a streamlined cab and chrome auto grilles; a 1939 60-ton for Mexico; and the 1940 65-ton standard model). His styling also appeared on the steam turbine–electric locomotive of 1939, and the so-called "Little Joe" electrics.

Arthur BecVar, who started in the Appearance Design Division in 1946, explained that Patten personally reviewed the work: "I was assigned to small appliances. Carl 'Fred' Schaus handled locomotives for Ray, then Bill Saenger took that assignment. I traveled to Erie with Saenger with models for 'workhorse' locomotives. The models for the streamlined locomotives went to Schenectady. If departments were outside Bridgeport, we would go there to meet with the engineering and marketing people."

BecVar became head of appearance design in 1948 after Patten's death. When GE built a separate manufacturing facility for major appliances in Louisville in 1951, BecVar and Saenger moved there. BecVar spent 33 years with GE before retiring.

Schaus, who was in the industrial products division in Schenectady, was primarily responsible for designing turbines, large motors and generators, switchgear, meters, and transformers. As a part-time consultant from 1950 to 1956, he conceived the contours and appearance of locomotives, as well as paint schemes. He traveled to Erie to get to know engineering managers and to see designs developed and built in the shop.

Schaus' designs included: GE diesel-electric locomotives of 1950 (1,500 horsepower for export with Alco engines and trucks); 1954 (a UD18 demonstrator for Mexico; the U9, U12, and U18 for export; and Erie demonstrator set No. 750); 1955 (XP24, 751 and 752, and U25B prototypes); and 1956 (U25B demonstrator with high nose); plus GE gas turbine–electrics for Union Pacific in 1948; the 4,500-horsepower experimental demonstrator 101 (UP 50); production turbines of 1952 and 1954; and the 8,500-horsepower turbines of 1958.

When Erie asked for more work than he had time for, Schaus suggested that it hire its own full-time industrial designer. James R. Chapin, the only industrial designer on the staff of locomotive engineering and marketing from 1956 to 1992, did all the appearance and ergonomic design for locomotives and multiple-unit commuter transit cars. John Gould prepared presentation paintings for railroad customers, and consultants did the renderings for transit car proposals.

Chapin's GE diesel road locomotives included: the 1961 U25B demonstrator paint scheme; the 1962 U25B and U25C low-nose cab design; the 1963 U50 cab for Union Pacific; the 1965 U50 C-C cab for Union Pacific; the 1967 U30CG passenger unit cab for Santa Fe; the 1978 BQ23-7 for Family Lines' first full-crew operator's cab; the 1980 C36-7 operator's cab; the 1982 C36-7 for China paint scheme; the 1983 C36-8 testbed; the 1986 DASH 8-40CM for Canadian National cab design and desktop operator consoles; the 1987 DASH 8-40CW North American Safety Cab; and the 1990 DASH 8-32BWH "Pepsi Can" for Amtrak.

Chapin's GE electric locomotives included: 1962's 4,200-horsepower units for Paulista Railway; the 1972 E60CP for Amtrak; the 1973 E-42C cab and paint scheme for Taiwan; the 1974 E60C cab and paint scheme for Mexico; and the 1975 E60C-2 cab and paint scheme for Deseret-Western. His GE industrial diesel-electric switchers were the 1974 standard switchers.

When Chapin retired in 1992, GE did not hire a replacement and has made made no substantial changes in the appearance of its road freight locomotives.

set up to oversee the allocation of strategic industrial materials for the war effort, took control of American locomotive production, limiting locomotive construction and reallocating some locomotive facilities and materials for military purposes. The War Production Board included representatives from various locomotive builders and significant parts suppliers to assist in the board's recommendations. The WPB divvied up locomotive production by type, in an effort to standardize procurement and, more importantly, to minimize problems with the production and supply of replacement parts.

The WPB directed the big steam builders—Alco, Baldwin, and Lima—to construct steam locomotives using established, tested designs, and the board greatly restricted the number of new designs. However, it also encouraged railroads to purchase steam locomotives, and severely curtailed diesel production in order to conserve crucial materials needed for military purposes. One valued commodity was copper, which is a primary component in electrical systems and traction motors. Since EMD had developed the most practical road freight locomotive, it was limited to the production of FTs. Baldwin and Alco were directed to build diesel-powered yard switchers and were largely restricted from selling road diesel models, although Alco was also allowed to produce some RS-1s and a few DL109s. Despite production limitations, there were no explicit restrictions on research and development, with the caveat that builders were not permitted to implement significant design changes on production models until the war's end.

After WPB restrictions were lifted, diesel builders scrambled to introduce new road models for North American railroads, as orders for steam locomotives dropped off sharply. EMD's line was at the forefront of the industry, followed by Alco-GE's. Both Baldwin and Fairbanks-Morse captured smaller amounts of the business. Alco-GE introduced several new models that used Alco's 244 engine, a design developed during the war. Like earlier Alco engines, the 244 was a four-cycle design. (The four cycles are: *intake*, the first downward piston stroke, in which air is forced into the cylinder; *compression*, the first upward stroke, in which air is compressed, greatly increasing the temperature; *power*, as the compression stroke nears completion, fuel is injected into the cylinder, igniting and forcing the piston downward; and *exhaust*, the second upward stroke in which burned gases are expelled from the cylinder.) The 244 engine used GE's RD1 turbocharger originally developed during the war for aircraft applications. In its original configuration, the 12-cylinder 244 engine idled at 350 rpm and worked at full speed at 1,000 rpm to produce 1,500 horsepower. It was used to power Alco-GE carbody road freight locomotives (types later assigned FA-1/FB-1 model designations; the latter a cabless booster) and RS-2 road switchers, models introduced to compete with EMD's F-units. John Kirkland indicates that the early FA models (specification numbers DL208 and DL209) used GE's GT564B traction generator and were equipped with either GE 726 or GE 731 traction motors. Using a standard 74:18 gear ratio, they were designed for 65 miles per hour maximum speed and would deliver 34,000 pounds continuous tractive effort at 13.5 miles per hour. These locomotives employed belt-driven auxiliary equipment. More advanced FA/FBs, (beginning with specification numbers DL208A and DL209B) and RS-2s (beginning with specification E1661A) were built starting in 1947. These later locomotives dispensed with belt-driven auxiliaries and employed more reliable motor-driven equipment. The traction generator type was upgraded to GE's GT564C model, and the GE 752 traction motor was introduced. This successful traction motor design has been a fundamental component used by thousands of GE locomotives since. Using the improved traction system greatly boosted tractive effort: FA/FBs with GE 752 motors delivered 42,550 pounds of continuous tractive effort at 11 miles per hour. In early 1950, Alco boosted the output of its 12-cylinder 244 engine to 1,600 horsepower, corresponding to like increases in power from Baldwin and Fairbanks-Morse. Later FA/FBs and RS-2s thus featured the higher rating. In mid-1950, Alco changed the model designation of its 1,600-horsepower road-switcher type from RS-2 to RS-3. Despite the change, the locomotives were virtually the same. Alco-GE's RS-3 operator's manual from September 1951 lists locomotive specifications:

Maximum height: 14 feet, 5-1/8 inches
Maximum width: 10 feet, 1-5/8 inches
Length (inside knuckles): 55 feet, 11-3/4 inches
Weight on drivers: 240,000 pounds

Alco's RS-2 and RS-3 road switchers were versatile machines designed to work singly or in multiple in freight, passenger, and switching service. They featured a semi-streamlined hood-unit configuration that was one of the more attractive road-switcher designs. Several railroads favored RS-2/RS-3s for suburban passenger operations, because they accelerated quickly and could maintain schedules better than other types. The Boston & Maine, New York Central, New Haven, Long Island, Pennsylvania, Reading, Erie, Central Railroad of New Jersey, and Rock Island all employed suburban service RS-2/RS-3 fleets.

In summer 1946, Alco-GE introduced a new high-horsepower, handsomely streamlined passenger locomotive that we today know as the Alco PA. Initially, Alco-GE did not use the PA/PB designations, instead describing these locomotives by their specification numbers. (The designation PA stands for Passenger, A-unit; the PB designation was used to describe the cabless booster.) The PA/PB was a full-carbody locomotive type that shared basic design elements with the Alco's FA freight diesel and embodied a well-balanced look. It featured a 6-foot-long "nose" section and used three-axle, four-motor trucks in an A1A configuration. (The center axle was unpowered for weight distribution.) John Kirkland indicates the PA measured 65 feet, 8 inches long over the couplers, while period sources give a slightly longer measurement of 66 feet, 2 inches.

Many observers have deemed Alco's PA as one of the finest-looking passenger locomotives of all time. Initially, the type was powered by a 16-cylinder 244 diesel using GE's RD2 turbocharger, which produced 2,000 horsepower. (Alco's primary competition was EMD's E-unit, which used a pair of 567 diesels instead of a single engine.) According to John Kirkland, the early PAs employed GE 746A2 traction motors and the GT566C1 traction generator. During the course of PA production, which ran from 1946 to 1953, Alco-GE introduced several improvements, including the GE 752 traction motor and a 250-horsepower increase per unit, giving the later PAs (often designated PA-2) a 2,250-horsepower rating. A total of 297 PAs were built for 16 different American railways. Among the type's best-known buyers were the Santa Fe, Southern Pacific, New York Central, Pennsylvania Railroad, New Haven, Lehigh Valley, and Erie.

During the massive postwar dieselization of American railroads, Alco-GE consistently held the position of number two diesel builder, with EMD remaining as the clear industry leader. However, according to Albert Churella in his book, *From Steam to Diesel*, Alco-GE commanded roughly 40 percent of the diesel-electric market in 1946, but slipped to only 15 percent by 1953. Churella illustrates a number of causes for this dramatic loss of business, some of which were a result of Alco's steam-era business practices. There were also issues of locomotive reliability. Although Alco-GE locomotives enjoyed favorable performance characteristics, offering higher horsepower per unit and greater tractive effort than comparable EMD products, many railroads found that Alco diesels required more maintenance than EMD products. A number of flaws were attributed to the 244 engine design, which was phased out in the mid-1950s when Alco introduced its more reliable 251 diesel engine. There were also difficulties with GE's Amplidyne electrical system. While Amplidyne control was intended to give a locomotive engineer more precise tractive control, it was more complex to operate than other "hands-off" electrical systems.

In 1953, GE terminated its joint production agreement with Alco, although the company continued to supply Alco with electrical gear for its diesel-electric locomotives. General Electric also continued to provide electrical gear for other builders, such as Fairbanks-Morse. Interestingly, while the Alco-GE arrangement was at its peak in the immediate postwar period, GE also built Fairbanks-Morse road diesels under contract at its Erie, Pennsylvania, plant. These large carbody locomotives were often known as Fairbanks-Morse *Erie-Builts*, to distinguish them from later locomotives built by Fairbanks-Morse at its Beloit, Wisconsin, factory. The Erie-Builts shared several common characteristics with the Alco-GE PA, which was designed about the same time.

GE Switchers

General Electric's original diesel locomotive market was for lightweight, low-output switcher types, and despite its agreement with Alco in the production of road locomotives, GE continued to produce its own line of switchers. In 1940, GE introduced new standard switcher models. The two most popular types used by domestic railroads were the 44-ton center-cab model and the 70-ton end-cab model. The 44-ton model was designed to comply with late 1930s legislation that permitted single-man operation

of locomotives weighing less than 90,000 pounds (45 U.S. tons). Heavier locomotives required both an engineer and fireman. Although several manufacturers built small center-cab switchers, GE's were the most common. Since the 44-ton label was a model designation, actual weight and output varied somewhat depending on individual locomotive configuration. The typical 44-tonner was powered by a pair of Caterpillar D17000 diesel engines, one at each end of the locomotive. These engines were rated between 180 and 200 horsepower each, providing between 360 and 400 total horsepower. The compact four-cycle V-8 design had a 5-3/4x8-inch bore and stroke and worked at maximum 1,000 rpm. A few 44-tonners used other engine types. A number of American Class I railroads, including the Boston & Maine, Pennsylvania Railroad, Santa Fe, and Burlington, employed 44-tonners in switching service, especially on light branchlines and industrial trackage, where heavier locomotives would damage track and

bridges. Shortline railroads embraced the type, using them to replace steam locomotives.

Numerous electric interurban railways had operated freight service over portions of their passenger lines, although by the 1940s many had dropped unprofitable passenger service and retained their freight operations. The 44-ton diesel-electric was an economical motive power solution for these lines. Many industrial lines and private companies also had GE center-cab switchers, including the 44-ton model. More than 350 44-tonners were built between 1940 and 1956.

The 70-tonner was designed for branchline work and allowed for relatively fast operation on very light track. Like the 44-tonner, it was acquired by both Class I and shortline railroads, where it was used to replace lightweight steam locomotives. Often 70-tonners were used where heavier diesels were banned because of weight restrictions. The 70-tonner was powered by a single six-cylinder Cooper-Bessemer

Allegheny Ludlum Steel Company's 65-ton GE switcher No. 18 makes a transfer run between its Natrona and Brackenridge, Pennsylvania, plants on May 13, 1988. Allegheny Ludlum hosts a fleet of radio-controlled GE center-cab locomotives. By the early 1980s, General Electric had built more than 5,700 diesel-electric switchers for use by railways and industrial customers in North America and around the world.
Patrick Yough

55

One of several 50-ton, 36-inch narrow gauge center-cab switchers works Bethlehem Steel's Bar, Rod and Wire Works at Johnstown, Pennsylvania. After Bethlehem Steel closed the Johnstown works, the narrow gauge locomotives were moved to Conrail's Juanita Locomotive Shop in Altoona, Pennsylvania, where they were to be rebuilt and shipped to South America. *Patrick Yough*

FWL6T diesel—the engine later developed by GE into the 7FDL-16—the prime mover used in most of its modern diesels. General Electric introduced its 70-tonner in 1946, and built more than 130 of them for the North American market over the next dozen years.

GE also built a great variety of switchers for industrial and military applications, as well as export. These ranged from small 25-ton units to locomotives weighing 110 tons or more. They were built to suit lines with a variety of different track gauges, and included a narrow gauge model for both industrial and shortline use. Although often eclipsed by GE's large, powerful, and high-profile locomotives, switchers were an important part of GE's locomotive business for many years. By the 1970s it had built more than 5,000 of them for service in

dozens of countries around the world. In 1944 and 1945, GE built 30 45-ton center-cab switchers for service in India. Similar to domestic types, these locomotives were 33 feet, 11 inches long and were powered by a pair of 190-horsepower Caterpillar diesels. They used four GE733 traction motors and a GT555 traction generator, and delivered 23,500 pounds starting tractive effort.

As most railways completed dieselization in the 1950s, the need for new switching locomotives dropped off. Switchers tend to have very long life spans, as evidenced by some of the earliest diesels that could still be found working more than 40 years after they were built. Also, the need for specialized lightweight engines declined as large railroads either abandoned branchlines or improved weight limits to

allow for the operation of heavier locomotives. The gradual shift from traditional carload traffic to intermodal operations, and the disappearance of traditional heavy industries such as steelworks, has also reduced the need for switchers.

In 1974, GE introduced a new line of industrial center-cab switchers. It offered three basic models for the domestic market: the SL80, SL110, and SL144—designations that roughly indicate the maximum weight in U.S. tons of each type. These locomotives have a more angular and utilitarian appearance than similar models from the 1940s and 1950s. Based on production figures published in *The Contemporary Diesel Spotter's Guide*, the combined domestic production for the three models over a 12-year period was just over 50 locomotives. In addition to its basic offering, GE built a variety of modern specialized switchers that varied in weight and

output to meet individual customer requirements. A pair of Cummins diesel engines powered nearly all of GE's late-era switching locomotives.

According to GE's specifications, the SL144 measures 45 feet long; 13 feet, 3 inches tall; and 9 feet, 6 inches wide, making it shorter, lower, and narrower than any modern American road locomotive. The locomotive can weigh between 230,000 and 288,000 pounds (115 to 144 U.S. tons) depending on the customer's needs. At the minimum weight, the locomotive will produce 69,000 pounds starting tractive effort. Most of the 1974 line switchers were purchased by industrial railways and have only made rare appearances on larger lines. GE has built very few switchers in recent years, and instead has focused locomotive production on its successful road locomotive line.

In modern times, General Electric has offered several center-cab models for industrial switching. The SL80, SL110, and SL140 models began production in the mid-1970s. This switcher is operated by GE's own East Erie Commercial Railroad. *Author collection, photographer unknown*

TURBINES

CHAPTER 3

Steam Turbine–Electric

The sudden and spectacular emergence of diesel-powered, high-speed streamlined passenger trains in the mid-1930s captured the collective imagination of American railroads. The novelty of new power sources and streamlining were the modes of the period, and they resulted in reactionary technological development as well as refinement in diesel-electric technology. General Motors' Electro-Motive Corporation was the driving force behind the development of internal combustion streamliners. In the spirit of these fast new trains, starting in 1936, General Electric worked with Union Pacific in the design and development of a "steam-electric locomotive," an oil-fired steam turbine–electric. General Electric planned to meld established stationary and marine steam turbine technology with electric locomotive designs to produce a new type of locomotive. Early GE specifications called for a streamlined turbine-electric locomotive with a net input of 2,500 horsepower "to the electric transmission for traction," and the ability to produce 81,000 pounds starting tractive effort. In GE lexicon, each unit was designated a 2-C-C-2–318/506–6GE725. The first part of the designation indicated the wheel arrangement (two guiding axles, two sets of three powered axles, and two trailing axles), while the last part reflected the traction motor arrangement of six GE 725 motors.

Opposite: General Electric's first gas turbine locomotive was a 4,500-horsepower double-cab unit numbered Union Pacific 50. It is portrayed here with a train of Pacific Fruit Express refrigerator cars at Sloan, Nevada, on Union Pacific's Los Angeles–Salt Lake route. Later gas turbines built for UP only had cabs at one end. *Union Pacific photo, John Gruber collection*

Initially, GE hoped to deliver the prototype steam-electric locomotive in 1937, but the machines were not ready for testing by Union Pacific until spring 1939. At that time the steam-electric locomotive attracted considerable attention in the trade press. Some viewed it as a potential successor to conventional reciprocating steam locomotive technology, as well as a challenge to the new diesel-electrics and an alternative to electrification. In the February 1939 issue of *General Electric Review*, the turbine was touted as having twice the thermal efficiency of a conventional steam locomotive and capable of operating at 125 miles per hour.

Two streamlined 2,500-horsepower units were built and designed to operate "elephant style," as opposed to back to back. Each machine weighed 548,000 pounds fully loaded, with 354,000 pounds on driving wheels, resulting in a 59,000-pound maximum axle load and allowing each unit to produce 86,500 pounds starting tractive effort, slightly more than originally specified. Continuous tractive effort had two ratings, depending on the amount of air supplied to cool traction motors: 32,000 pounds tractive effort with normal cooling or 40,500 pounds with greater cooling.

The locomotive used a 65:31 gear ratio to power 44-inch-diameter driving wheels. Guide and trailing wheels were just 36 inches in diameter.

The two locomotives featured styled and streamlined carbodies that shared a resemblance to EMC's Union Pacific streamliners of the period. The body was a lightweight truss type that used welded low-carbon, high-tensile steel frame supports and was covered with riveted sheet metal. Most of the skin and secondary supports were made from aluminum, except those used on the nose section, which were made of steel. An elevated cab was employed, similar to that used in EMC's M-10003 to M-10006 articulated *City* streamliners, and subsequently by E-unit passenger locomotives. This height afforded the operating crew a good forward view, while the substantial 9-foot nose section, which was significantly longer than that used by General Motors products, afforded protection in the event of a collision. Both sides of the nose also featured prominently placed General Electric builder's plates. Each unit measured 90 feet, 10 inches long and 15 feet, 3/4 inch tall, and was 10 feet wide at the cab.

A pair of General Electric steam turbine–electrics, Union Pacific Nos. 1 and 2, make their first run westward on UP's Lane Cutoff, west of Omaha, Nebraska, in April 1939. *Union Pacific photo, John Gruber collection*

The design of the steam turbine was largely based on contemporary powerplant technology of the time. Each unit employed a Babcock & Wilcox water-tube boiler that was fired and regulated automatically by specialized equipment built by the Bailey Meter Company. The boiler operated at 1,500 psi and 920 degrees Fahrenheit. By comparison, a late-era "superpower" steam locomotive, such as Union Pacific's own 800 series 4-8-4s, used a fire-tube boiler and had an operating pressure of just 300 psi. By removing impurities from the water and keeping it in a closed circuit, scale buildup was greatly reduced and the amount of water needed to operate the locomotive was kept at a minimum. Despite the closed circuit, there was some water loss during the heating cycle, and replenishment water was stored in tanks located in the locomotive nose section. Enough fuel oil was stored in tanks at the back of the locomotive to operate 500 to 700 miles between refueling.

Normally, the turbines worked at 12,500 rpm and turned a generator set using 10:1 reduction gearing. The generator set consisted of a self-ventilated, twin-armature DC generator to provide electricity for the traction motors;

a 220-volt, three-phase AC generator provided power for auxiliaries such as traction motor blowers and head-end power. (See discussion below.) The locomotives were equipped with dynamic braking, which used traction motors as generators. Today, dynamic brakes are standard on most diesel electric locomotives, but at the time of the steam turbine, the concept was unusual. Unlike modern diesel-locomotives, which expend all of the energy generated by dynamic braking, steam turbine locomotives directed water through resistor grids that allowed the locomotive to recoup some of the energy generated during periods of heavy braking.

The head-end power generator was also decades ahead of its time. Head-end electrical power is used to provide electricity to passenger cars for heat, light, and air conditioning. Most American passenger equipment continued to use conventional steam heat through the 1970s, and as a result many passenger diesels were equipped with steam generators. Only with the coming of Amtrak was steam heat finally dispensed with in favor of head-end power, which is now standard.

Union Pacific paraded the new GE steam turbines around the United States with a vintage 4-4-0 American-type steam locomotive to promote Paramount's 1939 film *Union Pacific*, which told the story of the building of the first transcontinental railroad. The film premiered at Omaha on the eve of the 70th anniversary of the Golden Spike Ceremony that joined the Union Pacific and the Central Pacific at Promontory, Utah, on May 10, 1869. *Union Pacific photo, John Gruber collection*

Officials pose with General Electric's steam turbine–electric at Erie, Pennsylvania, on October 24, 1938. When this machine was built, GE had great hopes for it; the steam turbine–electric was heralded as the successor to the traditional steam locomotive and a competitor of the diesel. *Union Pacific photo, John Gruber collection*

The steam-electric locomotives were delivered to Union Pacific in time for celebrations commemorating the seventieth anniversary of the completion of the first transcontinental railroad, which had occurred in May 1869. Union Pacific employed the locomotives on special trains that toured the railroad, giving the public a glimpse of them while providing railroad officials with a chance to see how they performed in service. In addition to service on the UP, the locomotives also made a tour of East Coast cities, traveling over the New York Central, New Haven, and Pennsylvania lines with a special UP train. The turbines featured excellent acceleration and maintained schedules faster than conventional steam-powered trains, but exhibited a variety of small failures. Most of these shortcomings were quickly corrected, but they discouraged Union Pacific officials, who became impatient with the turbines' failings.

Union Pacific considered using the turbines on a premier transcontinental passenger run but questioned their reliability. After just a couple of months of road testing in both passenger and perishable freight service, Union Pacific returned the locomotives to GE in June 1939, in the words of UP president W. M. Jeffers, "for necessary modification and/or reconstruction." Union Pacific remained interested in the steam-electrics for another two years, and Jeffers wrote that he believed the basic design principles were valid and the locomotives could be made to operate sufficiently reliably for UP's intended service. However, in December 1941, UP terminated its arrangement with GE. Among the reasons

cited for the change of position on the steam-electrics were what Jeffers described as "developments in other types of motive power." Specifically, Jeffers was referring to Union Pacific's 4-8-8-4 "Big Boy" type of steam locomotive, Electro-Motive's improved E-units, and the recently debuted FT freight diesels. Another factor in Union Pacific's waning interest in the steam-electrics may have been a regime change in the railroad's motive power department in the spring of 1939.

Despite Union Pacific's dissatisfaction with the steam-electrics, GE continued to work on them. In 1941, the locomotives operated in test service on the New York Central, primarily on its Water Level Route in New York State. Then in 1943, during the World War II power crunch, Great Northern operated the steam-electrics in heavy freight service between Spokane and Wenatchee, Washington. An article by Thomas R. Lee in Volume 10, Number 2, of *The Streamliner* indicates that by this time the turbines had been renumbered GE-1 and GE-2 and painted in a grayish black livery. Several sources, including *The Streamliner*, indicate the turbines provided good service on the GN. Steam locomotive historian Alfred W. Bruce concludes in his book *The Steam Locomotive in America* that GE's steam-electric was "one of the most exceptional steam locomotives ever built, and should be recognized as a pioneer because of its conception, design, and construction." Although GE shelved its steam turbine–electric some 60 years ago, the basic premise for this type of locomotive may someday be revived. Steam turbine technology has matured since the 1940s, and modern microprocessor technologies allow for a high level of precision control.

Gas Turbines

In the postwar environment, General Electric began development of a gas turbine locomotive type which, like the steam turbine, also attracted Union Pacific's interest. In 1948, GE built experimental double-ended gas turbine–electric No. 101, which became the prototype for one of the world's most unusual locomotive fleets. General Electric was neither the first to experiment with gas turbines nor the first to build a gas turbine locomotive, but it was the only company to build a fleet of them for heavy North American freight service. For decades, gas turbines had been built for use as stationary power plants. In *Modern Railway Locomotives*, P. Ransome-Wallis explains that since the 1920s various European locomotive builders had experimented with gas turbine locomotives. A successful machine was demonstrated in 1943, when Swiss manufacturer Brown Boveri unveiled a gas turbine with a 1-D-1 arrangement for Swiss Federal Railways.

Above: Union Pacific's 4,500-horsepower gas turbine locomotive No. 54 is seen in the shop, when the locomotive was brand-new. The equipment in front of the locomotive is a turbine power unit, presumably for No. 54. *Union Pacific photo, John Gruber collection*

Left: Union Pacific's first 10 production turbines were very similar to the prototype (GE 101, later Union Pacific No. 50), except they featured cabs only at one end. These machines were delivered in 1952 and numbered from 51 to 60. Turbine No. 60 is seen with a fuel tender and two Union Pacific EMD-built GP9s leading a westbound freight at sunset. *Otto Perry, Denver Public Library Western History Department*

By the late 1940s, the clear superiority of diesel-electric locomotives had sealed the fate of steam on most American railways, and Union Pacific was still looking for greater single-unit power than contemporary diesels could deliver. By virtue of its double-track route and relatively easy crossing of the Continental Divide, UP's mainline was, and is, one of America's primary east-west freight corridors. Across the Nebraska cornfields and the plains of Wyoming, Union Pacific freights can roll along largely unhindered for hundreds of miles. Even UP's grades in Wyoming and Utah are relatively mild in comparison to other transcontinental routes. It was in this wide-open territory that the gas turbine locomotive offered an advantage over diesel-electric operation. For two years Union Pacific tested the prototype, which was repainted for Union Pacific and designated UP No. 50. The railroad operated it for an estimated 106,000 miles in heavy service while General Electric worked out technical bugs and design hiccups. The locomotive's boxy-streamlined carbody design resembled those of Alco-GE cab diesels and GE's straight electric locomotives. It was 83 feet, 7-1/2 inches long; slightly more than 15 feet, 4 inches tall; 10 feet, 7 inches wide; and weighed an estimated 500,000 pounds. The locomotive used a B-B+B-B wheel arrangement, and its basic 4,500-horsepower rating (see below) was more than twice that available from single-unit diesel-electrics of the period. It delivered 77,800 pounds continuous tractive effort at 18.2 miles per hour.

The locomotive was powered by a GE gas turbine derived from contemporary aircraft engine design. It also employed a 15-stage axial flow compressor that directed airflow in a linear fashion along the shaft to compress filtered intake air to six atmospheres and then into six combustion chambers. The chambers were arranged radially around a central axis that contained the turbine shaft. Within the combustion chambers, compressed air was blended with fuel to burn at 1,400 degrees Fahrenheit (760 degrees Celsius), and the resulting gas was then directed through a two-stage (two sets of blades) turbine. Exhaust gases exited the turbine through roof vents at 850 degrees Fahrenheit at a speed of 150 miles per hour when operating under full load.

The output shaft was directly connected to the axial flow compressor and turbine, which turned four GE-576 electrical generators through a system of speed reduction gearing with a 65:18 gear ratio, allowing for 69 miles per

Top: A pair of 1952-built gas turbines brackets a fuel tender on a long westbound freight. These two turbines had a combined output of 9,000 horsepower; Union Pacific put them to work moving heavy freight over long distances at high speeds. Contemporary reports indicated the turbines could accelerate faster than diesel-electrics. Turbines burned low-grade petroleum, known as Bunker C oil, which was much cheaper than diesel fuel when the turbines were purchased. *Otto Perry, Denver Public Library Western History Department*

Above: Union Pacific's second order of GE turbines was numbered from 61 to 75. Mechanically, these were similar to the first order, but featured external catwalks that earned them the nickname "veranda turbines." The first of these, No. 61, is seen leading a freight with a fuel tender and a pair of EMD GP9s. *Otto Perry, Denver Public Library Western History Department*

Beginning in 1958, General Electric built for Union Pacific a fleet of more-advanced gas turbines that were rated at 8,500 horsepower. These later turbines were built in two pieces. Brand-new turbine No. 1/1B is seen with a fuel tender and a long freight under clear western skies. *Union Pacific photo, John Gruber collection*

hour maximum speed. (Reduction gearing was required because turbine output was greater than economically practical for electrical generation.) The gas turbine locomotive's electrical transmission system was very similar to that used by contemporary diesel-electrics and, in fact, used many common components, including traction motors. The GE-576 generators powered eight standard GE 752 nose-suspended traction motors, one for each axle.

Ambient temperature and atmospheric pressure affects turbine performance. As elevation increases, atmospheric pressure drops and turbine output decreases. Although Union Pacific No. 50's nominal output was rated at 4,500 horsepower, this must be clarified for accuracy. Technically, it generated 4,800 horsepower, when at its full load of 6,700 rpm, when working at 1,500 feet above sea level, with an ambient temperature of 80 degrees Fahrenheit. Of this output, 300 horsepower powered auxiliary functions, thus leaving 4,500 horsepower for traction. The locomotive used a six-cylinder Cooper-Bessemer diesel to provide auxiliary power for starting the turbine and moving the locomotive at slow speeds when gas turbine propulsion was not cost-effective.

A gas turbine locomotive only performs at optimum efficiency when operating at maximum load; compared with diesels, efficiency falls off dramatically when turbine speed is decreased. Union Pacific hoped to obtain cost-effective operation with the gas turbine locomotives by using them exclusively on long-haul heavy freight runs, where the machines could make the most of their enormous output. At maximum output, the gas turbine's fuel consumption was roughly twice that of a diesel locomotive set of similar output. Offsetting the turbine's high fuel consumption was the fact that it burned very cheap Bunker C fuel oil, the heavy oil that remains after high-value oils like gasoline and diesel have been distilled from crude petroleum. In order for the gas turbine to burn Bunker C, the oil needed to be heated to 200 degrees Fahrenheit and filtered prior to combustion, and the turbine was only fired on Bunker C oil after it had been brought up to speed using diesel fuel.

By 1950, GE and UP were sufficiently satisfied with the performance of the experimental turbine to put a fleet of locomotives in regular service. Among the advantages of gas turbine operation were greater output for the weight and length of the locomotive as compared with diesel-electrics, simpler mechanical components than diesel-electric locomotives (leading UP to anticipate greater reliability and lower maintenance costs), lower overall fuel costs, and the rapid acceleration of heavy trains.

Initially UP ordered 10 gas turbines, but placed a second order for 15 additional machines before the first batch was delivered in January 1952. The production locomotives were similar to the prototype, except they featured just a single-cab design. The first 10, numbered 51 to 60, featured a full carbody design. The subsequent 15 machines, delivered in 1954, incorporated technological advances and featured

Union Pacific's 8,500-horsepower turbine No. 2/2B is seen near Echo, Utah, in 1958. The later turbines used a pair of C-C units with a total of 12 traction motors. They were primarily assigned to Overland Route trains, on which UP could make the most of their high output. *Union Pacific photo, John Gruber collection*

external catwalks along the sides of the locomotive. For this reason, these machines, numbered 61 to 75, were popularly known as *veranda turbines*. They were 83 feet, 6 inches long, weighed 551,000 pounds, rode on 40-inch wheels, and produced 105,000 pounds continuous tractive effort (speed not indicated).

By 1957, UP boasted that as much as 11-1/2 percent of all its freight traffic was hauled by the gas turbine fleet. Turbines were primarily assigned to UP's main trunk, the heavily traveled Overland Route between Omaha, Nebraska, and Ogden, Utah. The most difficult challenges were the 0.82 percent westward ruling grade over Sherman Hill west of Cheyenne, Wyoming, and the eastward ascent of Utah's Weber and Echo Canyons. According to an article by Lester C. Harlow in the February 1955 issue of *Railroad Magazine*, turbine No. 57 hauled a 91-car freight weighing 4,200 tons between Rawlins and Green River, Utah, over the Continental Divide. He noted the working turbines produced enormous noise and described them as sounding something like a steam locomotive having its boiler blown down. The turbine's deafening roar earned them the name "Big Blows" by most railroaders. Their unacceptably high noise levels also proved a limiting factor in their operation.

Despite some difficulties, UP was sufficiently pleased with GE's gas turbines to invest in another 30 units of a more advanced design in the mid-1950s. These locomotives were bought in part to replace its 25 Big Boy steam locomotives that were reaching retirement age. Built in 1958, the later turbines used a two-section carbody arrangement with each section riding on C-C floating bolster trucks. The two sections measured a total of 132 feet, 6 inches long. In addition to the driver's cab and locomotive control equipment, the first section contained the auxiliary diesel engine and electrical generator, diesel fuel tank, batteries, air compressor and air reservoir (for braking), and dynamic braking resistor grids. The second unit contained the gas turbine, main traction generators, and related equipment. These machines employed a substantially more powerful gas turbine that featured a 16-stage axial flow compressor, 10 combustion chambers, and a two-stage turbine.

The arrangement of equipment was somewhat different. With the older turbines, the power shaft came out of the exhaust casing, but on the new machines the power shaft exited on the compressor end of the turbine. Full load was achieved at 4,860 rpm. These gas turbines were almost twice as powerful as the first-generation machines and their service condition rating was 8,500 horsepower at 6,000 feet above sea level with an ambient temperature of 90 degrees Fahrenheit. In an article in the May 1957 issue of *Diesel Railway Traction*, General Electric's R.M. Smith compares the output of the two turbine types, explaining that at 1,500 feet above sea level and 80 degrees Fahrenheit, the newer turbines could produce a nominal rating of 10,700 horsepower. He also notes, however, that the machines only had sufficient electrical capacity to accommodate 8,500 horsepower. To overcome complaints of inadequate control with the earlier turbines, the 8,500-horsepower machines used a 20-notch air-actuated driver's throttle. As with the 4,500-horsepower locomotives, the 8,500-horsepower gas turbines employed four generators operating at 1,050 rpm each, reduced from the turbine power shaft through gearing.

However, instead of eight traction motors on the 4,500-horsepower units, these generators powered 12 GE 752 traction motors, each engaging one axle using a 74:18 gear ratio. With this gearing combined with 40-inch wheels, the 8,500-horsepower gas turbines were designed for 65-mile-per-hour operation. Ransome-Wallis indicates they delivered 240,000 pounds starting tractive effort and 145,000 pounds continuous tractive effort at 18 miles per hour. By comparison, a single 1,500-horsepower Alco FA-1 weighing 228,500 pounds and using 40-inch wheels and a 74:18 gear ratio delivered 60,000 pounds starting tractive effort and 34,000 pounds continuous tractive effort at 13-1/2 miles per hour.

Another change on the later turbines was the pre-filtering of Bunker C oil rather than filtering fuel on board the locomotive. To give the turbines greater range between refueling, Union Pacific equipped them with 23,000-gallon fuel tenders remanufactured from steam locomotive tenders.

The Gas Turbine's Demise

Although Union Pacific built an experimental coal-fired gas turbine in 1959, ultimately it gave up on its gas turbine fleet in favor of modern diesel-electric locomotives. A variety of factors contributed to the turbine's demise. Turbine efficiency drops dramatically when operated at less than full load, so when UP was not keeping trains at top speeds, turbines were much less efficient than diesel-electrics, which were still reasonably efficient at slower speeds. Although the gas turbines were supposed to offer greater reliability and lower maintenance costs, an article by Union Pacific's Ross C. Hill in the July 1957 issue of *Diesel Railway Traction* suggests otherwise. In his article, Hill states that the 4,500-horsepower turbine's reliability was hampered by a variety of auxiliary system failures. More serious problems, the article says, included blade erosion in the main axial flow compressors that required re-blading after about every 15,000 hours of service. The use of Bunker C oil was also a difficulty. The ability to burn this cheap oil had been anticipated as one of the primary advantages of the GE turbines, but the fuel proved difficult to burn and caused greater wear to turbine blades than more refined fuel. Today, operators of stationary turbines would only consider Bunker C oil as a fuel of last resort.

Finally, by the 1960s, significant improvements in diesel-electric technology closed the performance gap between gas turbines and diesels. Diesel engines were improved to burn lower grades of fuel than had been possible in the 1940s. By 1960, GE had entered the heavy diesel-electric business, and 4,500-horsepower gas turbines were traded in for U50 diesels in 1963. The 8,500-horsepower turbines met a similar fate a few years later, when they were turned in for GE U50Cs.

Union Pacific's 8,500-horsepower turbines used the common GE 752 traction motor. More modern variants of this standard motor can be found beneath modern General Electric DC-traction diesels. *Union Pacific photo, John Gruber collection*

Union Pacific gas turbine No. 11/11B leads an EMD DD35 and two DD35Bs (eight-motor double-diesels) eastbound near Hermosa, Wyoming, as a westbound train passes on the lower track. *Union Pacific photo, John Gruber collection*

UNIVERSAL LINE

G eneral Electric was one of the foremost suppliers of electrical components for locomotives during the formative years of American dieselization, and a significant producer of lightweight diesel-electric switchers and industrial locomotives. As previously described, GE worked closely with Alco from 1940 until 1953 in the production and marketing of heavy diesel-electric locomotive designs. The three decades following the introduction of Central Railroad of New Jersey No. 1000 saw revolutionary change in the American locomotive market. The diesel had evolved from an experimental switching locomotive into *the* preferred and dominant machine for railroad transport. In the early 1940s, when Alco and GE had cemented their relationship, the situation was still in flux. While the diesel-electric had demonstrated great capability, some in the industry believed that there was still a place for steam locomotives alongside diesels, while for others the large-scale electrification of American railways seemed to be just on the horizon.

At the time, the diesel-electric was seen as the latest form of motive power, but still too new to declare the greatest. Despite this view, the overwhelming superiority of diesel power for American heavy-haul applications resulted in an unprecedented wide-scale switch from steam to diesel power. In the March 1947 issue of *Diesel Railway Traction*, it was noted that Alco had spent an estimated $20 million on the

Opposite: Erie-Lackawanna U33C No. 3308 sits at an engine terminal in Port Jervis, New York. General Electric built 16 U33Cs for Erie-Lackawanna in the late 1960s. *Jim Shaughnessy*

research and development of diesel-electric locomotives and expected that 93 percent of its production capacity would be in diesel-electric manufacturing. But even as railroads undertook large-scale dieselization at a rate faster than even optimistic estimates had anticipated, many projected that steam power would still be in use through the mid-1960s.

Albert Churella, author of the book *From Steam to Diesel*, notes that as late as 1947, even Alco executives still believed that a portion of their business would be derived from the production of steam power. By 1954, however, dieselization was nearing completion; several large railroads were already completely dieselized and most were only a few years away from dispensing with their last steam locomotives. Even Norfolk & Western, America's last large steam holdout, was on the verge of abandoning steam. Serious talk of large-scale electrification had quieted.

During this steam-to-diesel transition, Electro-Motive had become America's largest locomotive supplier, producing the vast majority of diesel locomotives while traditional locomotive builders fell on hard times. As dieselization neared completion in the mid-1950s, there was a sharp decline in the new locomotive market, forcing out the weakest builders, Baldwin and Fairbanks-Morse. Railroads had embraced the many operational advantages of diesel-electric

operation, including much lower maintenance costs; substantially better thermal efficiency, which translated to lower fuel costs; and the fact that they were less damaging to track. In addition, the ability to operate diesels in multiple, combined with high tractive effort from a start, allowed the railroads to operate much longer and heavier trains.

Locomotive manufacturers had offered a variety of diesel models to suit railroads' various needs. Switching engines were built for light work; streamlined cab units were built for freight and passenger work; high-speed passenger diesels, such as the EMD E-unit and Alco PA, were designed for streamlined passenger services; and heavy, slow-speed transfer locomotives had been built for heavy yard transfers and mineral service. By the late 1940s, the road-switcher type was gaining popularity, and by the 1950s EMD's "General Purpose" road-switcher types had become the best-selling locomotives in the United States. In the late 1950s, railroads were clamoring for higher-horsepower general-purpose types that would provide operational flexibility while requiring fewer locomotives to haul heavy trains.

Fast freight service was the premier market as railroads faced ever-greater highway competition. EMD and Alco introduced new high-power designs in the late 1950s in response to market demands. These models were largely

adaptations of existing designs, as the essential technology had not evolved much since the late 1930s. By that time, many of the oldest diesels—those sold during World War II and in the immediate postwar period—were reaching the end of their expected service lives. To sell new models, Alco and EMD encouraged railroads to trade in older locomotives as credit on new ones.

General Electric Diesel Development

In reaction to industry developments, General Electric made a well-timed entry in to the American heavy locomotive market. In 1953, GE formally dissolved its arrangement with Alco on the production of road locomotives and began developing its own locomotive line. Perhaps no other North American company was in a better position to develop a locomotive than GE. The company had all the resources it needed on hand: large-scale locomotive construction facilities, excellent locomotive engineering experience, and sufficient financial resources to fund research and development. Unlike Alco and EMD, which were battling for immediate market share, GE could take the time to develop locomotive technology free from immediate competitive forces. Competitive pressures had rushed diesel development in the 1940s, resulting in design errors.

GE's engineers surveyed experienced railroaders to learn their views about the performance and reliability of contemporary diesel locomotives. Using this input, they looked to provide a better locomotive, and undoubtedly hoped to avoid some of the problems that plagued Alco, Fairbanks-Morse, and Baldwin products. General Electric

In the mid-1950s, General Electric debuted its Universal Line, which directly competed with both Alco and EMD for lucrative export sales. General Electric's primary export markets were in Third World countries that did not possess railway technology of their own. A GE U11B is seen at the Pacific Railway Station in San Jose, Costa Rica, on the Ferrocarriles de Costa Rica. *William D. Middleton*

On the afternoon of February 5, 1977, Southern Pacific U25B No. 6722 works as a rear-end helper on an eastbound ascending California's Beaumont Hill, east of the Ordway Crossovers. *J.D. Schmid*

The first U25Bs featured high-short hoods. Southern Pacific was the first railroad to receive U25Bs with low-short hoods, the style for which the model is best remembered. Southern Pacific 3100 was built in 1963 as No. 7508. Today, the locomotive is preserved at the Orange Empire Museum in Perris, California. *Brian Solomon*

designers sought to build a better, simpler, and potentially more powerful locomotive than any available on the American market at that time.

David P. Morgan pointed out in *TRAINS Magazine* (September 1962) that GE's Universal Line had a basic advantage over existing diesel-locomotive designs, because it was developed new, as opposed to suffering from the restraints of evolutionary development. Morgan credits the work of GE's John C. Aydelott, who coordinated the design of a new diesel-electric locomotive free from the prejudice of existing designs.

A potential disadvantage for GE in marketing its new diesel line was that its locomotives did not have a track record, while those of Alco and EMD were well known. Yet, General Electric was already well respected in the industry, and by taking time to work through engineering problems before selling its product, it hoped to deliver a well-designed machine that would deliver high output and good reliability while requiring only minimal maintenance.

New York Central U25B No. 2501 leads an eastbound train on the former Boston & Albany mainline at State Line Tunnel near Canaan, New York. General Electric diesels have been regularly used on the B&A route for the better part of half a century. *Jim Shaughnessy*

But a diesel-electric locomotive is not a simple machine. It uses many different components that must work together flawlessly in harsh operating conditions. Electro-Motive, with its mass-produced 567 series diesel, had set very high standards for reliability.

Working from its strengths, GE set out to build a machine with a much simpler electrical system. During the 1940s and 1950s, GE refined its already excellent traction motor designs while consolidating motor production facilities at its Erie, Pennsylvania, plant. GE also worked through the other elements of locomotive design, carefully choosing an appropriate prime mover and designing an effective airflow and air-filtering system. Its Universal Line locomotives used far fewer components than competing models, and its railroad traction equipment was the most respected in the industry—even EMD traction motors emulated GE designs.

Cooper-Bessemer Engine

General Electric chose the Cooper-Bessemer V-type diesel as the basis for its new engine. In the early 1930s, the U.S. Navy had funded the research and development of diesel-engine design in order to procure better submarine propulsion.

Several different compact, high-output diesel designs resulted, including the Winton 201A two-cycle diesel, initially used by Electro-Motive; the Fairbanks-Morse opposed-piston engine; and the Cooper-Bessemer. Since the 1920s, General Electric had used a variety of diesel engines in its locomotives. It had used six-cylinder Cooper-Bessemers since the 1930s and was very familiar with the engine's performance. Morgan wrote in the September 1962 issue of *TRAINS Magazine* that GE examined some 46 different diesel engine designs before settling on the Cooper-Bessemer. While this may be true, it should be noted that the Cooper-Bessemer design had several fundamental similarities with Alco's engine designs, with which GE was also familiar. From an engineering perspective, it is often better to work with a familiar system than to attempt to design something completely new. Both the Cooper-Bessemers and the Alco engines were turbocharged, four-cycle V-types that operated at moderate rpm. By comparison, EMD's 567 engine was a supercharged two-cycle V-type diesel, and Fairbanks-Morse's engine was a two-cycle opposed-piston design.

General Electric contracted for the use of the Cooper-Bessemer design and expanded it into a larger, and thus more powerful, engine capable of substantially higher output than initially required. GE initially built locomotives with a maximum output of 2,000 horsepower and less but anticipated the need for a single-unit, single-engine locomotive that could develop as much as 4,000 horsepower. The engine was designed to meet these future needs, and it has proven to be a very good design. Today a 7FDL-16 produces 4,500 gross horsepower, and its inherent fuel economy advantage over EMD's two-cycle engines has given GE an edge in a highly competitive market.

In 1954, General Electric built four experimental diesel-electric locomotives that it used as testbeds to further road locomotive design. They were built in a traditional carbody style with two cab units and two boosters operated in A-B-B-A fashion. The cabs shared a styling treatment similar to that used by the Alco FA and GE electrics, such as the New Haven EP-5, built about the same time. One noticeable styling difference was the use of fluted sides. One cab and booster set used eight-cylinder C-B engines to generate 1,200 horsepower per unit; the other set used 12-cylinder C-B engines to develop 1,800 horsepower per unit. The entire four-unit set was initially numbered 750, painted

A Family Lines–painted U23B leads an eastbound CSX coal drag toward Allegheny Summit on the old Chesapeake & Ohio at Tuckahoe, West Virginia, on the bright clear morning of October 29, 1987. Family Lines was a pre–Seaboard System grouping of railroads that are now components of CSX. *J.D. Schmid*

in the Erie Railroad's blue-and-yellow livery, and operated on the Erie in freight service. In 1959, after GE was through experimenting, each of the four units was rebuilt with 12-cylinder C-B engines rated at 2,000 horsepower each and sold to Union Pacific.

Initially, General Electric was interested in expanding its export sales, and in 1956 debuted its new Universal Line for sales overseas. By the mid-1950s, the export market was larger than the waning domestic market. American manufacturers led the world in diesel-electric technology, and GE competed directly with EMD and Alco for lucrative export sales. EMD's exports included its G12, a 12-cylinder 1,200-horsepower model with a B-B wheel arrangement, and its G16, a 16-cylinder 1,600-horsepower locomotive with a C-C wheel arrangement. Alco offered its "World Locomotive" in various power configurations. GE's exports, like those of EMD and Alco, were designed to operate on significantly lighter track than American locomotives, and thus featured low axle weights. For this reason, six-axle models, both in A1A-A1A and C-C arrangements, were favored for export models. Additional axles spread out locomotive weight, keeping axle weight down. With the Universal Line, GE consolidated its export line and thus re-duced engineering costs by producing standard models. In this respect, GE emulated one of the most successful elements of EMD's approach toward locomotive production.

At first, GE focused its exports toward developing nations that did not possess the ability to develop diesel-electric technology. In April 1959, GE advertised: "Because of their greater horsepower, tractive effort and versatility, GE diesel-electric locomotives *do more work faster*; fewer units are needed, and investment is kept to a minimum."

The Universal Line was built in several different models using FDL series Cooper-Bessemer diesels in 8- and 12-cylinder configurations. The FDL was an inter-cooled, turbocharged four-cycle diesel with dual camshafts and 9x10-1/2-inch (bore and stroke) cylinders, each with 667-ci displacement. The engine worked at 1,000 rpm. Cylinders and cylinder heads were individual assemblies, rather than single cast-iron blocks. Electrical components consisted of standard GE items, such as the 752 series traction motor.

Domestic Aspirations

General Electric quickly established its Universal Line as a practical export locomotive, enhancing the company's

75

credibility as a diesel-electric locomotive manufacturer, while giving it practical experience with locomotives in service. Working out design bugs takes time, and many problems only manifest themselves after many hours of rigorous service.

By the late 1950s, the American market was again ripening for increased sales. The September 1957 issue of *Diesel Railway Traction* reported that EMD general manager N.C. Dezendorf estimated that during the following five years, some 7,750 American diesel-electrics would be due for major rebuilding, and that both EMD and Alco were planning to accommodate such work. The builders also hoped that many railroads would take the opportunity to trade in diesels in the 1,350- to 1,500-horsepower range for new more powerful models.

Looking to capture its share of the expanding domestic market, General Electric advanced the FDL engine to a 16-cylinder design in 1958. Then in 1959, it built two experimental 2,400-horsepower units. Louis Marre indicates in *Diesel Locomotives: The First 50 Years* that they were initially designated model XP24-1, indicating the type was intended as an eXPort model. Each of these high-hood road switchers was powered by an FDL-16 diesel rated at 2,400 horsepower. As with the 1954 experimentals, these locomotives tested on the Erie Railroad for the better part of a year, running approximately 100,000 miles in heavy service to give GE time to refine its designs and work out engineering problems. By 1960, GE was confident of its product and in April publicly announced its new domestic road locomotive, the U25B. Rated at 2,500 horsepower, the four-axle, four-motor U25B was the most powerful single-engine diesel-electric on the market at that time.

Only a few railroads attempted to extend the service lives of Universal Line locomotives. In 1977, Southern Pacific contracted Morrison-Knudsen of Boise, Idaho, to rebuild four U25Bs with Sulzer engines. They were re-designated TE70-4S models and painted in an attractive adaptation of SP's famous "Daylight" livery. Unfortunately, the units, nicknamed "popsicles" for their bright paint scheme, were not mechanically reliable, and they served out their days on the flat track of Oregon's Willamette Valley between Portland and Eugene. Here, two of the TE70-4S units lead 99 cars and a caboose westbound at Alford, Oregon, on the afternoon of May 25, 1979. *J.D. Schmid*

In the years after the Penn-Central merger, General Electric locomotives from the Pennsylvania, New York Central, and New Haven often shared assignments, along with newer GE units bought by PC. Unusual lash-ups were common sights, such as this set bringing a westbound freight around Horseshoe Curve in the summer of 1972. A former PRR U25C and a former NYC U30B are creeping up the grade, keeping the train moving as a crewmember attends to a failed GP40 in the consist. *Jeremy Plant*

Rather than introduce various models designed for different types of traffic, GE initially focused its domestic efforts on the U25B, the one model that it believed would be the best-selling type. To promote its U25B, GE built high-hood demonstrator sets that traveled from railroad to railroad as rolling examples. The U25B used an FDL-16 rated at 2,500 horsepower that was coupled to a GE GT-598 generator to provide DC current to four GE 752 traction motors, one powering each axle. In the standard configuration, the U25B used a 74:18 gear ratio designed for 65 miles per hour. David P. Morgan, in an article in the August 1960 *TRAINS Magazine*, indicated that GE would offer the U25B in a variety of different gear ratios, allowing maximum speeds between 65 and 92 miles per hour, a common practice that allowed railroads to obtain optimum performance for their desired service. While EMD locomotives used standard eight-notch control, the U25B came with a 16-notch control stand to allow for more precision control. The U25B measured 60 feet, 2 inches long; 14 feet, 7 inches tall; and

On June 2, 1973, Penn-Central U33B 2900 leads an Alco C628, GE U25B, and three EMD GP40s with the westbound TV-7 through Buffalo, New York. No. 2900, five years old in this view, was built for PC in 1968. *Doug Eisele*

The Burlington Northern merger of 1970 brought together an eclectic collection of locomotives, including a good sampling of GE units. Three six-axle "U-boats" of Northern Pacific and Burlington heritage—two U25Cs followed by a U33C—led a unit coal train bound for the powerplant at South Joliet, Illinois, under the semaphores at Joliet in early April 1971. The train is on the Gulf, Mobile & Ohio mainline, which ran parallel to the Santa Fe at this busy location. The GEs are renumbered for their new owner, but they still carry the colors of their predecessor lines. *Jeremy Plant*

On April 6, 1980, three Southern Pacific U30Cs leading the LAOAF (Los Angeles to Oakland forwarder) climb Cuesta Pass between Chorro and Serrano, west of San Luis Obispo, California. Time was running out for SP's six-motor GEs; most were taken out of service during the economic recession in the early 1980s. *Don Marson*

10 feet, 3 inches wide, and weighed between 260,000 and 264,000 pounds. Using a 74:18 gear ratio, it delivered 81,000 pounds starting tractive effort. As with most diesel-electrics of the period, the U25B was intended to operate in multiple, thus allowing flexibility in the amount of power railroads assigned to trains.

The U25B demonstrators toured in 1961, and GE began accepting orders. The first sales were high-hood types, four to Union Pacific and eight to the Frisco. By the early 1960s, locomotives with low-short hoods (often described as a *low-nose*) were taking favor with American lines. This arrangement offered greater forward visibility and soon was standard with most new locomotives, including the

U25B from 1962 onward. This difference had little effect on locomotive performance, but made a significant difference in appearance. Southern Pacific was the first railroad to receive U25s with low-short hoods, two locomotives completed by GE in March 1962 and numbered 7500 and 7501. Ultimately, SP was one of the largest buyers of early GE products, purchasing 68 U25Bs.

General Electric's Universal Line earned the nickname "U-boats." *TRAINS Magazine*'s J. David Ingles has hinted that the first use of the moniker came from the Rock Island, one of GE's U25B customers. The nickname is an interpretation of GE's model designation system, which coincidentally mimicked that of the German navy's designation for its World War

The Michigan iron ore hauler Lake Superior & Ishpeming acquired a small fleet of former Burlington Northern U30Cs in 1989 and 1990 to replace older six-motor GE and Alco diesels in heavy service. On August 21, 1995, a pair of LS&I U30Cs wearing BN's Cascade Green livery crosses the Morgan Creek trestle at Eagle Mills, Michigan. *John Leopard*

In the 1980s, Guilford acquired a single former Detroit Edison U30C, which it numbered 663. It is seen leading DHT-4, an eastbound Sealand double-stack train, on the former Erie Railroad through the Canisteo River Valley near Cameron Mills, New York, at 12:30 P.M. on May 7, 1988. It was known colloquially as the "S.S. *Bickmore*" and for several years was the only six-motor GE on Guilford. It survived into the mid-1990s. *Brian Solomon*

II–era submarines, which were also known as U-boats. However, the designation may have also conveyed the claustrophobic confines of the GE's diesel cabs and low, narrow cab doors, which made them unpopular with some railroad crews. Another connotation may stem from GE's seemingly stealthy entry into the heavy locomotive market. To some observers, the U25B seemed to have appeared on-scene suddenly, as if it emerged from deep waters to torpedo the competition.

According to Marre's *Diesel Locomotives: The First 50 Years*, GE sold 476 U25Bs in a seven-year period ending in 1966, making the U25B one of GE's most successful single locomotive models up to that time. It had sold more of them in just a few years than its total production of mainline electrics for domestic railroads since 1900! More to the point, the U25B greatly outsold Alco's domestic offerings of the time. The combined domestic production totals of

General Electric's second round of double-diesels were U50Cs built for Union Pacific. They resembled the U50s of the early 1960s but featured the common C-C six-motor arrangement and were powered by a pair of 12-cylinder diesels. Wheeling past the sandstone cliffs beneath Windy Knoll, UP U50C No. 5026 leads an eastbound freight through Utah's Echo Canyon on June 12, 1974. *Tom Kline collection, photographer unknown*

General Electric U36B demonstrator locomotives are seen leading a Delaware & Hudson freight at Mechanicville, New York, in August 1968. This train is bound for Binghamton, New York; trailing the GEs are Erie-Lackawanna Alcos and EMDs. *Jim Shaughnessy*

Alco's 2,400-horsepower RS-27, 2,400-horsepower C-424, and 2,500-horsepower C-425—models that were comparable to the U25B—was less than 200 units. Even if Alco's 1,800-horsepower RS-36, 2,000-horsepower RS-32, and 2,000-horsepower C-420 were added in, Alco's four-motor domestic sales totals for the 1961–1966 period numbered less than 400 locomotives. GE had outdone its onetime partner in the road-locomotive business. GE's sales comparison with EMD, however, is less favorable. Between 1961 and 1963, EMD's 2,250-horsepower GP30 outsold GE's U25B better than 2 to 1; EMD's 2,500-horsepower GP35 sold nearly three times as many units as the U25B in less than three years. General Electric had a long way to go to match General Motors' sales, but its U25B gave it a solid foothold in the domestic market.

In 1963 GE brought out a six-motor version of the U25, designated U25C (C to indicate the three-axle trucks). Similar to the four-motor U25B in most respects, the U25C was designed for heavy freight service. It developed greater tractive effort at slow speed and was considered a specialized machine, as six-motor diesels were not yet standard road power. GE sold just 113 units of the U25C in a little more than two years. During the 1960s, high-horsepower six-motors gained popularity, and by the early 1970s were more popular than four-motor types.

U28B and U28C

The U25B established GE as a heavy-diesel builder, and in a 15-year period it built more than 3,100 Universal series locomotives for American railroads. During the 1960s, competition resulted in a rapid increase in the maximum horsepower output of new locomotives, as well as in design improvements to improve reliability. At the end of 1965, GE boosted the output of its U-boat from 2,500 horsepower to 2,800 to match increases by EMD and Alco. The 2,800-horsepower U28B and U28C were produced for a little more than a year before GE boosted its standard output to 3,000 horsepower. The first U28Bs closely resembled U25Bs in that they used the same body style. Later U28Bs featured a different body style with a shorter nose section and did not feature a large step along the running boards toward the back of the locomotive.

Until the mid-1990s, Squaw Creek Coal used a pair of secondhand U33Cs to move unit coal trains in southern Indiana. The lead locomotive in this view is former Southern Railway No. 3809, originally constructed with a high nose. After Southern traded in 3809 to GE, it was rebuilt with a low nose and later resold to Squaw Creek in 1992. The trailing locomotive was formerly Burlington Northern 5752. These two, among the last U33Cs in regular service in the United States, are moving a coal train north of Yankeetown, Indiana, on October 26, 1994. Squaw Creek operated between the Ayrshire Mine near Booneville to docks on the Ohio River near Yankeetown, where the coal was transloaded onto barges. *John Leopard*

During U28 production, GE implemented a significant electrical change by switching to an AC-DC transmission system. The new system used an alternator rather than a generator and employed silicon diodes to rectify alternating current to the direct current needed by traction motors. This reduced the number of components, decreased maintenance, and, most significantly, allowed for higher output to traction motors. To increase output, all three manufacturers made the switch to AC-DC transmission systems during the mid-1960s.

A passenger variation of the U28C, designated U28CG, was built for Santa Fe. Ten U28CGs utilizing steam generators to provide heat and electricity were painted in Santa Fe's warbonnet livery. Although geared for faster service, they closely resembled standard freight service U28Cs.

U30B and U30C

General Electric boosted its output again at the end of 1966, when it introduced the U30 models. As the model designation conveys, the U30 delivered 3,000 horsepower. Although, GE would introduce more powerful U-series locomotives, the U30B and U30C remained in continuous production for the better part of 10 years. The two models equaled the horsepower output of EMD's standard GP40 and SD40 models, which were among that builder's most popular models of the period. Nearly 600 U30Cs were sold to American railroads, making it the most popular of all U-series models.

A standard U30B measured 60 feet, 2 inches long, just over 15 feet tall, and slightly more than 10 feet, 3 inches wide. It weighed 254,800 pounds, used an FDL-16 engine

General Electric built 25 cowl-body P30CHs for Amtrak in 1975 and 1976. These unusual locomotives were Amtrak's only GE road diesels until the early 1990s, when it ordered 20 DASH 8-32BWHs. On September 25, 1981, Amtrak P30CH 719 leads a two-car *Blackhawk* across the Rock River at Rockford, Illinois. The *Blackhawk* was an Amtrak service that connected Chicago and Dubuque, Iowa, using an Illinois Central Gulf routing. *John Leopard*

with an 81:22 gear ratio, and 40-inch wheels allowed it to deliver 54,100 pounds continuous tractive effort at 12 miles per hour. It was designed for 75-mile-per-hour operation and, like the U25B, was intended for fast freight work.

Technically, the U30C was largely the same as its four-motor counterpart but was slightly longer and heavier. It measured 67 feet, 3 inches long—the standard length for most GE six-motor U-series—and was slightly more than 15 feet, 4 inches tall. Its standard weight was 363,000 pounds and, using a 74:18 gear ratio, could deliver 90,600 pounds continuous tractive effort at 9.6 miles per hour. The U30C was designed for heavy freight operation and was often assigned to drag freights and mineral service. Burlington Northern operated the largest fleet, painted in the railroad's standard Cascade-green livery with white lettering and often assigned to Alliance, Nebraska, for Powder River coal trains originating in Wyoming. Santa Fe ordered a semi-streamlined cowl version of the U30C with a steam generator for passenger service.

In the mid-1970s, Amtrak ordered a 3,000-horsepower cowl type from GE, designated P30CH. These boxy machines measured 72 feet, 4 inches long and used a small auxiliary diesel engine and generator to provide head-end power rather than take power from the prime mover, as was done with other passenger diesel-electric types. The P30CHs were not a common sight, and for most of their service lives were assigned to Lorton, Virginia–Sanford, Florida, *Auto Train* service and to the *Sunset*, Amtrak's tri-weekly run over Southern Pacific's Sunset Route between New Orleans and Los Angeles.

High Horsepower U-Boats

General Electric met the demand for very high-horsepower diesels by increasing the output of its FDL diesel engine. Unlike EMD, which used a larger version of its 645 diesel to obtain greater output, GE made relatively minor adjustments to the FDL-16 engine, primarily adjusting the fuel rack to increase output and modifying the electrical and

Very few domestic Universal Line locomotives were regularly used in passenger service, making the fleet of U34CHs used on former Erie-Lackawanna lines radiating from Hoboken, New Jersey, especially unusual. New Jersey Transit U34CH No. 4172 sits below Hoboken Terminal's vintage Bush train sheds on October 11, 1992. *Brian Solomon*

At 6:33 A.M. on July 21, 1988, New Jersey Transit U34CH 4164, working in "push" mode, shoves its consist past Howells, New York, toward Hoboken. In regular operation, the U34CHs work in push-pull service, with the locomotives situated on the west end of passenger consists. *Brian Solomon*

cooling systems to accommodate greater output. The larger "bat-wing" radiators at the rear of the 3,300-horsepower U33B and U33C and the 3,600-horsepower U36B and U36C distinguish these models from 3,000-horsepower locomotives, but the basic layout of the locomotive and primary dimensions remained unchanged.

In addition, a U34CH model was built for passenger services on Erie-Lackawanna routes radiating from Hoboken Terminal in New Jersey. This was similar to the U36C, but diverted some output for head-end power. Marre indicates that the U34CH had 3,430 horsepower available for traction. They were paid for by the New Jersey Department of Transportation and delivered in a blue-and-silver variation of the Erie-Lackawanna paint scheme, featuring both the Erie-Lackawanna herald and the NJDOT logo. In the early 1980s, New Jersey Transit was created to operate New Jersey's suburban passenger trains, and many U34CHs were repainted in NJT's silver scheme. The U34CHs were regularly paired with lightweight Pullman-Standard coaches, and in their early years were occasionally used by Erie-Lackawanna in weekend freight service, when they were not required for passenger duties.

Delaware & Hudson U30Cs are seen at Mohawk Yard in Glenview, New York, just across the river from Schenectady. In the late 1970s, D&H sold its 12 U30Cs for operation in Mexico. *Jim Shaughnessy*

U23 and U18

Following the introduction of new high-output diesel-electrics, both EMD and GE brought out more moderately powered diesels. The primary application for high-output, four-motor diesels was hauling priority fast freights; they are unnecessary for slower trains such as local and branchline freights, and for lower-priority "drag" freights. Lower-output locomotives cost less to operate.

General Electric's moderately powered four-motor locomotive was the 2,250-horsepower U23B, powered by a 12-cylinder 7FDL engine. Externally, the U23B appears nearly identical to the more powerful U30B, but the catalog U23B weighed 242,000 pounds (11 tons less than the U30B) and developed 57,200 pounds continuous tractive effort at 11.9 miles per hour. Commercially, the U23B was one of GE's most successful Universal types—465 were sold for North American service, nearly as many as the U25B—and it remained in regular production until 1977. The basis for the successful B23-7 design, the U23B was also one of the longest surviving U-boats, with some models serving for more than 25 years.

The U23C was built for specialized service. Like the U23B, this locomotive used a 12-cylinder 7FDL to produce 2,250 horsepower, but developed considerably more tractive effort. Using the 74:18 gear ratio, a U23C developed 85,800 pounds at 7.3 miles per hour. Railroads such as Penn-Central used them for heavy yard work, where high tractive effort at slow speeds was needed, and a high-output diesel engine would have been unnecessary. The U23C shared common dimensions with the U30C, but with standard options weighed slightly less. Although the type remained in GE's catalog for a number of years, just over 50 were built for domestic purposes between 1968 and 1970, making it one of the more unusual GE types.

Another fairly unusual model was the low-output U18B, which used an eight-cylinder 7FDL to produce 1,800 horsepower. Seaboard Coast Line and Maine Central (MEC) were the primary domestic buyers. Some U18s made use of recycled components from old EMD models traded in to GE, and many U18Bs rode on EMD's Blomberg trucks, as did some other GE four-motor types built during the same

period. Bought to replace Maine Central's aging Alco road switchers, the U18Bs were delivered on the eve of the American bicentennial and thus designated as the railroad's "Independence Class." They were painted in an attractive bright yellow livery with a green stripe and adorned with large, stylized American eagles on the nose. Each locomotive was named in tribute to Revolutionary War heroes and locations. Maine Central assigned its U18Bs to road freights, and often used them on its legendary Mountain Division that connected Portland, Maine, to St. Johnsbury, Vermont, crossing over New Hampshire's Crawford Notch. Some of MEC's U18Bs remained in service for more than 25 years and later wore the gray-and-orange paint of MEC's owner, Guilford, which also operated the Boston & Maine (and the Delaware & Hudson from 1984 to 1988).

While the U18B was the lowest-rated domestic Universal model and was only built between 1973 and 1976, General Electric had offered a variety of low-output models for export after the 1950s. The U17B, for example, used an eight-cylinder 7FDL engine, but was only 46 feet, 4-1/2 inches long (almost 8 feet shorter than the U18B) and weighed just 164,000 pounds, in order to accommodate lines with very low axle weights. General Electric's low-output export C-C Universal models, such as the 1,550-horsepower U15C and the 1,820-horsepower U18C, were also much lighter than domestic locomotives. They were offered in a variety of different gauges and built to a substantially lower profile, measuring just under 12 feet, 6 inches tall. The least powerful Universal Line exports were powered by Caterpillar diesels instead of Cooper-Bessemer FDL engines.

The U10B—one of several models that remained in GE's export catalog for years after domestic production had switched to the Dash-7 line—used a Caterpillar D379 engine to produce 1,050 gross horsepower with 950 available for traction. Its electrical transmission system was of a fairly simple direct current design and employed GE's GT 602 generator and GE761 traction motors.

U50

Union Pacific was the first railroad to purchase the U25B, but it only operated a relatively small fleet of 16. Yet, Union Pacific was impressed with GE's road diesel and prompted the builder for something more powerful. Greg McDonnell relates that UP's motive power chief, David S. Neuhart, convinced GE, as well as EMD and Alco, to develop massive double-diesel types. In GE's case, UP wanted to replace its first-generation turbines. What GE came up with was effectively a double U25 that incorporated recycled components from the turbines, including Association of American

Above: On the first day of winter 1979, Maine Central U18B No. 406 leads the eastbound YR-1 over the Mountain Division at Crawford Notch. Maine Central was one of the few railroads to purchase GE's 1,800-horsepower U18B. *Jim Shaughnessy*

Right: In 1969 the Delaware & Hudson purchased 16 U23Bs, the first and only four-axle GE units on the railroad. Originally numbered 301 through 316, they were renumbered 2301 through 2316 in 1971. In October 1974, during peak autumn color, a matched set of four clean U23Bs slowly grinds up Kelley's Grade (0.8 percent) at Delanson, New York, on the line from Schenectady. The train has just picked up a block of heavy ore cars at Mohawk Yard and is being assisted by another U23B and an Alco RS11 working as a helper at the rear of the train. *Jeremy Plant*

Railroads (AAR) Type B trucks in the unusual B-B+B-B arrangement. The U50s were 83 feet, 6 inches long, weighed 558,000 pounds, and used a pair of 7FDL-16 diesels to produce 5,000 horsepower. The cab rode higher than on other diesel-electric types and featured a distinctive front end with a much smaller nose section than was typical of American diesels. Union Pacific took delivery of 23 U50s between 1963 and 1965. Southern Pacific, which at the time was also experimenting with high-output imported Krauss-Maffei diesel-hydraulics, bought three U50s that were built in spring 1964. They featured minor differences from the UP's, weighing about 3,000 pounds less and featuring doors on the nose section and variations in their braking and wheel slip–control equipment. SP based its U50s at Taylor Yard in Los Angeles and often assigned them to Sunset Route services. Both UP and SP regularly used U50s in combination with other locomotives, including U25Bs.

In the late 1960s, Union Pacific encouraged further development of double-diesel types. GE answered with a new variation of the U50 type that rode on C-C trucks from the 8,500-horsepower turbines and were appropriately designated U50Cs. Union Pacific bought the entire production run of 40 built between 1969 and 1971. In addition to different trucks, these later U50s featured several other significant differences from the first batch of U50s. Advances in the FDL engine design permitted GE to use a pair of 12-cylinder engines to develop 5,000 horsepower. As a result, the U50C was shorter and lighter, measuring 79 feet long and weighing 141,000 pounds less than the U50 type. Another change was the use of aluminum wiring, which unfortunately resulted in serious electrical difficulties. McDonnell indicates that several U50Cs suffered fires that caused their premature retirement.

Maine Central U18Bs are seen at Bangor, Maine, on a cold winter night, February 17, 1976. Maine Central regularly assigned its U18Bs to road freights, working them in consists with the railroad's EMDs and Alcos. *Don Marson*

DASH-7

From the beginning, American railroad locomotive purchases have followed a cyclical pattern, typically providing builders with a feast-or-famine marketplace. When the economy is doing well and traffic is up, railroads are hungry for new power and place large orders for new motive power; when economic conditions cool, new locomotive orders drop off precipitously. Peak times result in the largest numbers of new locomotives, but traditionally the times of the poorest locomotive sales have resulted in the most significant developments in locomotive technology. Smart builders wait out lean years by planning for the next boom. During times of low production, builders have the opportunity to experiment and test new concepts, advance new technology, and design new locomotives with minimal pressure from the market. The Great Depression, for example, saw the advancement of the diesel-electric locomotive, while the economic slowdown of the late 1950s and early 1960s, which coincided with the completion of dieselization, resulted in the development of substantially more powerful diesel-electrics and gave GE the opportunity to enter the road-diesel market.

The mid-1970s saw another period of slow economic activity. An article by Kenneth Ellsworth in the January 31, 1977, issue of *Railway Age* summed up the climate in its opening sentence: "Final returns aren't in yet, but it looks as if 1976 was the worst year since 1961 for the installation of new locomotives by the railroads."

Opposite: New England–based Providence & Worcester was one of the few smaller railroads that bought new GE locomotives. It ordered a single B23-7, No. 2201, which was delivered with an expanded lighting package that included an oscillating headlight. In later years, P&W acquired a sizable fleet of secondhand GEs, including U23Bs, B30-7ABs, and Super 7s. On December 6, 1993, P&W B23-7 No. 2202 and a U23B lead a freight at Old Saybrook, Connecticut. *Brian Solomon*

General Electric has historically had the foresight to use slow periods to great advantage. In recent decades, every economic recession has allowed GE to advance its designs and produce even better machines that have permitted the company to capture greater shares of the domestic locomotive market.

The recession of the mid-1970s came with its share of special circumstances. The fuel crisis of 1973 and 1974 had driven up the price of crude oil and consequentially the price of diesel fuel. While fuel efficiency had always been a locomotive design concern, fuel efficiency suddenly became a major issue. The fuel crisis gave GE a distinct market advantage over EMD, because General Electric's four-cycle 7FDL diesel engine is inherently more fuel-efficient than EMD's two-cycle 645 design. GE hoped to play this design strength to its advantage and use it to gain market share. However, as Alco had found out a decade earlier, fuel efficiency alone does not sell locomotives. Despite Alco's advertisements and demonstrations of better fuel economy, EMD continued to dominate the locomotive market, as a result of its higher reliability and lower maintenance costs—railroads wanted fuel efficiency combined with high reliability.

During the 1960s and early 1970s, General Electric's Universal Line captured a significant share of the new locomotive market, and in the mid-1970s GE sought to improve its reputation for lower reliability than comparable EMD products. By addressing specific railroad concerns and stressing its locomotives' superior fuel consumption, GE captured a greater share of the market when the economy picked up at the end of the decade. According to period advertisements and articles in *Railway Age*, GE sought advice from the railroads on how to improve locomotive design for its "New Series" of locomotive. GE wasn't just looking to spiff up its Universal Line, but to debut a whole new line. One ad in a 1976 *Railway Age* read:

"Early in 1974, General Electric began interviewing top railroad mechanical officers to seek an answer to an innovative question: given the opportunity, how would railroads themselves design a better locomotive?

"The result was an evolutionary program, which led to 58 design and component advances. An additional 20 have also become standard on the New Series locomotive."

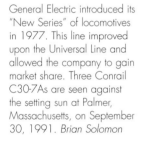

General Electric introduced its "New Series" of locomotives in 1977. This line improved upon the Universal Line and allowed the company to gain market share. Three Conrail C30-7As are seen against the setting sun at Palmer, Massachusetts, on September 30, 1991. *Brian Solomon*

Three Conrail B23-7s lead a freight at CP Draw in Buffalo, New York, on April 22, 1989. GE's B23-7 was a moderately powerful model designed for road and switching work. Railroads such as Conrail used them as general workhorse locomotives, assigning them to yards, local freights, and road freights, as needed. Conrail's B23-7s were equipped with Association of American Railroad (AAR) trucks, a traditional design used on a great many models over the years.
Brian Solomon

The basics behind General Electric's new locomotive line remained the same: They used the 7FDL diesel—the latest variation of the 752 traction motor—and other primary components that had proven their reliability. GE avoided major design changes that would introduce a host of new primary components, which railroads may have avoided until they were proven. While the new locomotives retained their fundamental components, GE implemented numerous small changes to produce a more refined, higher-quality machine that would better suit the everyday needs of railroads. Among these improvements was a redesigned engineer's cab that followed Association of American Railroads (AAR) guidelines. The new cab featured a standard location for the conductor's emergency brake valve release, a more convenient toilet, Lexan (safety glass) on the side windows, better sun visors, better access to locomotive number lights and headlights, and hinge guards on the doors. The electrical compartment arrangement was improved by separating the high-voltage and low-voltage equipment. A walk-in low-voltage compartment, situated behind the engineer's cab, featured a user-friendly control arrangement and diagnostic equipment that made the correction of malfunctions simpler

and easier. High-voltage electrical control equipment was located in cabinets below the cab. Other improvements included a better arrangement of auxiliary equipment such as the air compressor, water tank, and oil filters at the back of the locomotive. Some equipment, such as blowers, that were formerly located at the front of the locomotive were relocated to the back to accommodate the cab rearrangement. On Universal Line locomotives, the air compressor, used to generate air for the air brake, had been located in the radiator compartment. To minimize the compressor's exposure to oil and oil vapors, and to ensure that it was properly ventilated, it was relocated to a sealed-off section of the engine room on the New Series locomotives.

The changes paid off—GE soon enjoyed increased sales and an improved reputation. The crowning achievement of this investment occurred in 1983 when General Electric outsold EMD for the first time.

Dash-7 Designations and Details

Initially, GE called its new line the "New Series." However, later company documents referred to the post–Universal Line locomotives as the "Series-7." Since the introduction

of the DASH 8 line in the mid-1980s, the Series-7 locomotives have been commonly referred to as "Dash-7s," referring to the revised designation system that GE introduced with the "New Series." In this revised nomenclature, the first letter in the model name was either a B or a C to signify the number of axles/motors (B=four axles/four motors and C=six axles/six motors). The letter was followed by a two-digit number to identify the horsepower, then a dash, and finally the number 7 to indicate that the locomotive line was introduced in 1977. Thus, a six-axle 3,000-horsepower road switcher described in the Universal Line as a U30C was designated a C30-7.

Although GE had altered the platform somewhat to provide a better arrangement of essential locomotive systems, the outward appearance of the Dash-7 closely resembled Universal Line locomotives. For locomotive watchers, one of the few spotting differences that clearly identifies Dash-7 models is a subtle step in the width of the hood toward the rear of the locomotive. GE's Universal Line locomotive hoods featured a smoother profile between the engine cab and the radiator cab.

The Dash-7 Catalog

General Electric initially offered its Dash-7 series in about a dozen different model configurations that ranged in output from 1,800 to 3,600 horsepower and came in four-motor/four-axle and six-motor/six-axle arrangements. Of these models, only the B23-7, B30-7, B36-7, C30-7, and C36-7 were built for domestic use. Models like the B18-7, C23-7, and C28-7, which corresponded to similar Universal Line locomotives, as well as to comparable EMD products, were listed in GE's catalog but never constructed for use in

Left: Sometimes a photographer just gets lucky! On October 28, 1992, an eastbound CSX mixed freight led by a pair of DASH 8-40Cs descending Sand Patch meets a westbound intermodal train charging upgrade through the Falls Cut Tunnel (Pennsylvania) with a set of four B36-7s. Seaboard System, a component of CSX, received its fleet of B36-7s from GE in 1985. *Brian Solomon*

Below: Four CSX B36-7s lead a westbound intermodal train west of Meyersdale, Pennsylvania, on the afternoon of October 22, 1992. *Brian Solomon*

the United States. The C23-7, for example, would have been a six-motor 2,250-horsepower locomotive powered by a 12-cylinder 7FDL diesel.

Typical Universal Line locomotives used GE 7FDL diesels in either 12- or 16-cylinder configurations depending on the locomotive model. All domestic Dash-7 locomotives used the latest versions of the proven GE 752 traction motors. Forty-inch driving wheels were standard with most domestic Dash-7s.

Over the course of Dash-7 production, GE implemented a variety of additional improvements intended to further boost reliability and result in better fuel efficiency. For example, later Dash-7s were equipped with an eddy-current clutch (an electromagnetic clutch activated electrically) to operate the radiator fan. On previous locomotives, the radiator fan was mechanically driven from the engine and therefore operated continuously whether or not the engine (or, more specifically, the radiators) needed cooling. Additional fuel-saving features were the introduction of a new fuel injection pump, known as the 18-millimeter double-helix design (describing the diameter of the pump plunger)

Right: Conrail regularly assigned high-horsepower, four-motor locomotives to its fast intermodal trains. In September 1988, three B36-7s race eastward near School Road in Batavia, New York, along the old New York Central mainline, the route of the famous *20th Century Limited*. *Brian Solomon*

Below: A westbound Conrail "Trailvan" crosses a small deck bridge on the former New York Central Water Level Route near Palmyra, New York, in May 1989. Conrail had a fleet of 60 GE B36-7s, numbered 5000 to 5059. They were equipped with GE's "floating bolster" trucks, designed for high adhesion. *Brian Solomon*

to supplant an earlier model. The new pump varied fuel injection timing with the quantity of fuel injected and thus lowered fuel consumption when the locomotive was operating in the lower throttle positions.

General Electric Dash-7 production saw other changes that were not a direct result of the new line but reflected other contemporary changes in the industry. In the late 1970s, because locomotives needed to comply with more stringent federal sound emissions standards, later Dash-7s were equipped with more effective engine mufflers. This is the reason later Dash-7s sound less impressive than earlier GE models—instead of a pronounced, throaty chugging sound, muffler-equipped models emit a softer tone. To reduce smoke emissions and improve fuel economy, GE also introduced a modified throttle position arrangement described as the "skip three, double seven" schedule. This refers to the traditional eight-position AAR throttle, wherein position one is the lowest and position eight is the highest.

"Skip three, double seven" revised the diesel engine speed and load schedule, running it at higher crankshaft speeds than in the earlier AAR schedule.

An external change was the loss of the extra side windows in the locomotive cab. Traditionally, GE models featured two smaller, unopenable windows bracketing the main window on the side of the cab. According to Union Pacific locomotive historian Don Strack, the introduction of more expensive shatterproof Lexan glass discouraged railroads from spending extra money, leading to the discontinuation of side windows. In some Dash-7 models, the spaces for these windows remained in the cab but were covered with sheet metal. Later models didn't provide a space for the extra windows.

B23-7

This intermediate output B23-7 was basically an improved version of the U23B and was intended for the same type of

service. Slightly longer than the U23B, it measured 62 feet, 2 inches and used a 12-cylinder 7FDL diesel that produced 2,250 horsepower. The typical B23-7 weighed 280,000 pounds and produced 70,000 pounds starting tractive effort (based on 25 percent adhesion). The model was offered with three different gear ratios, but the 83:20 ratio designed for 70 miles per hour was probably the most common. This gearing allowed the locomotive to deliver 63,250 pounds continuous tractive effort at 10.7 miles per hour.

The B23-7 was built with several different types of trucks, depending on customer preference. Some locomotives, such as those ordered by Conrail, used AAR's Type B truck; others, such as those used by the Norfolk Southern predecessor Southern Railway, employed GE's floating bolster truck; a third option was recycled EMD Blomberg trucks that came in with EMD trade-ins. Most B23-7s were

Southern Railway always bought road switchers with high-short hoods, and continued to order new locomotives with this arrangement until years after most other railroads switched to the low-short hood configuration. High-hood Southern B23-7 No. 3972 leads train 173 at Ruffin, North Carolina, in the autumn of 1986. *Doug Koontz*

Among the more unusual domestic GE models were 10 BQ23-7s built for CSX predecessor Family Lines. These locomotives featured "Quarters Cabs" designed to accommodate a larger crew and allow for some of the first caboose-less operations. Family Lines BQ23-7 No. 5134 leads the Ringling Brothers Barnum & Bailey Circus train at Wingate, North Carolina, on March 3, 1983. *Doug Koontz*

The sun momentarily pierces the cloud cover over Buffalo, New York, on March 19, 1989, to reveal a pair of Seaboard System–painted C30-7s paused with a Detroit-Buffalo freight at CP 437 in front of the abandoned Buffalo Terminal. At this time, CSX regularly operated its Detroit-Buffalo freight via Ontario. The once-magnificent Buffalo Terminal building was designed by Fellheimer and Wagner, and was inspired in part by the main station in Helsinki, Finland. *Brian Solomon*

A scorecard is needed to decipher the complex arrangements of railroad operations in the eastern United States. In 1988, New York, Susquehanna & Western was appointed designated operator of bankrupt Delaware & Hudson, a line formerly under control of Guilford. To cover for a motive power shortage on D&H, NYS&W borrowed a fleet of Norfolk Southern (former Norfolk & Western) C30-7s. On September 9, 1988, this NS C30-7 and a former Burlington Northern SD45 lead a westbound D&H freight through the Canisteo River Valley on trackage rights over Conrail's former Erie-Lackawanna, née Erie Railroad, mainline. Brian Solomon

Above: A C36-7 and DASH 9-40CW lead a loaded coal train through Coopers, West Virginia, on Norfolk Southern's former Norfolk & Western mainline on March 12, 1999. N&W was one of the last major railroads to build and operate mainline steam locomotives in the United States, with steam surviving on some lines until 1960, more than a decade after other railroads had completely dieselized. T.S. Hoover

ordered with low-short hoods, but Southern Railway ordered the model with high-short hoods. An unusual variation of the model was the BQ23-7, 10 of which were ordered by Family Lines. This model featured a large boxy cab designed to accommodate a three-man crew. The BQ23-7 was a temporary solution offered by the railroad in the late 1970s, when the line was trying to get rid of its cabooses.

According to figures published by Louis A. Marre and Paul K. Withers in *The Contemporary Diesel Spotter's Guide*, 446 B23-7s (including the BQ23-7s) were built for North American service. This figure includes a large order of locomotives assembled by GE's Brazilian affiliate for the National Railways of Mexico.

B30-7 and B36-7

These high-horsepower Dash-7 models corresponded to the Universal Line U30B and U36B, and like those locomotives were intended for high-priority, fast freight services, such as intermodal trains. In many respects, these models closely resembled the B23-7 except for minor variations in external vents on the sides of the locomotives. The primary difference was that they were powered by a 16-cylinder 7FDL diesel rated at 3,000 or 3,600 horsepower for the B30-7 and B36-7, respectively. The combined production total of these two models was 421, just under that for the domestic production of B23-7s.

These locomotives were the hot rods of the industry when they were new, and they were assigned to some of the fastest trains in the country. Conrail and Santa Fe used them to haul their transcontinental piggyback trains, such as the TVLA/QNYLA, which ran from the New York area to Los Angeles on an expedited schedule. Santa Fe was legendary for its fast freights operating on passenger-train-like schedules, some of which ran from Chicago to Los Angeles in just 52 hours. Likewise, Southern Pacific and its affiliate, Cotton Belt, used its B30-7s and B36-7s on the ultra-hot *Blue Streak* and *Memphis Blue Streak* intermodal runs. The *Blue Streak* was originally conceived as a fast less-than-carload (LCL) train connecting St. Louis and Texas and was intended to help SP/Cotton Belt to win back business lost to trucks during the 1920s. By the late 1970s this train had become SP's premier freight and one of the best-known freight trains in America.

C30-7

During the 1970s and early 1980s, the best-selling locomotive types were 3,000-horsepower six-motor machines. While EMD's SD40/SD40-2 types were by far the most numerous, General Electric sold a respectable number of its U30C, and later its C30-7. According to *The Contemporary Diesel Spotter's Guide*, GE built more than 1,100 C30-7s for North American service, making it GE's best-selling locomotive up to that time. Some were sold to Mexico as kits and assembled there. Burlington Northern, Union Pacific, and Norfolk Southern, and CSX predecessors bought large numbers of C30-7s for heavy freight service, commonly using them on unit coal trains. Moving slow-speed heavy trains was one of the strengths of GE's locomotive design and the C30-7s were known for their excellent lugging abilities. A standard C30-7 was powered by a 16-cylinder 7FDL diesel that produced 3,000 horsepower. Fully loaded, a typical C30-7 weighed 420,000 pounds and could deliver 105,000 pounds starting tractive effort (assuming dry rail with a 25 percent factor of adhesion). In later years, Union Pacific listed its C30-7s as weighing 395,000 pounds, more than 12 tons less than GE's specifications for a new locomotive. Assuming standard weight, 40-inch wheels, and 70-mile-per-hour gearing using an 83:20 ratio, a C30-7 would deliver 96,900 pounds continuous tractive effort at 8.8 miles per hour. As with other GE six-motor diesels, the C30-7 rode on a 67-foot, 3-inch platform.

C36-7

The most powerful locomotive in General Electrics' Dash-7 line was its C36-7. Significant technological changes were implemented during the production run to make later C36-7s near cousins of GE's DASH 8 locomotives. The C36-7 was introduced in 1978 as a 3,600-horsepower model, but later examples featured enhanced engine output rated at 3,750 horsepower. The C36-7 uses virtually identical mechanical equipment as the C30-7; the models employ the same platform, the FDL diesel engine, and other primary components. GE obtained greater output from the engine through adjustments to the fuel rack and related systems.

GE C36-7s built after 1983 incorporated sophisticated electronic control systems that had been tested on pre-production DASH 8 locomotives and were actually built alongside the classic DASH 8 models. Later C36-7s provided greater tractive effort because of improved adhesion made possible by GE's SENTRY adhesion control system. According to GE promotional literature, the SENTRY system used traction-motor shaft speed sensors in place of older axle-mounted systems. The motor shaft sensors were as much as six times more sensitive to speed fluctuations, allowing for more detailed corrections to wheel slip and a better application of sand to the rail. Depending on the severity of wheel slip, the SENTRY system would automatically sand the rail

Continued on page 108

In 1985, Union Pacific's Missouri Pacific component took delivery of hybrid C36-7s that incorporated some DASH 8 technology and were rated at 3,750 horsepower instead of the lower 3,600 rating assigned to early C36-7 models. This view features 9016 at North Platte, Nebraska, in September 1989. Notice the DASH 8–style dynamic-brake grids on the hump-like box behind the cab. In 2002, some of these locomotives were rebuilt and re-gauged by GE for service in Estonia. *Brian Solomon*

GE IN ESTONIA

It is July 2002. Sitting among a host of curious-looking, Russian-built M62 diesels is a pair of glistening burgundy-and-gold GE C36-7s waiting to head east on a 60-car freight. This is a long way from North Platte; we're in Tallinn, Estonia—what are big GEs doing here?

Following the dissolution of the Soviet Union, the three Baltic States—Estonia, Latvia, and Lithuania—regained their independence. In the decade that followed, Estonia has been one of the most progressive former Soviet states, adopting Western-style business practices, while preening for inclusion in an expanded European Union. Part of this process has led to the sectorization and semi-privatization of the national railway network. The Estonian National Railway (known locally as Eesti Raudtee, or by its initials EVR) is the semiprivate company responsible for moving freight; EVR is a major outlet for Russian freight traffic. In 2001, a consortium of American, British, and Estonian interests known as Baltic Rail Services purchased a majority interest in EVR. Leading this transnational effort is American Ed Burkhardt of Rail World. Burkhardt is well known and respected in both American and international circles for his ability to transform freight railroads. In the 1980s and 1990s, the recently formed Wisconsin Central flourished under his leadership.

To make the Estonian effort succeed, Burkhardt and his team needed to find ways to reduce operating expenses in order to make EVR more profitable. By American standards, the railway has an excellent market share and moves a great volume of

In 2002, General Electric rebuilt former Union Pacific C36-7s for service on Estonian Railways. These locomotives received the modified designation C36-7i. In order to accommodate the broader gauge used in Estonia, GE cast new trucks for 5-foot gauge. *Brian Solomon*

traffic, primarily Russian oil. EVR's trains are heavy by European standards and operate on frequent headways. However, EVR's motive power was a collection of inefficient and unreliable Soviet-era diesels. After surveying various options to buy new and used diesels, EVR turned to General Electric to supply a fleet of secondhand motive power. GE offered refurbished units at a very good price, and EVR agreed to purchase 55 former Union Pacific (originally Missouri Pacific) C36-7s and 19 former Conrail C30-7As.

After more than 16 years of hauling Union Pacific freight across the mountains, plains, and deserts of the American West, UP's C36-7s had nearly reached the end of their natural service lives. Yet, GE and Burkhardt's team at EVR felt that with some overhaul and modifications, they were ideally suited for heavy service in Estonia. General Electric overhauled and re-gauged the units; because Estonian railways use the Russian 5-foot track gauge, new trucks were cast. Other modifications included equipping them with Russian-style SA3 knuckle couplers and fitting class lamps on the nose sections. To improve performance and reliability, the locomotives were equipped with GE's Bright Star high-adhesion computer system, which maximizes output while protecting electrical equipment from overloading. The refurbished GEs were painted in Burkhardt's preferred livery colors of burgundy and gold, similar to those he had used on Wisconsin Central and the British-based freight operation, the English-Welsh-Scottish Railway. The EVR logo is a variation of the "wheel with

reliable and less maintenance intensive than the Russian diesels that EVR management experts will be able to drastically curtail shop expenses while improving locomotive productivity and overall efficiency. A single C36-7i can handle a 6,700-ton train of Russian oil from the Russian frontier to the port of Tallinn, replacing a set of semi-permanently coupled 2M62 diesels. Typically, EVR freights had been limited to about 60 cars, but with the GEs, EVR has experimented with running trains up to 90 cars long, hauled by just two C36-7is.

GE has impressed and astounded Estonian railroaders and these C36-7is have performed better than anything that has ever operated here before.

Eesti Raudtee (Estonian Railways) C36-7i Nos. 1509 and 1520 were rebuilt by General Electric in May 2002. They are seen here shortly after entering service in Estonia, at the shops in Tallinn. Eesti Raudtee No. 1509 began service as a Missouri Pacific (Union Pacific) locomotive. To the right of the GEs is a Russian-built M62 diesel-electric of the type the C36-7s were bought to replace. *Brian Solomon*

In Estonia, freight trains are typically limited to 60 cars and weigh about 5,600 U.S. tons. While relatively small compared to some American freights, they are still much heavier than those operated in Western Europe. On July 25, 2002, a pair of freshly rebuilt GE C36-7s leads a westbound Eesti Raudtee freight from Narva (on the border with Russia) to Tallinn, Estonia. *Brian Solomon*

wings" theme that is found throughout railways in Eastern Europe, from Austria to Russia.

A variety of technical and political hurdles needed to be overcome before the American GEs could be operated in Estonia. The refurbished C36-7s (now designated C36-7i) were shipped by boat to Tallinn starting in May 2002. By July, they were hauling freight to and from the Russian frontier. The C36-7s represent a technological revolution on Estonian rails. Built new in 1985, the same time as many of the M62s they were bought to replace, they are having the same effect on Estonian motive power that the first mass-produced diesels—EMD F-units and Alco-GE FAs—had on steam power in America. The GEs are so much more

Union Pacific C36-7 No. 9006 leads an empty potash train at the base of Telocassset Hill east of Union Junction, Oregon, at 4:25 p.m. on June 13, 1993. The Missouri Pacific C36-7s were re-lettered for Union Pacific in the late 1980s. *Brian Solomon*

Class H insulation and other design refinements allowed GE to wrap more copper on the armature coils and obtain a 6 percent increase in motor rating (presumably over the GE 752E8 motor, a previous design that GE used as a basis for comparison). To minimize power losses attributed to eddy currents, motor armature coils used a pair of conductors in parallel in place of a single conductor. Additional motor improvements included a better gear-case design and better insulation on motor field coils intended to give better moisture resistance and superior performance in high temperatures.

General Electric built 129 C36-7s between 1978 and 1985 for North American service. Many of these machines were the later, more powerful models with SENTRY adhesion control. These transitional models were some of the first to employ microprocessor controls.

General Electric specifications for the late-era C36-7 indicate a fully loaded locomotive weighing 420,000 pounds could deliver 105,000 pounds starting tractive effort (based on 25 percent adhesion), the same as the C30-7. However, with 70-mile-per-hour 83:20 gearing and 40-inch wheels, a C36-7 could deliver 96,900 pounds at 11 miles per hour, rather than 8.8 miles per hour as with a C30-7. In other words, the C36-7 could move the same tonnage continuously at greater speeds.

Some of the most advanced C36-7s were an order of 60 built for the Missouri Pacific in 1985. By that time, MoPac had become a part of the Union Pacific system, as a result of the 1981 Union Pacific–Missouri Pacific–Western Pacific merger. These big GEs were delivered in Union Pacific paint with Missouri Pacific lettering, but were generally assigned to road service all across the Union Pacific system. Don Strack indicates that in the late 1980s, the C36-7s were re-lettered for Union Pacific.

Among the microprocessor advances used on these locomotives was what GE described as a Motor Thermal Protection panel, which electronically monitored the conditions of the traction motors while calculating the effects of ambient temperature and automatically regulating the current supplied to them to avoid damage from overloading. On older locomotives, the engineer needed to watch the ammeter on the control stand to monitor traction motor conditions and use personal judgment when working in short time ratings. The Motor Thermal Protection

Continued from page 105
and make small, calculated reductions to motor output. The system was specially designed to aid locomotive traction in poor weather conditions.

Another improvement related to the SENTRY system was the GE 752AH traction motor, the latest variation of the traditional 752 family of motors. In its promotional literature, GE stated the GE 752AH has a higher continuous current rating than earlier 752 motors. Using advanced

12-Cylinder Economy

In the early 1980s, General Electric offered 3,000-horse-power models with a 12-cylinder 7FDL diesel in place of a 16-cylinder engine. These locomotives received an "A" designation after their normal model number to distinguish them from ordinary 16-cylinder models. The theory behind the 12-cylinder models was that better fuel economy could be obtained by employing an engine with fewer cylinders. Since the output of the 7FDL diesel had been boosted dra-

system was a real advantage for Union Pacific, which operates trains in some the most extreme weather conditions in North America.

matically since its introduction, GE found it could easily push a 12-cylinder design to produce 3,000 horsepower. Between 1980 and 1983, GE produced several variations of B30-7As in a production run totaling just over 200 units. Among these were 120 cabless B30-7ABs built for Burlington Northern in 1982 and 1983. Although BN didn't order similar Dash-7 models with cabs, in later years it often operated these "B-units" with its LMX GE B39-8 lease fleet, running them in A-B and A-B-A sets.

In 1984, Conrail ordered a fleet of 50 C30-7As that used 12-cylinder engines. Numbered 6550 to 6599, these Dash-7s were intended for high-tractive-effort, moderate-speed applications where good fuel efficiency

In 1984, GE built 50 C30-7As for Conrail. The C30-7A uses a 12-cylinder 7FDL diesel instead of the 16-cylinder engine used in standard C30-7s. At 10:10 A.M. on June 18, 1988, Conrail TV-9 (Boston-to-Chicago Trailvan), led by C30-7A and two C32-8s, overtakes a laden ballast train powered by three C30-7As at Chatham Center, New York, on the former Boston & Albany mainline. *Brian Solomon*

107

Northbound Alberta RailNet (ARN) train No. 458 is seen along the Wildhay River Valley on September 21, 2002. ARN operates on former CN and Northern Alberta Railway trackage, using a fleet of secondhand four- and six-axle GEs to haul coal. These two former Norfolk & Western C30-7s are leading a former Santa Fe SF30C. Other locomotives in the ARN fleet were originally built for the Louisville & Nashville, Frisco, and Southern. Most are leased from the Livingston (Montana) Rebuild Center.
John Leopard

Conrail had one of the most diverse fleets of General Electric locomotives, variously consisting of more than 20 different models. Its 25 C36-7s, built in 1985, operated in the railroad's general road pool. The first in the series was locomotive 6620 (numbered after the C32-8s) seen here at Frontier Yard, Buffalo, New York, in 1988.
Brian Solomon

was a significant objective. They were frequently assigned to Selkirk Yard, south of Albany, New York, for service on the rugged Boston Line, the former Boston & Albany mainline. In their early years, the C30-7As were typically assigned in sets of three and sometimes mixed with the similarly powered C32-8 prototypes (see Chapter 6). In later years, it was more typical for Conrail to operate the C30-7As in sets of four and to occasionally mix them with other modern GE six-motor types.

C36-7s for Export

By far the largest order for C36-7s was for an export variety built during the early and mid-1980s for operation in China. At the time, the first Chinese order was the single largest order GE had ever received. It was a savvy move by GE that kept its production levels up at a time when domestic production was at a low ebb. Ultimately, the China Ministry of Railways bought 422 C36-7s, a number nearly three times the total of all C36-7s used by railroads in North America. GE not only provided China with the locomotives but also the technology needed to rebuild them.

Although the basic equipment of the Chinese C36-7 is the same as the North American locomotives, several specifications were modified to accommodate differences

on Chinese railways. Lower maximum axle weights in China meant that the maximum base weight (subject to minor adjustments depending on modifications) of the locomotives fully loaded was just 304,235 pounds, about one-third (or 150,000 pounds) less than a standard American C36-7. This allowed for a maximum axle load of 50,705 pounds, a little more than 25 U.S. tons. Lower engine weight translates to lower tractive effort, but GE's formula for calculating starting tractive effort on Chinese C36-7s is based on 30 percent adhesion—as a result, GE specifications give the locomotives 91,270 pounds starting tractive effort. The locomotives use an 82:21 gear ratio for 73-mile-per-hour service, allowing for continuous tractive effort of 89,350 pounds at 13.8 miles per hour. The wheelbase is the same as North American locomotives (13 feet, 7 inches) but overall locomotive length is shorter—65 feet, 4 inches. Height is about the same, and the locomotives are nearly 7 inches wider. The Chinese C36-7s also feature a different cab profile with a significantly lower nose and larger forward windows. In addition, the radiators feature a slightly different profile. Another peculiarity of these units is the use of removable driving wheel tires, which was a standard steam locomotive practice.

A close-up of the fuel rack on a 7FDL-16 diesel engine. *Brian Solomon*

DASH 8

In the early 1980s, General Electric advanced diesel-electric technology to the next stage of development by introducing onboard microprocessor controls on the DASH 8 line. Locomotive electrical control systems had utilized advances in technology, gradually progressing from traditional relay controls to solid-state electronic modules and finally to microprocessors. Using microprocessor control, GE refined locomotive component performance and improved fuel efficiency, reliability, and overall performance, as well as performance for specific applications. The successful introduction of microprocessor controls is considered one of the most significant technological advancements of the late twentieth century. Through the successful application of microprocessor controls, General Electric secured its position as the foremost builder of diesel-electric locomotives in North America.

Third or Fourth Generation?

Annalists of diesel locomotive development often classify the DASH 8 line as a member of the diesel-electric locomotive's third generation. By this assessment, the first generation comprised the machines that replaced steam: the cab units, switchers, and road switchers of the 1930s, 1940s, and 1950s. The second generation, then, were the high-horsepower locomotives starting in the 1960s, including EMD's first turbocharged diesels, such as the GP20 and SD24, as well as GE's Universal Line and Alco's Century Series.

CHAPTER 6

Opposite: General Electric's DASH 8 line was the company's key to becoming America's foremost locomotive manufacturer. On a July 1991 afternoon, a General Electric LMX B39-8 and a Burlington Northern B30-7AB lead a westbound Burlington Northern intermodal train on the Montana Rail Link east of Sand Point, Idaho. Montana Rail Link operates former Northern Pacific lines in Montana and Idaho, and handles through traffic for Burlington Northern. *Brian Solomon*

Writers such as John Kirkland, author of *The Diesel Builders* series, however, offer a different generation breakdown. In this line of thought, the diesel-electric's first generation comprised the early and experimental machines of the prewar period, while the second generation were the mass-produced postwar diesels. The introduction of AC-DC transmission in the mid-1960s is considered the third generation of development, and the DASH 8 microprocessor locomotives are deemed the fourth generation.

While these categories can help us understand the various stages of diesel development, they do not necessarily form rigid locomotive groups. Diesel manufacturers, after all, do not set out to design a "new generation," but rather look for ways to advance technology to produce more reliable and better-performing locomotives. If one manufacturer introduces an innovative cost-saving technology, other major builders are quick to follow. In microprocessor control, GE led the way, introducing its DASH 8 line a couple years ahead of EMD.

In the autumn of 1984, General Electric provided Conrail with 10 C32-8 pre-production locomotives for road testing and evaluation. These locomotives, numbered 6610 to 6619, were based in Selkirk, New York, and were largely assigned to trains using the old Boston & Albany mainline. On May 24, 1987, three C32-8s lead the eastbound SENH (Selkirk, New York–to–New Haven, Connecticut) near Washington Summit at Hinsdale, Massachusetts. Also in consist are two GE B23-7s and an EMD SW1500 destined for New Haven local service. *Brian Solomon*

Testbeds and Classics

According Greg J. McDonnell in his November 1988 *TRAINS Magazine* article, "General Electric: A Prophecy Fulfilled," GE began work on what became its DASH 8 line in 1980 and built its first experimental DASH 8 in the fall of 1982. This 3,600-horsepower machine carried the number 606 and, like earlier GE road diesels, used a 16-cylinder 7FDL diesel engine and a variation of GE 752 traction motors. However, it featured an entirely new control system and a host of new components and newly designed auxiliary systems. A second experimental machine was built in 1983, a six-motor locomotive rated at 3,900 horsepower. Following more than a year of testing, GE moved to the next stage of DASH 8 development by building four small fleets of prototypes for extensive in-service road testing on North American railroads. Each of the four fleets comprised different locomotive configurations, and all were painted in their host railroads' respective liveries.

Locomotive testing is an important element of the design process. While GE typically tests new locomotives for many hours on its East Erie Commercial Railroad, this does not necessarily replicate the circumstances that locomotives will be subjected to in actual service. History has many examples of locomotives that performed well in laboratory tests, yet failed in day-to-day service. Extensive road testing by the railroads also gave GE an opportunity to learn which features railroaders liked and disliked before incorporating them into production designs.

By taking this somewhat unusual approach, General Electric collected valuable data on real-life locomotive performance in a variety of different applications while allowing prospective customers to experiment with the locomotives without obligation to buy them. (After the test period, several railroads opted to purchase the prototypes.)

Burlington Northern received three B32-8s numbered 5497 to 5499. Each of these four-axle/four-motor (B-B wheel arrangement) units was powered by a 12-cylinder 7FDL diesel. They were rated at 3,150 horsepower, weighed 280,000 pounds fully loaded, and delivered 70,000 pounds starting tractive effort (based on 25 percent adhesion). Santa Fe received three similar B-B locomotives that were powered by 16-cylinder 7FDL engines and rated 3,900 horsepower. They carried Santa Fe numbers 7400 to 7402. Conrail had the largest test fleet, consisting of 10

Santa Fe tested three of GE's pre-production DASH 8s, model B39-8. These, like other early DASH models, were known at GE as "Classics" to distinguish them from later "Enhanced" models. Classics featured a lower-profile curved cab that gave them a humpback appearance. In January 1991, Santa Fe 7402 basks in the winter sun near Ash Hill in California's Mojave Desert. *Brian Solomon*

In 1984, Norfolk Southern tested a pair of GE C39-8 pre-production prototypes numbered 8550 and 8551. Impressed with this model, the railroad ordered the first fleet of DASH 8s. Norfolk Southern's preferred operating practice was long hood forward, and in their early years the railroad's Classic DASH 8s were normally operated nose to nose, radiator first. On Halloween morning 1987, a pair of C39-8s catches the sun while descending Attica Hill westbound on Conrail's Southern Tier Line near Dixons, New York. *Brian Solomon*

six-axle/six-motor (C-C wheel arrangement) C32-8s. These locomotives shared common characteristics with the 50 C30-7As that were built for Conrail at about the same time. They were powered by 12-cylinder 7FDLs rated at 3,150 horsepower, and fully loaded weighed 420,000 pounds and delivered 105,000 pounds starting tractive effort (based on 25 percent adhesion). Norfolk Southern received the most powerful test locomotives, a pair of C39-8s that used the 16-cylinder engine to produce 3,900 horsepower. Their weight and starting tractive effort was the same as that of the C32-8.

Conrail's C32-8s were delivered in autumn 1984 and carried the numbers 6610 to 6619. Both the C32-8s and C30-7As were based at Conrail's Selkirk Yard, located south of Albany, New York, and in their early years were largely assigned to trains on the heavily graded former Boston & Albany mainline. The B&A route is a tortuous line that traverses the rolling Berkshire Hills and has had a long history of serving as a testbed for new locomotive designs.

On May 4, 1989, Norfolk Southern C39-8 No. 8574, running long hood forward, leads an eastbound freight on the former Nickel Plate Road mainline at Lackawanna, New York. In the distance, a pair of South Buffalo Alco-GE switchers leads a local freight across a bridge over the NS train. Although long-hood operation was initially preferred, in later years, NS C39-8s were arranged to run short hood forward. *Brian Solomon*

(This is the same grade where New York Central and Lima tested the legendary 2-8-4 steam locomotive type in 1924, the first of Lima's so-called "superpower" locomotives and a type later christened the "Berkshire.") It was a perfect place for GE and Conrail to test the merits of the DASH 8 in daily heavy service. Initially the C32-8s worked in matched sets of three, producing 9,450 horsepower, enough to lift most freights over the Berkshires. Conrail eventually acquired the locomotives and throughout the 1980s and early 1990s, the 10 C32-8s were commonly used on the B&A, although they often wandered and could be found just about anywhere on the Conrail system. At times, like the other DASH 8 test fleets, they were used off-line for demonstration purposes. Conrail retained the locomotives until the railroad was broken up by Norfolk Southern and CSX in 1999, after which the unusual locomotives were finally retired. Their curved cab-roof lines and boxy hump located immediately behind the cab gave the early pre-production DASH 8s a distinctive appearance. At General Electric they were known as "Classics."

Although the 12-cylinder B32-8 and C32-8 did not attract production orders, General Electric built several fleets of pre-production DASH 8s based on the B39-8 and C39-8 designs at Erie in the mid-1980s alongside late-era Dash-7 locomotives. Conrail received a fleet of 22 C39-8s, built in summer 1986, numbered 6000 through 6021, while Norfolk Southern amassed a fleet of 139 C39-8s that included their two test locomotives. Norfolk Southern C39-8s were routinely operated long hood forward, as was contemporary NS practice. NS has since become one of GE's largest customers, and its "Classic" DASH 8s were some of the longest lived of the type. As of this writing in late 2002, there were still some Classics in service on the railroad. By contrast, the BN and Santa Fe test fleets were out of service by the early 1990s.

DASH 8 Technology

A 1984 General Electric DASH 8 promotional brochure boasted, "It's All Here, Reliability . . . Performance . . . Fuel Economy." GE explained that its design objective was to substantially reduce locomotive failures and produce a 30 percent increase in reliability. Performance was enhanced through the introduction of a better 752 traction motor and more advanced excitation control and wheel-slip control

In 1987, Union Pacific started ordering DASH 8s from GE, and eventually assembled a large fleet of DASH 8-40Cs. In November 1989, UP DASH 8-40C No. 9305, built in January of that year, leads a westbound through California's Feather River Canyon on the former Western Pacific mainline. *Brian Solomon*

115

On September 26, 1993, a matched set of three Union Pacific DASH 8-40Cs leads the SLPA-Z, a priority intermodal train, westbound in the Feather River Canyon at Pulga, California. *Brian Solomon*

Below: General Electric builder's plate on a brand-new Conrail DASH 8-40C. *Brian Solomon*

systems, while computer-activated auxiliaries would lower the draw on the engine to reduce fuel consumption.

In the DASH 8 designs, General Electric employed the latest and most refined versions of its primary components: the FDL diesel engine and 752 traction motors. Decades of continuous development and improvements from road service experience had made these the foundation for GE's success. The FDL engine had powered GE locomotives for more than a quarter-century, while the modern 752 nose-suspended motor was the fruit of roughly a century of continuous research and development. In its literature, General Electric highlighted the motor's design qualities and noteworthy performance characteristics, including a broad speed range, low continuous operating speed, and the ability to deliver high tractive effort. It is a simple motor to maintain, with easy-to-inspect brushes and sealed armature bearings that do not require regular lubrication. With its modern motors, GE advertised that it had reduced operating temperatures significantly while providing greater resistance to moisture. By employing a specialized

Conrail DASH 8-40Bs Nos. 5060, 5061, and 5062 were only a few days old when they were photographed on the former New York Central Water Level Route at Wayneport, New York, at 4:53 P.M. on May 4, 1988. Conrail 5060 is the class leader of an order for 30 DASH-40Bs built for Conrail in spring 1988. *Brian Solomon*

epoxy varnish insulation, GE motors also offered superior heat transfer, while experiencing minimal moisture absorption without suffering from unwanted grounding. GE explained that its traction motors employed a Teflon "creepage band" and "motor frame flash ring" combined with glass banding on the commutator end of the armature to limit potential damage from motor flashover. This is a serious electrical short that can occur in traction motors at higher speeds when current fails to follow the normal desired path. The 752AG motor introduced with the DASH 8 exhibited further improvements that enabled GE to boost continuous tractive effort ratings by 5 to 11 percent on the DASH 8 locomotives over early models.

Among the other significant advances of the DASH 8 line was the development of a sufficiently powerful traction alternator/rectifier that is capable of supplying high voltage and high current to motors without the need for transition switching. In earlier locomotive designs the alternator could not supply both sufficient current for starting and the voltage needed for high speeds. To overcome this inadequacy,

an electrical transmission was needed to match output characteristics of the alternator (or generator in pre–AC-DC rectifier locomotives, such as the U25B) with the needs of the motors. This transmission serves a function similar to that of a mechanical gearbox in an automobile, although electrical steps are used instead of mechanical gears. As the speed of the locomotive increases, so does the need for voltage. To accommodate the need for greater voltage, motors are reconfigured—a process known as *transition*—through various arrangements of series and parallel connections. In early diesels, such as the Alco-GE RS-2, the locomotive engineer manually initiated the transition; in later locomotives, transition functions were automated. In most GE locomotives, transition takes place in the motor connections, although in some late-era Dash-7s, transition functions are accomplished by a switch-gear in the traction alternator.

Because the need for transition was a compromise, the system had several drawbacks. As is the case of shifting gears using a clutch in a manual automotive gearbox, there is a momentary power drop during transition. Different locomotives

working together in a consist enter transition independently based upon each machine's design characteristics. While similar locomotives should enter transition in harmony with one another, dissimilar locomotives may have different transition characteristics and enter transition at different times. While this doesn't necessarily result in lower efficiency, it can produce a rough ride. In the most extreme circumstances, as when a heavy train ascends a steep grade, rough transitions can result in broken knuckle couplers when locomotives and cars slam together. Overcoming the need for transition in DASH 8 locomotives allowed GE to wire the locomotives in full parallel, providing superior adhesion characteristics—locomotives no longer needed to drop load while performing transition functions. Also, since the complex electrical switch-gear required to make transition was eliminated, the DASH 8 was a simpler machine electrically.

Microprocessor control was the key to the DASH 8 design. Although computers had been around for many years, it wasn't until the early 1980s that technological advances made possible powerful computers that were both

Above: Union Pacific DASH 8-40Cs Nos. 9180 and 9292 run "elephant style" (nose to tail) and catch the glint of the evening sun at Reno Junction, California, in November 1989. Union Pacific assigned its fleet of high-tech GEs to road service on its transcontinental routes, making them a common sight along the old Western Pacific, a railroad that UP had absorbed at the end of 1981. *Brian Solomon*

Right: On the morning of April 28, 1989, a matched set of three Conrail DASH 8-40Bs leads double-stack container train TV-200 eastward along the Delaware River near Hancock, New York. Conrail 5073 features a recently applied nose banner, featuring a stylized image of shaking hands and promoting better labor-management relations. *Brian Solomon*

small enough and sufficiently rugged to fit on a locomotive and endure the harsh conditions imposed by a railroad environment. Only a few years prior to the development of the first DASH 8 prototypes, serious computers had been large machines that filled entire rooms and required constant attention and careful climatic control in order to perform properly. The initial DASH 8 models employed three different computers that were situated in the locomotive's electrical cabinet. Each computer had its own specialized functions and managed specific locomotive systems to achieve optimum performance. Computer controls constantly compared input data collected from a multitude of sensors, analyzed the data, and accordingly regulated individual system performance through electrical adjustments. One computer oversaw overall locomotive performance, another strictly managed the excitation of the main alternator, and the third regulated the auxiliary systems.

On the DASH 8, the computers are designed to prevent component damage by de-rating or shutting down systems before perceived flaws get out of control. For example, computers sense symptoms that precede traction motor flashover and introduce corrective action before flashover can occur, minimizing the instances of this destructive event.

Another advantage of DASH 8 computer control is a detailed set of diagnostic tools that gives operators and mechanics the ability to diagnose and keep track of flaws. Diagnostics also provide a detailed record of a locomotive's performance history, making preventative maintenance easier and allowing mechanics to overcome problems before they become serious. It also helps GE track reoccurring problems in the event of flawed components or other system inadequacies.

On DASH 8 locomotives, computer diagnostic panels are located on the rear cab wall. The interactive diagnostic

In June 1988, New York, Susquehanna & Western took delivery of four DASH 8-40Bs for intermodal service. This was an unusual order for a regional railroad, since by the 1980s few smaller lines were acquiring new locomotives. In April 1989, NYS&W No. 4002 leads DHT-4C, a Sealand double-stack container train, past an antique Union Switch & Signal semaphore on the former Erie Railroad mainline near Cameron Mills, New York, in the Canisteo River Valley. Technically, this was a Delaware & Hudson train running on trackage rights over Conrail. *Brian Solomon*

In spring 1989, backed by CSX, the New York, Susquehanna & Western placed a second order for GE DASH 8-40Bs. These locomotives were needed while NYS&W was the designated operator of the bankrupt Delaware & Hudson. Seen on April 28, 1989, NYS&W 4020 was fresh out of GE's Erie Plant when it was photographed in the morning sun at "BD" in Binghamton, New York, after running overnight from Buffalo. *Brian Solomon*

Overpressure"; and "SHUTDOWN: Electrical Control Problem." Less serious messages include: "Load Limited: Low Oil Pressure"; "Load Limited: Traction Motors Cut Out"; and "May Reduce Load: Radiator Fan Problem."

On DASH 8 locomotives, GE also introduced an entirely new method to drive auxiliary equipment such as the electrical equipment blowers, air compressor, radiator fan, and dynamic brake fans. On Universal Line and Dash-7 locomotives these auxiliaries were mechanically driven from a large shaft off the FDL engine. (As mentioned in the previous chapter, later Dash-7 models employed an eddy-current clutch on the radiator fan that was only operated when needed.) The disadvantage with this arrangement is that auxiliaries operate continuously regardless of whether they are needed or not, causing a drain on the engine and wasting fuel. It also results in unnecessary wear to auxiliary systems that reduces reliability and increases maintenance. With the DASH 8, the 7FDL diesel engine drives an auxiliary alternator that produces three-phase AC current to provide power for auxiliary systems that are powered by three-phase motors. (The auxiliary alternator also provides power for charging batteries and alternator excitation.) The AC motors are maintenance-free, as they do not require brush changes and are carefully regulated by computer and only switched on when conditions require. For example, pre–DASH 8 locomotives used a single mechanically driven equipment blower that ran continuously at a rate governed by engine speed. On the DASH 8, three separate blowers are employed: one for the alternators, rectifier diodes, and excitation regulators, and two to cool traction motors and related equipment with one blower for each truck.

Symphony of Sounds

A DASH 8's automated auxiliary controls result in the locomotive producing a variety of sounds at different times. The sounds produced are a peculiarity of GE's modern technology, but they seem more prevalent because the mufflers used on DASH 8s keep traditional engine noises at a minimum. If you listen to a DASH 8, or other modern GE idling, you will note several distinct sounds that reveal what is going on inside the locomotive.

The constant *ticka ticka ticka* is the noise made by engine valve gear at low cylinder pressure. The valves continue to make noise when the locomotive is throttled up,

readout, known in GE terminology as a Diagnostic Display Panel and abbreviated DID, replaces a multitude of conventional warning lights used on earlier locomotives. In situations where a serious system flaw or component failure occurs (what GE terms a *fault*), the computer sounds an audible alarm to warn the locomotive engineer. Unlike on earlier locomotives, on which an alarm could indicate a variety of problems that the crew would then have to troubleshoot, on DASH 8 locomotives the alarm bell is typically accompanied by a description of the problem. GE lists potential faults in order of severity. Among the most serious alarm messages are: "WARNING! Air Compressor Does Not Pump"; "SHUTDOWN: Low Oil Pressure"; "SHUTDOWN: Crankcase

but these sounds are usually drowned out by exhaust roar. Periodically, the locomotive will produce a distinctive space-age *Vhoooop!* This is the big radiator-fan motor starting, indicating that the engine requires cooling. A *pfft pfft pfft* spitting sound is made by water purge valves expelling water from the air reservoir. This tends to be more prevalent on damp days. Lastly, GE's motor-driven air compressor kicks in from time to time when air pressure drops below an established threshold. When this happens, the locomotive issues a sudden *Budda gidda gidda . . .Pffscht!*

DASH 8 Production

GE used a modular approach in the construction of its DASH 8 locomotives. Although several different models were offered, they were basically different configurations of established modules. According to Greg McDonnell in "General Electric: A Prophecy Fulfilled," from the November 1988 issue of *TRAINS Magazine*, this approach eased construction, reduced building time, and improved component testing. In 1987 and 1988, GE built two fleets of four-motor, high-horsepower locomotives that carried the B39-8 designation. These locomotives were more advanced than the early pre-production units and incorporated several external changes such as boxy, squared-off cabs, and angled radiator vents. GE distinguished these locomotives from the "Classics" by calling them "Enhanced" DASH 8s. *The Contemporary Diesel Spotter's Guide* designates these locomotives B39-8Es to reflect the differences between the Enhanced production units and Classic B39-8 prototypes painted for Santa Fe. GE built 40 of these locomotives for Southern Pacific (which designated them B39-8), and 100 for General Electric's LMX subsidiary for use as a lease fleet. These latter locomotives were painted gray, white, and red (similar to some other GE demonstrators) and lettered for GE and LMX, and were leased to Burlington Northern on a "power by the hour" basis. With this arrangement, the railroad only pays for the work done rather than the whole locomotive. The LMX fleet was the first full-service maintenance contract won by General Electric. The maintenance facility was located at the former Burlington shop in Lincoln, Nebraska. This set an important precedent. Today, GE maintains most of its modern GE fleets at shops all across North America.

Southern Pacific B39-8s (SP class GF439) make a rare appearance on Donner Pass on June 7, 1992. Against a stormy sky, SP No. 8007 leads the second RORV-M (Roper Yard, Utah, to Roseville, California). This 4,433-ton train is descending the Sierra Nevadas on the original 1860s alignment at Yuba Pass, California. Four-motor GEs were more commonly assigned to the Sunset Route. *Brian Solomon*

B39-8 and C39-8 models, respectively. Despite this official change, many railroads continued to list GE locomotives by the older designation system, thus referring to a DASH 8-40C as C40-8. During the first few full years of DASH 8 production, beginning in 1987, the majority of locomotives were either four- or six-motor 4,000-horsepower models. With these two basic types, GE claimed and held the title as America's most prolific domestic locomotive manufacturer.

The DASH 8-40C was initially the most popular model and *The Contemporary Diesel Spotter's Guide* indicates that 581 were sold domestically. The locomotives featured the boxy conventional cab profile exhibiting the "meaner," more linear appearance of the production DASH 8 line. According to GE data, it shared the same external dimensions with the C39-8 and exhibited most common performance characteristics, while producing slightly higher horsepower.

At the end of 1987, Union Pacific, which had neither experimented with nor ordered any of the early DASH 8 models (instead acquiring hybrid C36-7s through Missouri Pacific), ordered the first and largest fleet of DASH 8-40Cs. As is often the case with new diesel acquisitions, Union Pacific traded in worn-out locomotives for the latest model; in this case UP sent GE its well-used U30Cs. General Electric recycled some components, and the first UP DASH 8-40Cs rode on refurbished U30C trucks. Union Pacific's DASH 8-40Cs weighed just 391,000 pounds, several tons less than GE's published maximum of 420,000 pounds for the model. Ultimately, Union Pacific placed five orders for this model, consisting of more than 255 locomotives that were numbered in the 9100 to 9350 series. Union Pacific's DASH 8s were assigned to its general road pool, but in their early days were typically operated in matched sets of two to four units. In the late 1980s, they were a common sight on UP's busy Overland Route, where they could be found hauling long drags and grain trains across Nebraska and Wyoming, as well as leading intermodal trains, such as priority APL (American Presidents Line) double-stack trains to West Coast ports.

Conrail acquired a relatively small fleet of just 25 DASH 8-40Cs (which had C40-8 printed on their sides below the road number) that were delivered in spring 1989. Conrail was one of GE's best customers throughout the 1980s, and these six-motor locomotives joined the railroad's

To the thrill of a child, a Chicago & North Western DASH 8-40C blasts eastward toward Chicago at Sterling, Illinois. *Brian Solomon*

As the DASH 8 line matured, several standard types were offered and a new designation system was developed. Taking advantage of the higher quality conveyed by its DASH 8 line, GE incorporated the "DASH" in its new designations. Concurrent with this change, General Electric also boosted the output of its 16-cylinder models to an even 4,000 horsepower. The resulting models were the DASH 8-40B and DASH 8-40C, which replaced the already GE-intensive road fleet. Initially, they tended to operate in matched pairs, but could soon be found in combination with other types and were used in a great variety of road service.

In 1989, CSX bought DASH 8-40Cs, its first DASH 8s, and the first in a long line of high-tech General Electric locomotives that have dominated that railroad's fleet ever since. Since this first DASH 8 order, CSX has been a very steady GE customer and in recent times has only sampled EMD products. As a testimony to the DASH 8 design, GE won another longtime EMD customer in 1989. Chicago & North Western—which, with the exception of seven U30Cs, had ignored General Electric road diesels—bought a fleet of DASH 840Cs based on the UP's experience with them. At first, these locomotives were assigned to C&NW's Powder River coal services. They were restricted from many C&NW routes, because their unusually heavy axle loads put them above existing limits and they lacked necessary signaling equipment for mainline service. C&NW placed successive orders for DASH 8-40Cs, and in later years operational limitations were overcome, allowing the locomotives to be used in a variety of mainline services.

While the six-motor DASH 8-40C dominated orders for new locomotives, GE had considerable success selling the four-motor DASH 8-40B, as well. This model shared external characteristics with the DASH 8-40C and had common dimensions with the B39-8, which it superseded. The DASH 8-40B was nominally heavier and had slightly better traction characteristics than the B39-8. According to GE specifications, it delivered 69,200 pounds at 18.6 miles per hour. As with other high-horsepower, four-motor diesels, the DASH 8-40B was intended for fast freight. Intermodal giant Conrail was the first railroad to purchase the model. Its first DASH 8-40Bs were delivered to the railroad at Erie, Pennsylvania, at the end of April 1988 and were immediately dispatched westward on a high-priority intermodal train. Conrail's DASH 8-40Bs were numbered in the 5060 series following the B36-7s delivered a few years earlier. Conrail initially operated the DASH 8-40Bs (which it designated B40-8) in three-unit sets, providing intermodal trains with a high horsepower-per-ton ratio and thus the fast acceleration needed to maintain tight schedules. Conrail's intermodal network typically operated on passenger-train-like scheduling and was one of the most impressive high-speed

freight networks in the United States. Gradually, the DASH 840Bs were mixed with the B36-7s and EMD-built GP40-2s in intermodal service. A few months after delivery, Conrail affixed to the noses of the DASH 8-40B fleet white banners that featured a pair of stylized shaking hands and proclaimed "Labor/Management Project. Working Together for Safety Service Success."

Santa Fe and Southern Pacific, also major intermodal carriers operating significant fleets of high-horsepower GE four-motor diesels, both ordered DASH 8-40Bs, as well. Santa Fe's were among the last new locomotives painted in its blue-and-yellow scheme. These locomotives were well suited to Santa Fe's "intermodal expressway" that connected Chicago and California cities with a regular parade of fast

Chicago & North Western had been a solid EMD customer for decades, until GE developed the DASH 8 line. From that time onward, C&NW bought only GE locomotives, assembling a sizable fleet of DASH 8, DASH 9, and AC4400CWs. Initially, its DASH 8-40Cs, such as No. 8548, were limited to Wyoming coal service. In later years they were cleared for mainline work and were common on the transcontinental route to Chicago. *Brian Solomon*

piggyback trains. Southern Pacific's DASH 8-40Bs were adorned in its standard gray and scarlet paint, and were typically operated with its B39-8s. SP's DASH 8s were primarily Sunset Route power, where they were assigned to high-priority intermodal trains, including double-stacks operating east of Los Angeles. These locomotives were occasionally assigned to other routes but were only rarely operated on SP's Overland Route between Oakland, California, and Ogden, Utah.

The smallest fleet of DASH 8-40Bs was acquired by the Northeastern regional railroad New York, Susquehanna & Western. The NYS&W achieved some notoriety in 1945 as the first Class I carrier to complete dieselization, which it accomplished with a small fleet of Alco-GE S model

switchers and RS-1 road switchers. It was also one of the few Northeastern lines to escape inclusion in Conrail in 1976. In the early 1980s NYS&W expanded its operations by acquiring former Lackawanna lines north and west of Binghamton, New York, along with haulage rights over Conrail's former Erie Railroad Southern Tier Route to Binghamton from NYS&W's operational base in Little Ferry, New Jersey. In the mid-1980s, NYS&W became the eastern terminus for intermodal stack train traffic by teaming up with the Delaware & Hudson and CSX to offer an alternative to Conrail. Initially, NYS&W hauled double-stack trains using a fleet of secondhand Alco C430s acquired from Conrail. Later, it purchased a fleet of ex–Burlington Northern SD45s and F45s that proved more reliable and more capable of handling the railroad's growing intermodal traffic. Typically, NYS&W locomotives operated west of Binghamton to Buffalo, New York, over the former Erie mainline using Delaware & Hudson trackage rights. In the spring of 1988, NYS&W acquired four new DASH 8-40Bs built to Conrail specifications to haul its stack trains. These locomotives were evenly numbered from 4002 to 4008 in accordance with Susquehanna practice, in which the first two digits reflected horsepower output. They were painted in the railroad's attractive yellow-and-black livery, giving them a traditional appearance.

Coincidental with this acquisition was the bankruptcy of Delaware & Hudson in June 1988. D&H had been operated by Guilford since 1984, but in the summer of 1988, Susquehanna was appointed the designated operator of the D&H, which put the railroad in a need for more heavy motive power. In the short term, NYS&W leased locomotives from a variety of sources, including Norfolk Southern, which leased a small fleet of C30-7s. NYS&W, with financial assistance from CSX, ordered an additional 20 DASH 8-40Bs, and for a couple of years, NYS&W's DASH 8-40Bs were standard road power on D&H freights. Although Susquehanna was among the bidders for control of the D&H, ultimately Canadian Pacific acquired the property, at which time CSX assumed ownership of the second 20 NYS&W DASH 8-40Bs. These were quickly repainted in CSX's colors and numbered in the 5900 series after that line's B36-7s. The remaining four NYS&W GEs continued to work for their original owner.

Another fleet of four-motor DASH 8s comprised 45 DASH 8-32Bs ordered by Norfolk Southern in 1989. These locomotives were nearly 3 feet shorter and weighed about 2 tons less than the DASH 8-40Bs. They were rated at 3,200 horsepower and powered by a 12-cylinder 7FDL engine.

New Santa Fe DASH 8-40BWs lead train 197 past vintage Union Switch & Signal lower-quadrant semaphores on the Southern Pacific's Tucumcari Line at Torrance, New Mexico, on May 5, 1991. Rerouted due to a derailment on the Santa Fe's El Paso subdivision, this expedited train of auto parts and merchandise is detouring over its competitor's rails to reach El Paso. The undulating profile of this high-desert mainline will be no match for this high-horsepower trio of locomotives.
Photo by Tom Kline

Santa Fe train 199, the line's premier Chicago–Bay Area intermodal, glides through Franklin Canyon at Christie, California, behind five DASH 8-40BWs on the afternoon of March 18, 1993. *Brian Solomon*

In January 1991, four Santa Fe safety-cab DASH 8-40BWs and one standard-cab DASH 8-40B lead a once-weekly Maersk double-stack train across the Mojave Desert near Goffs, California. Combined, these five GEs produce a total of 20,000 horsepower. Santa Fe reintroduced its famous warbonnet livery in 1989 on its Super Fleet locomotives. *Brian Solomon*

Four Santa Fe DASH 8-40BWs, running "elephant style," lead an eastbound intermodal train across the desert east of Holbrook, Arizona, in the evening of October 20, 1995. Santa Fe transformed its Chicago-California passenger route into one of America's premier intermodal corridors. Now operated by BNSF, this line remains one of the most heavily traveled freight routes in the western United States. *J.D. Schmid*

The Widecab Revolution

In recent years, American diesel-electrics have taken on a new appearance. Since 1989, nearly all railroads have adopted an improved cab style known as the *North American Safety Cab*, and frequently referred to as *widenose cabs* or *widecabs*. Though not specifically related to DASH 8 technology, GE implemented the design during the height of DASH 8 production. The root of the North American Safety Cab stems from the elimination of the caboose in the mid-1980s and other changes in labor practices, including the extension of crew districts to cover hundreds of miles. One of the most progressive railroads in implementing new crew arrangements was the Santa Fe. It offered concessions to operating personnel, including an improved working environment—specifically a better locomotive cab. In "Cab of the Future" (December 1990, *TRAINS Magazine*), Steve Schmollinger listed objectives that Santa Fe and its crews desired from a new cab design, including a safer, quieter space with more ergonomic arrangements for the locomotive engineer. Modern road locomotives had

evolved from the road-switcher type first developed in the 1940s. However, since modern operations often require long mainline runs that do not require switching, the cab and control stand arrangement that made sense for a road switcher was deemed inadequate by engineers who faced forward for hours at a time. Schmollinger noted that Santa Fe borrowed a modern Canadian National EMD SD50F for evaluation while drawing inspiration from its own cowl types in the design of the new, modern cab. Although Santa Fe considered a modern cowl-type locomotive along the lines of those used by Canadian roads, it decided against it and instead worked with both General Electric and EMD in the design of a new cab that incorporated soundproofing, desktop controls, a better forward view, and greater structural safety to protect crews in the event of a collision.

In 1988, GE outfitted its four-motor DASH 8 testbed as a safety-cab prototype. However, EMD sold the first modern safety-cab locomotives to an American line, building SD60Ms for Union Pacific in 1989. General Electric followed about a year later with its DASH 8-40CW (W to

General Electric built 20 four-axle safety-cab locomotives for Amtrak in December 1991. Although the DASH 8-32BWH was unique to Amtrak, the type shared many common attributes with Santa Fe's DASH 8-40BWs, and externally the two types are nearly identical. The Amtrak locomotive uses a 12-cylinder engine and produces 3,200 horsepower. It also has an additional alternator to generate head-end electricity for passenger cars. *Author collection, photographer unknown*

reflect the wider cab design), which also was first sold to Union Pacific. Within a few years most of GE's customers were purchasing locomotives with North American Safety Cabs, and only a few lines, such as Norfolk Southern, continued to order the traditional cab design.

Warbonnets

Soon after Union Pacific's first safety cabs, Santa Fe bought fleets of high-horsepower, four-axle locomotives from both EMD and GE. Santa Fe had recently reintroduced its colorful red, yellow, black, and silver "warbonnet" livery—a color scheme that was designed by Electro-Motive artist Leland A. Knickerbocker and which had graced its passenger locomotives from the 1930s until the end of passenger service in 1971. From 1990 until Santa Fe merged with

Burlington Northern in 1995, all of its new road locomotives were dressed in the warbonnet scheme and assigned to the railroad's premier Super Fleet, a name coined to recall the days of the railroad's best-known passenger train, the *Super Chief.*

Between 1990 and 1992, GE built a fleet of 83 DASH 8-40BWs for Santa Fe, a model unique to the railroad. Numbered in the 500 series, they were assigned to the railroad's fastest high-priority intermodal trains, including the famous QNYLA, a transcontinental run between the New York City metro area and Los Angeles and operated in conjunction with Conrail, and the 199/991 trains that connected Chicago and the California Bay Area. These trains operated on passenger-train-like schedules and were among the fastest freight trains in the world, based on end-to-end timing. In order to keep its priority trains moving, Santa Fe used a very high horsepower-to-ton ratio and ensured that the premier trains were assigned the very best locomotives. Typically, four or more DASH 8-40BWs were used on the 199/991 train. The 500 series GEs were preferred on this run, because they exhibited superior traction qualities when climbing through California's Tehachapis, an especially steep and sinuous mountain crossing. When Santa Fe's DASH 8-40BWs were new, they were among the best-performing locomotives in the United States.

Similar to Santa Fe's 500 series were 20 DASH 8-32BWHs built for Amtrak, which Amtrak interestingly also numbered in the 500 series. These locomotives share most external dimensions with the Santa Fe 500s but feature a few significant internal differences. The DASH 8-32BWH uses a 12-cylinder engine instead of a 16-cylinder and produces 3,200 horsepower for traction. An extra alternator is

Above: "Quality" was the buzzword of the 1990s, which many American railroads incorporated into their corporate vocabularies. A new Conrail DASH 8-40BW features a "Quality" variation of the Conrail livery. *Brian Solomon*

Left: The first North American Safety Cab locomotives ordered by a major eastern carrier were General Electric DASH 8-40CWs for Conrail in 1990. In September 1991, Conrail BUOI (Buffalo, New York, to Oak Island, New Jersey) sports a new DASH 8-40CW at Linden, New York, on the former Erie mainline. *Brian Solomon*

used to produce head-end power for passenger cars (thus the H at the end of the designation). Amtrak dressed the locomotives in an entirely new livery, a radical and refreshing change from the staid and well-worn "red-white-and-blue stripes on platinum mist" livery that had adorned the majority of Amtrak's F40PH locomotives since the 1970s. The scheme was compared to the coloration used by Pepsi on its 12-ounce cola cans, leading to the DASH 8-32BWH's unofficial "Pepsi Can" moniker. Some pundits have claimed this was the most attractive of all Amtrak liveries. The locomotives were initially assigned to Amtrak's West Coast services and were commonly used on the *Coast Starlight*, *San Joaquin*, and *Capitol* trains. Amtrak's order for DASH 8-32BWHs was a prelude to the development of the GENESIS type.

Super 7

By the late 1980s, trends in locomotive development had produced high-horsepower, high-tech models at a relatively high price. In order to expand its market, General Electric developed its Super 7 line of inexpensive and moderate-horsepower diesel-electrics. Initially GE intended to assemble Super 7 models using recycled components from older U-series Dash-7 locomotives. By melding traditional components with modern control systems and other technological advances, GE could offer a high-quality locomotive with greater fuel efficiency and better reliability than its older designs. Externally, Super 7s resembled contemporary DASH 8 locomotives; they featured the larger, boxy cab and DASH 8–style radiators, among other DASH 8 elements. By using DASH 8 electronics, GE estimated a 10 to 20

percent improvement in fuel efficiency over its 1970s-era Universal Line and Dash-7 locomotives. Super 7 locomotives used SENTRY wheel-slip control for improved tractive effort; and operator amenities such as a bigger and more comfortable cab, a modern toilet, and built-in refrigerator improved the working environment offered by traditional GE road locomotives. The total cost of the locomotive was kept down by using recycled 7FDL prime movers, GE 752 traction motors, trucks, and locomotive platforms, all of which are among the most expensive individual components in a new GE locomotive.

The first commercial Super 7s were built for the Pennsylvania-based Monongahela Railway in 1989, using components from retired Western Pacific U23Bs. They were built at the old Montreal Locomotive Works plant in Montreal, a facility in which many Alco-GE locomotives had been built in the late 1940s and early 1950s. Monongahela received 11 Super 7-B23s (sometimes described as B23-Super 7) rated at 2,250 horsepower. The railroad was closely involved with the development of the Super 7 and, according to the book *Monongahela* by Harry Stegmaier and Jim Mollison, the railroad's president, Paul Reistrup, suggested the Super 7 branding to GE.

General Electric offered two primary Super 7 models for the domestic market—the Super 7-B23 and Super 7-C30—and built demonstrators of both types. The external

Being tested on Southern Pacific's heavy trains in the Gulf Coast region, GE's Super 7 demonstrator No. 3001 prepares to depart Galveston, Texas, on August 24, 1996, with a molten sulfur drag. *Tom Kline*

131

dimensions of locomotives can vary depending on the recycled platforms used in the manufacture of different machines. The figures here are based on GE's published data. The Super 7-B23 is a four-axle/four-motor machine and measures 60 feet, 2 inches long; 14 feet, 11-1/2 inches tall; and 10 feet, 3 inches wide. It uses 40-inch wheels and a standard 83:20 gear ratio for 70-mile-per-hour operation. Maximum weight is 272,000 pounds, and the continuous tractive effort rating is 64,000 pounds at 10.2 miles per hour. The engine is GE's standard 12-cylinder 7FDL rated at 2,250 horsepower.

The Super 7-C30 is a six-motor machine and has nearly the same external dimensions as the C30-7, although it's slightly wider and shares styling with DASH 8 types. It uses the same size wheels and same gearing as the Super 7-B23. Based on 410,000 pounds maximum weight, a Super 7-C30 develops 96,000 pounds continuous tractive effort at 9.1 miles per hour. It uses a 16-cylinder 7FDL rated at 3,000 horsepower.

One of the largest orders for Super 7s came from Mexican railway Ferrocarriles Nacionales de México, which was so impressed with the type that it ordered a large fleet of 3,000-horsepower units using all new components rather than recycled parts. They were painted in the railroad's attractive two-tone blue and received its five-digit numbers.

Overall, the market for new-built (or remanufactured) moderate-horsepower locomotives remained comparatively soft through the 1990s. This may be attributed to the large numbers of third-party leased locomotives in the 3,000-horsepower range already available to North American railroads. These locomotives became available as the largest railroads bought large numbers of new locomotives and sold older locomotives to leasing companies, including GE subsidiaries, instead of trading them in or scrapping them, as had previously been common practice.

Amtrak's unique DASH 8-32BWHs were typically assigned to western trains. On April 21, 1994, a pair leads Amtrak's *Coast Starlight*. The train is seen on Southern Pacific's Coast Line, just past the east switch of the siding at Harlem, California, in the agriculturally rich Salinas Valley. *Brian Solomon*

General Electric's Super 7 line offered an affordable locomotive that was manufactured from recycled Dash-7 and Universal components while taking advantage of increased reliability and performance, made possible by state-of-the-art microprocessor controls developed for the DASH 8 line. Mexican railway Ferrocarriles Nacionales de México was so impressed with the Super-7 that it ordered a large fleet of S7N30Cs (3,000 horsepower) using all new components. *Author collection, photographer unknown*

DASH 9

General Electric introduced its DASH 9 line in 1993. Whereas the DASH 8 had implemented a variety of significant design changes, the DASH 9 was largely a marketing tool used to distinguish GE's latest direct current–traction locomotive line that reflected a refinement of existing design. The DASH 9 was all about making a good locomotive design even better. This is a significant distinction, but one that should not be confused with GE's AC4400CW (its first alternating current–traction diesel-electric) that was introduced shortly after the DASH 9's debut.

In most respects, DASH 9 locomotives appeared and performed much like late-era DASH 8s. It expanded on DASH 8 technology in order to provide a more capable locomotive with lower lifecycle costs. After the introduction of the DASH 8 in 1984, GE implemented a number of evolutionary improvements to its locomotive line. Some innovative improvements, such as electronic fuel injection and split cooling, were offered as options on late-era DASH 8s and became standard features with DASH 9 locomotives. With the DASH 9, General Electric introduced its new and distinctive-looking HiAd (high-adhesion) truck designed to improve traction. Another change introduced with DASH 9 was the number of traction-equipment blowers. While the DASH 8 uses three blowers (one for the alternator and related equipment, and two for the traction motors with one blower directed at each truck), the DASH 9 uses only two blowers, with one large traction blower for

Opposite: Burlington Northern Santa Fe has amassed a large fleet of DASH 9-44CWs to haul merchandise and intermodal freights. Two BNSF freights pass at Darling, Arizona, on September 27, 2002. The near train is an eastbound intermodal; the far train is a westbound merchandise freight with DASH 9s working the back as Distributed Power Units (DPUs)—today's terminology for remote-control helpers. Many railroads assign DPUs in graded territory to ease operations with long, heavy trains and eliminate the need for manned helpers. *Tim Doherty*

all traction motors. Nominal external changes include a more ergonomic step and handrail arrangement for improved crew safety and comfort.

Electronic Fuel Injection and Split Cooling

Electronic fuel injection (EFI) replaced a conventional mechanical fuel injection system. EFI allows for more precise control of the diesel engine, improving power output, reducing fuel consumption, and lowering exhaust emissions. In addition, EFI enabled GE to eliminate traditional components used by mechanical fuel injection in order to improve reliability and lower maintenance costs. Years ago, exhaust emissions were only a nominal consideration in engine design. However, in recent years, more stringent governmental regulations have made lower locomotive emissions a significant goal with new designs. In order to comply with these regulations, GE improved several elements of its engine design. Introducing radiators with the split cooling arrangement is an important part of this strategy. The term *split cooling* refers to the dual water circuits used for greater cooling of diesel engine intercoolers. Improved intercooler performance allows for lower engine air-intake temperatures, reducing harmful gas emissions. In conjunction with split cooling, GE also employed a coalescer in the crankcase ventilation system to filter oil vapors from exhaust

gases. One external characteristic that identifies GE locomotives with split cooling is slightly thicker radiator wings at the back of the locomotive. The wings house the radiator cores, which are 9 inches thick, 3 inches thicker than earlier designs.

HiAd Truck

Perhaps the most identifiable feature that distinguishes DASH 9 models from DASH 8 models is GE's HiAd truck, a bolsterless truck (a bolster is a mechanical weight-bearing surface on which the wheels pivot beneath the locomotive body) designed to both reduce weight transfer and permit easier maintenance. Reducing weight transfer improves wheel-to-rail adhesion, thus the term *high-adhesion truck* from which GE coined the name HiAd. The high-adhesion truck is identifiable by its boxy, uncluttered appearance and winged journal boxes.

High Power

Higher output was also a notable feature of the DASH 9 line. Standard 16-cylinder DASH 8 locomotives had been rated at 4,000 horsepower until the early 1990s, when GE gradually increased engine output. In 1993 and 1994, GE built DASH 8-41CW locomotives, for Union Pacific and Santa Fe, featuring 4,135-horsepower output. Externally, they appeared

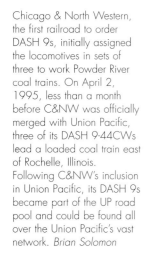

Chicago & North Western, the first railroad to order DASH 9s, initially assigned the locomotives in sets of three to work Powder River coal trains. On April 2, 1995, less than a month before C&NW was officially merged with Union Pacific, three of its DASH 9-44CWs lead a loaded coal train east of Rochelle, Illinois. Following C&NW's inclusion in Union Pacific, its DASH 9s became part of the UP road pool and could be found all over the Union Pacific's vast network. *Brian Solomon*

the same as the DASH 8-40CW. DASH 9 locomotives used GE's most modern DC-traction motor, the 752AH, which GE advertises as "equipped with roller support bearings and oil-filled gear cases," features designed to improve motor reliability. This motor did not make its debut on the DASH 9, however, as many late-era DASH 8s also used it.

DASH 8 Hybrids

Among the last domestic DASH 8s were a fleet of 53 locomotives built for CSX in 1994. These locomotives are best viewed as DASH 8–DASH 9 hybrids. As with the case of the late-era C36-7s, such as those ordered by Union Pacific–Missouri Pacific, the CSX DASH 8s embody features

from two locomotive lines. Numbered in the 9000 series, they incorporate DASH 9 features: split cooling and 4,400-horsepower output. However, they do not feature other notable DASH 9 characteristics such as the HiAd truck. While some sources, including CSX, list these locomotives as DASH 9s, others, such as *The Contemporary Diesel Spotter's Guide*, list them as DASH 8s.

DASH 9 Production

The first DASH 9s are normally considered those ordered by Chicago & North Western at the end of 1993. These locomotives were designated DASH 9-44CWs and use a 7FDL-16 engine to produce 4,380 horsepower (often listed

On October 20, 1994, a CSX westbound climbs through the horseshoe curve at Mance, Pennsylvania, on the Sand Patch grade. Leading the train is one of CSX's 9000-9052 series GEs, locomotives that contain some defining features of both the DASH 8 and DASH 9 series. For this reason, these unusual machines are best viewed as hybrids. *Brian Solomon*

as 4,400 horsepower). Based on information in Sean Graham-White's article "AC Revolution," published in the January 1996 issue of *Pacific RailNews*, a DASH 9-44CW with standard options and featuring 40-inch wheels with a 83:20 gear ratio can produce 140,000 pounds maximum tractive effort and 108,600 pounds continuous tractive effort (calculated using a 27 percent factor of adhesion). In the first half of 1994, Southern Pacific and Santa Fe also bought new DASH 9s. Santa Fe's were numbered in the 600 series. Following the merger with BN in 1995, BNSF made the DASH 9 its staple locomotive for its general freight pool, ordering hundreds. BNSF's typical DASH 9 uses 42-inch wheels, weighs 415,000 pounds, and delivers 105,640 pounds tractive effort at 12.9 miles per hour. BNSF applied several different paint liveries to its DASH 9 locomotives, reflecting schemes used by its heritage railroads, including Santa Fe and the Great Northern. The most recent of these

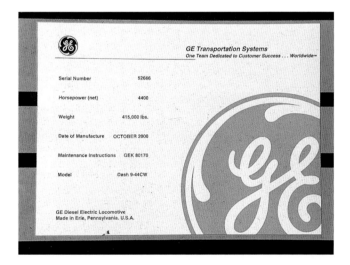

Above: Burlington Northern Santa Fe has experimented with a variety of liveries on its new locomotives. BNSF DASH 9-44CW No. 968 was the first locomotive painted in the "Heritage I" scheme shown, so named because it incorporates elements of several heritage railroad liveries. *Author collection, photographer unknown*

Right: The styles of locomotive builders' plates have evolved over the years. Compare the plate on BNSF DASH 9-44CW, built in October 2000, with the plate on a C&NW locomotive of the same model built in April 1994. *Photos by Tom Kline and Brian Solomon*

paint schemes, the so-called "Heritage II" livery, is a blend of the Santa Fe warbonnet and Great Northern schemes.

In 1994, Canadian National purchased DASH 9s with a Canadian safety cab; these are designated DASH 9-44CWL, the L indicating the four front windows of the Canadian cab. These locomotives were numbered in CN's 2500 series. While their performance characteristics are roughly the same as the BNSF models, the locomotives are slightly lighter, weighing just 390,000 pounds, and they use a slightly smaller fuel tank. BC Rail also acquired DASH 9-44CWLs. Later Canadian National DASH 9s feature widecabs with the more common two-piece windshield.

Norfolk Southern has been one of the largest users of GE DASH 9s. However, while other North American lines ordered models in the 4,400- to 6,000-horsepower range, NS specified locomotives with the more nominal output of just 4,000 horsepower. The basic building block for Norfolk Southern's modern fleet is the GE DASH 9-40CW, a DC-traction locomotive model that, as of this writing in late 2002, is only utilized by NS. In its highest throttle notch, a

Above: The engineer's desktop controls on BNSF DASH 9-44CW No. 998. The black-and-white box on top of the stand to the left is for the control of Distributed Power Units (remote-control helpers) that allow individual control of helpers using the same desktop controls used to operate the lead engines. *Tom Kline*

Left: On September 11, 2002, three BNSF DASH 9-44CWs lead an eastbound stack train along the Libby Bypass, which follows the Fisher River near Jennings, Montana. Working hard upgrade in the Flathead Mountains, these high-horsepower units maintain maximum track speed as they climb toward the Flathead Tunnel. *Tom Kline*

139

Canadian National still prefers DC-traction locomotives, rather than new models with three-phase AC-traction systems. While CN's early DASH 9s featured cabs with four-piece windshields, the line's later DASH 9s feature a "Canadian cab" with just a two-piece windshield. Both varieties are designated DASH 9-44CWL. Note that this unit does not feature the six-piece step that characterizes domestic DASH 9s. CN 2587 is eastbound with a stack train at St. Lambert, Quebec, on July 13, 2002. *Tim Doherty*

4,400-horsepower locomotive burns more fuel than a 4,000-horsepower model. NS does not want to pay for greater locomotive performance than it needs to move its trains, and sees a 4,400-horsepower locomotive as an unnecessary use of resources. Considering that NS operates hundreds of locomotives, even nominally lower fuel consumption adds up to considerable savings.

Norfolk Southern was also the only railroad to order DASH 9s with conventional cabs, designated DASH 9-40Cs. NS adopted the North American Safety Cab as a result of changes in locomotive-building cost structure. When the safety cab was introduced, it was offered as an option, and locomotives that used it cost more than comparable machines with conventional cabs. By the mid-1990s the situation was reversed—because most railroads were buying new locomotives with safety cabs, it became standard and the conventional cab became a specialty option. Unlike most safety-cab locomotives, Norfolk Southern DASH 9-40CWs feature conventional control stands, rather than electronic desktop controls. Desktop controls make reverse running awkward, and NS often requires road locomotives to make switching moves, so it is advantageous for locomotive engineers to be able to run comfortably in both directions.

Mechanically, Norfolk Southern's DASH 9-40CWs are basically the same as standard DASH 9-44CWs. The primary difference is in the locomotive's engine governing unit (EGU), the onboard computer that runs the diesel engine. By using a different software strategy, Norfolk Southern DASH 9 EGUs limit maximum output in "Run-8" (the highest throttle position). There is no appreciable difference in output in the lower throttle positions. Furthermore, a key-operated switch behind the engineer can be used to revert the EGU software strategy to that of standard 4,400-horsepower maximum output. Norfolk Southern's conventional-cab DASH 9-40Cs are designed for a maximum weight of 410,000 pounds, but in actual service normally weigh slightly less.

Spotting DASH 9s in Action

General Electric introduced its AC4400CW just a year after the first DASH 9, and the two model lines have been built concurrently for more than eight years. Several railroads have preferred direct current locomotives, while others prefer ACs. The many external similarities between the DASH 9 and AC4400CW lines may be confusing to the casual observer. In most respects, these machines, despite their

significantly different traction systems, share the same external appearance. One of the best spotting features, which clearly distinguishes the DASH 9 and AC4400CW, is the larger box behind the cab on the fireman's side (right-hand side when viewed head on) of the AC4400CW that contains the AC inverters. The DASH 9s do not use inverters, as the equipment is a part of AC locomotive technology.

Above: Norfolk Southern has a large fleet of DASH 9-40Cs and DASH 9-40CWs, which it uses in all types of road service. Here, a pair of DASH 9-40CWs leads a loaded coal train on the old Norfolk & Western at Bluefield, West Virginia, on October 16, 1999. *T.S. Hoover*

Right: Three Norfolk Southern DASH 9-40CWs working at full throttle lead an eastbound loaded coal train on the former Pennsylvania Railroad mainline at Lilly, Pennsylvania, in May 2002. At the rear of the train is a set of former Conrail SD40-2s. *Brian Solomon*

AC Traction

I n the early 1990s, to meet the demands of the market, both General Electric and General Motor's Electro-Motive Division independently developed modern diesel freight locomotives with three-phase alternating current traction. This advancement in North American locomotive technology required an intensive investment of time, skills, and resources, and required a substantial advance commitment to the purchase of AC locomotives on the part of American railroads. In this respect, the development of AC traction is different than most other stages of American locomotive development. As explained in previous chapters, the typical pattern of development follows the "feast or famine" purchasing cycles that have characterized locomotive acquisition since the steam era.

Technological advancement has been largely financed by individual locomotive builders during periods of slow locomotive sales in order to obtain greater market potential when economic conditions improve. By contrast, AC-traction technology was developed at a time when locomotive purchases were already robust, and in effect was financed in advance by railroads guaranteeing large AC locomotive purchases.

The development of AC traction is closely tied to the movement of unit coal trains, a big business for railroads. Modern railroads haul coal using heavy unit trains that operate directly from mines to domestic powerplants for consumption or

Opposite: CSX's commitment to General Electric enabled the builder to refine three-phase alternating current technology for American heavy-haul applications. On October 18, 2002, a CSX AC4400CW leads empty coal cars westward at Keyser, West Virginia. *Brian Solomon*

to ports for export. Coal trains have special motive power requirements, because they are extremely heavy and often operate in heavily graded territory. However, coal trains are less time sensitive than other types of rail traffic, and their cargo is not perishable. Provided coal trains are handled on predictable schedules, they don't need to be expedited, and for this reason railroads can assign less horsepower per ton.

Since economical transport is key to profits in coal transport, the large coal-hauling railroads have considered various motive power solutions that would potentially lower operating expenses. One solution was electrification. Several smaller coal-hauling lines, such as the Deseret Western, have followed this path. While large common carrier railroads have variously considered electrification, they have not embraced it because of the high costs of implementation and the inflexibility of operation. Another possibility was the development of alternative locomotive types. In the early 1980s, Burlington Northern and CSX considered the potential of a modern coal-powered locomotive. They encouraged the ACE 3000 program, which explored the redevelopment of steam locomotive technology using microprocessor controls to optimize performance. In a related program during the mid-1980s, General Electric experimented with coal-fueled diesel technology and encouraged renewed interest in turbine locomotives. By the late 1980s, however, interest in these technologies had waned, and while the job of moving coal was left to conventional diesel-electric locomotives, the desire to reduce operating costs remained.

AC Advantages

The operating characteristics of three-phase AC motors, which are well suited to slow-speed heavy service, have been known to railroads for many years. As illustrated in Chapter 1, Great Northern selected three-phase AC traction

Southern Pacific was one of the first large users of GE's AC4400CW. It acquired them primarily for its Central Corridor and used them on heavy mineral trains operating to and from Colorado and Utah, as well as for merchandise services. In August 1995, two westbounds are powered by brand-new AC4400CWs at Pando, Colorado. A mixed freight led by No. 121 holds the siding, while a loaded iron ore train led by 186 overtakes it. At this time, SP was running roughly 20 freights a day over the former Denver & Rio Grande Western's Tennessee Pass crossing. *Brian Solomon*

for its first Cascade electrification. Yet the complexity of controlling three-phase AC had limited railroad traction applications, and for the most part DC-traction motors were the standard for most modern applications.

The inherent characteristics of three-phase AC motors make them virtually free from the overheating that plagues DC motors operating at maximum load. Where DC-traction locomotives are limited by short-time motor ratings to keep them from overheating when operating at maximum load, AC locomotives can operate at maximum load at virtually any speed with minimal risk of motor damage or stalling. In addition, three-phase AC motors offer greatly improved wheel-slip control and extended-range dynamic braking, both of which aid in operating heavy trains in graded territory while reducing costs. For example, DC-traction locomotives can only use dynamic brakes to slow a train down to about 10 miles per hour without risking motor damage. However, with AC traction, dynamic braking can be used to virtually a complete stop. This improves train handling and greatly reduces brake-shoe wear.

In addition, advanced motor control and wheel-slip control has allowed for much higher adhesion with three-phase AC traction than was possible with conventional DC traction. Traditionally, tractive effort was calculated on DC locomotives using a 25 percent factor of adhesion. Through the micromanagement of wheel slip, GE's AC diesels have dry-rail adhesion factors close to 40 percent. This translates to much higher tractive effort ratings for AC locomotives than was possible with DC locomotives of the same weight, which gives AC locomotives much greater pulling power at slow speeds.

While three-phase AC motors have been used for more than 100 years, traditionally the difficulties in controlling the motors made them impractical for most railroad traction purposes. Advances in microelectronics, however, enabled engineers to overcome motor control problems, and developments in Europe and Japan in the 1980s demonstrated the capabilities of modern three-phase traction systems, both for high-speed passenger services and relatively light freight services. In the mid-1980s, GE's competitors experimented with AC traction for heavy freight locomotives in Canada and later in the United States. By the 1990s, advances with the technology convinced American railroads to commit to adapting it for heavy service.

CSX No. 1, a GE AC4400CW, leads a loaded coal drag at the 21 Bridge east of Keyser, West Virginia, on October 17, 2002. Since buying its first AC4400CWs, CSX has assembled one of the largest fleets of AC-traction diesels in the United States. *Brian Solomon*

Burlington Northern, in effect, sponsored EMD's development through the purchase of a large fleet of SD70MACs for its Powder River coal service operations. In the summer of 1993, GE built a single AC prototype and by the end of the year, CSX—one of GE's largest customers—agreed to purchase 250 AC-traction locomotives from GE. This large order, like BN's with GM, allowed GE to refine its AC-traction technology.

GE's AC Approach

General Electric and EMD had very different approaches to the way they went about developing AC technology. EMD was the first to introduce a commercial AC-traction diesel, delivering its first BN SD70MACs at the end of 1993. It had teamed with the German firm Siemens to develop an AC-traction system based on that company's past success. General Electric, meanwhile, had already pioneered modern AC-traction technology for passenger rail and transit applications, and it simply adapted its existing technology to a heavy diesel locomotive application.

Above: General Electric's AC4400CW prototype was painted for the company and used in promotional literature. *Author collection, photographer unknown*

Right: On July 20, 1995, a pair of brand-new Southern Pacific AC4400CWs leads the first section of a westbound taconite pellet train between the remote sidings of Floy and Solitude along the former Rio Grande in the Utah desert east of Green River. The second section of the train will follow with another pair of GEs in about an hour. The iron ore was transported on a dailybasis between Minnesota's Iron Range and steelworks at Geneva, Utah. *Brian Solomon*

Above: The combination of a prolonged 3 percent eastward climb at very high altitudes and heavy trains made Colorado's Tennessee Pass one of the greatest challenges in modern railroading. This Southern Pacific coal train seen climbing through the Eagle River Canyon east of Red Cliff, Colorado, has three AC4400CWs leading, followed by four more in the middle of the train and two shoving on the rear. The two sets of helpers are controlled remotely from the cab as Distributed Power Units. *Brian Solomon*

Right: A set of four SP AC4400CWs works as mid-train Distributed Power Units on an eastbound loaded coal train seen ascending Colorado's Tennessee Pass east of Pando in September 1996. *Brian Solomon*

When EMD had the first heavy-haul, AC-traction diesel-electric on the market, it encouraged General Electric to develop a more innovative design to secure a market advantage. The two primary electrical differences between General Electric's AC-traction system and EMD's are the inverters—the banks of high-tech electrical equipment that convert direct current to a form of three-phase alternating current for traction. AC-traction motor control is accomplished by modulating current frequency using sophisticated electronic thyristor controls. Advances in semiconductor technology had permitted the development of practical frequency control equipment. Where the EMD-Siemens AC control system uses two inverters, one for each truck (one inverter controls three motors), General Electric uses six inverters per locomotive. This permits individual axle control and thus enables higher tractive effort and affords greater reliability. GE's system regulates power to each axle individually. With EMD's system, in order to prevent wheel slip, power must be reduced to three axles simultaneously, resulting in a greater loss of power. GE's control system also

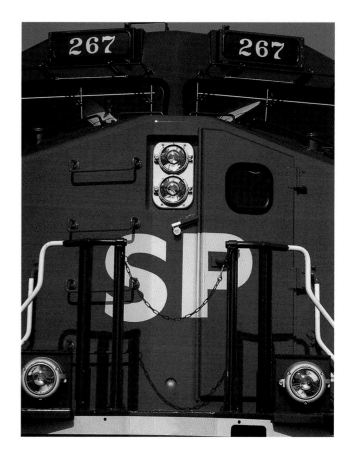

Above: A pair of CSX AC4400CWs leads an empty coal train off the North Mountain subdivision on the former Chesapeake & Ohio at JD Cabin, east of Clifton Forge, Virginia, on February 24, 2002. *T.S. Hoover*

Right: Southern Pacific AC4400CW No. 267 was brand-new and had yet to work in revenue service when photographed here on July 1, 1995. *Brian Solomon*

On January 26, 2002, a pair of clean CSX 500 series AC4400CWs lead empty coal cars across the Potomac River bridge at Harpers Ferry, West Virginia, on the former Baltimore & Ohio mainline. Because the 500s have more weight, when rail conditions decline they outperform any other EMD or GE. However, their maximum tractive effort on dry rail is the same as that of other AC4400s with the same software. They are routinely assigned to coal service out of Grafton, West Virginia, where they are needed to conquer the rugged grades on the old B&O West End between Grafton and Keyser.
T.S. Hoover

allows for greater variance in wheel diameter, which provides a maintenance advantage. Because of this, General Electric's six-inverter system offers a distinct reliability advantage over EMD. A single inverter failure on an SD70MAC (or other EMD AC) can cut locomotive output by as much as 50 percent. However, with GE's AC locomotives, a single inverter failure will result in a maximum traction loss of 12 percent. However, in most situations a single inverter failure on a GE will not result in an appreciable change in output, because the remaining inverters have sufficient capacity to compensate for the loss of power.

The second design distinction between EMD and GE inverters is the method of cooling. Where EMD uses a chemical cooling system to disperse the intense heat generated by the inverters, General Electric uses an air cooling system. The latter is less harmful to the environment and requires less maintenance, and is therefore more economical for the user.

AC4400CW

The development of GE's AC traction immediately followed its introduction of the DASH 9 DC-traction line. Like most DASH 9 locomotives, GE's initial AC offering, the AC4400CW, was rated at 4,400 horsepower. With the exception of the traction system, most components are common between the two locomotives, and in most respects they appear quite similar. (Visual differences between the two models are discussed in Chapter 7.) The AC4400CW provided General Electric a valuable product that it used to better serve its customers and expand its customer base. In addition to securing large AC4400CW orders from CSX and Union Pacific, railroads that already operated large GE fleets, GE also took its first orders for road diesels from Canadian Pacific and Kansas City Southern, both longstanding EMD customers. GE has also sold AC models to recently privatized Mexican railways and to lines in Australia.

Left: The two large Canadian railroads have different philosophies on locomotive acquisition and application. Canadian National has remained committed to traditional DC traction, while Canadian Pacific has embraced three-phase AC technology and began acquiring AC4400CWs in 1995. *Author collection, photographer unknown*

Below: Canadian Pacific's bright red AC4400CWs are a visual treat in the scenic splendor of the Canadian Rockies. A trio of GEs leads a grain train near Canmore, Alberta, on June 28, 1998. *Eric T. Hendrickson*

Since the AC4400CW made its commercial debut in 1994, GE has continuously adjusted its design to improve performance and increase reliability. One of the early advantages offered by EMD's SD70MAC was its so-called *radial truck*, which steered through curves to reduce wheel and rail wear while improving adhesion. To match this feature, GE developed its "steerable" truck and offered it as an option on new locomotives in place of the HiAd truck introduced with the DASH 9. Several railroads have adopted the steerable truck, including CSX, Kansas City Southern, and Canadian Pacific. Another change was the introduction of Sampled Axle Speed computer software in place of the older True Ground Speed Sensor (TGSS). The new system works by monitoring individual axle speed, and is a more reliable way of controlling wheel slip than the Doppler radar employed by TGSS. According to GE, the AC4400CW is 73 feet, 2 inches long and 15 feet, 4.6 inches tall, and weighs 412,000 pounds fully serviced. It uses six 5GEB13 three-phase AC-traction motors and is geared for 75 miles per hour using 42-inch wheels.

One variation of the AC4400CW is CSX's 500 series AC4400CW. These are designed to develop more tractive effort in poor rail conditions. They are unusual in CSX's GE fleet because they have an extra 10 tons of ballast to boost their tractive effort, making them more effective in slow-speed mineral service on very steep grades. However, the maximum tractive effort on dry rails is the same as normally ballasted AC4400s with the same software package, because maximum tractive effort is limited by the software. Initially, these heavy locomotives were primarily assigned to the old Baltimore & Ohio West End grades between Grafton and Keyser, West Virginia, where a combination of multiple steep summits and very heavy unit coal trains have long presented a difficult operating environment. Kansas City Southern's AC4400CWs were built with steerable trucks and feature dual language (English and Spanish) diagnostic controls.

The AC4400CW has been one of GE's most successful locomotives, with hundreds of the type operating all over North America. While introduced as coal service locomotives, many railroads now use AC4400Cs in a variety of road services.

AC6000CW

One advantage of AC traction is the ability to produce a substantially more powerful single-unit locomotive than is

Three Canadian Pacific AC4400CWs lead train No. 874, carrying metallurgical coal destined for Chicago, past a grain elevator at Ernfold, Saskatchewan, on September 11, 1998. Canadian Pacific's early AC4400CWs used the HiAd truck, later models, such as these, use GE's "steerable" truck with 44-inch wheels. *John Leopard.*

Union Pacific acquired three new AC4400CWs built in November and December 1994, numbers 9997 through 9999. It bought additional AC4400CWs in 1996, numbered in the 6700 to 6800 series. These, combined with the former Chicago & North Western and Southern Pacific units, gave UP a fleet of over 830 AC4400CWs. Union Pacific 6779 was only two months old when photographed on the former C&NW mainline at Nelson, Illinois, in July 1996. *Brian Solomon*

A pair of Kansas City Southern AC4400CWs leads train No. 92 across the Illinois River at Watts, Oklahoma, on September 26, 2000. This 112-car coal train also sports a single remote-control AC4400CW helper shoving on the rear. *Tom Kline*

possible with traditional DC-traction motors. General Electric believed it had reached the zenith of DC-traction output with the DASH 9 and needed new technology to build a 6,000-horsepower single-engine locomotive.

Interest in 6,000-horsepower locomotives stemmed in part from the cost advantages made possible through unit reduction. In the 1960s, railroads had purchased large numbers of 3,000-horsepower locomotives in order to replace older 1,500-horsepower units on a two-for-one basis. Likewise, a 6,000-horsepower locomotive would permit a similar replacement of 1960s- and 1970s-era

3,000-horsepower machines—by the mid-1990s, most American railroads had large fleets of 3,000-horsepower locomotives nearing retirement. Both manufacturers anticipated a blossoming market for 6,000-horsepower diesels, and EMD developed its SD90MAC, while GE produced its AC6000CW. In both cases, the builders needed to develop compact diesel engines capable of producing substantially higher output.

When GE expanded the Cooper-Bessemer engine in the late 1950s, it anticipated that the design would eventually need to deliver up to 4,000 horsepower, and at 4,400

horsepower the engine had reached its maximum practical output. To obtain 6,000 horsepower, GE teamed up with the German engine manufacturer Deutz MWM to build a new diesel engine. Known as the GE 7HDL, like the 7FDL it is a four-cycle design using a 45-degree V configuration operating at 1,050 rpm.

The AC6000CW uses a larger carbody featuring much larger radiators than any earlier GE locomotive. The massive wings at the rear of the locomotive house the radiators that are designed to accommodate 550 gallons of coolant.

Several railroads were interested in the AC6000CW when the locomotive was still in its design stage. Union Pacific—which has pushed for the most powerful locomotives on the planet, from the steam turbine–electrics of the 1930s to the gas turbines of the 1940s and 1950s and the double-diesels of the 1960s—placed orders for the new 6,000-horsepower locomotives with both manufacturers well in advance of production. Perpetually power-hungry, the UP did not want to wait until GE's new 7HDL was

ready. In the mid-1990s, the UP ordered a number of AC6000CW "convertible" locomotives from GE, as well as upgradeable locomotives from EMD. These AC6000CW convertibles featured the larger carbody designed to accommodate the HDL, but were initially powered with a standard 4,400-horsepower 7FDL diesel engine. (Union Pacific classified these locomotives C44/60AC.) In this way, UP could satisfy its immediate power needs, while having the option of converting the GEs to more-powerful locomotives when the new engine was ready. Later, Union Pacific and CSX both took delivery of new AC6000CWs with the 7HDL engine. CSX's locomotives are 76 feet long and 15 feet, 5 inches tall, and weigh 432,000 pounds fully serviced. Based on an article in *Diesel Era* (Volume 9, Number 6) titled "Shoving with 12,000 Horsepower" by Jay Potter, CSX's AC6000CWs were rated at 166,000 pounds continuous tractive effort using a factor of adhesion of 39.5 percent.

The AC6000CW is intended for high-priority, intermodal-type services in which railroads can make use of high

CSX AC6000CWs with westbound freight symbol Q423 (Framingham, Massachusetts, to Selkirk, New York) crests Washington Summit on October 18, 2001. Since 2000, pairs of General Electric AC6000CWs have been standard motive power on the old Boston & Albany mainline.
Brian Solomon

output. Initially, CSX experimented with its AC6000CWs in coal service, using them on both the head end and as helpers. Since the year 2000, many of CSX's AC6000CWs were assigned to service on former Conrail lines radiating from out of Selkirk, New York. They are commonly assigned in pairs to Water Level Route trains and those operating on Boston Line (former Boston & Albany) trains. On the latter route, pairs of the big GEs displaced EMD SD80MACs (5,000-horsepower AC units) and GE C30-7As, which had been assigned there by Conrail.

Working at 1,050 rpm, the four-cycle HDL engine sounds similar to FDL-powered GEs, although the character of the HDL sound is deeper and carries farther than that of the smaller engine.

Neither GE's nor EMD's big 6,000-horsepower locomotives have enjoyed the success of the lower-powered AC-traction diesels. For several reasons, the builders' anticipation of large-scale unit reduction schemes has not come to fruition. One has been the overwhelming success of modern 4,000- and 4,400-horsepower locomotives, machines

CSX AC6000CW rolls through CP 83 at Palmer, Massachusetts, in May 2002. These big locomotives feature GE's new 7HDL engine. *Brian Solomon*

that have demonstrated excellent reliability, dependability, and versatility. Also, a 4,000- to 4,400-horsepower unit gives a railroad greater flexibility in assigning power to a train, while a pair of 6,000-horsepower units is often either too much or too little power. In the interests of timeliness and efficiency, railroads, of course, prefer to match the power requirements as closely as possible to a train's operating needs. Assigning a train too much power is a waste of resources, but giving it too little power may cause it to stall or struggle over the line at reduced speed. Another issue is the reliability of 6,000-horsepower locomotives. Since fewer locomotives are assigned to a train, if a locomotive fails en route, the train has to make do with substantially less power. If, for example, CSX sends three 4,000-horsepower locomotives up a grade and one fails, the train still has 8,000 horsepower with which to make it over the road; but using just a pair of 6,000-horsepower units, a failure leaves 6,000 horsepower, just half the assigned power. And, the high cost of new diesels precludes overpowering trains to

cover for potential failures. As a result, 6,000-horsepower locomotives must have higher reliability expectations than lower-power models. While GE's AC6000CWs work daily in demanding services, hauling heavy trains up the Boston Line's Berkshire grades, their reliability has not always met expectations. As of this writing in late 2002, it seems that in the short term, railroads will prefer to acquire locomotives with lower output, and the anticipated economy offered by unit reduction will have to be met by other means.

In December 2002, General Electric announced the introduction of its new "Evolution Series" locomotive line, which incorporates a new engine design. Although specifics of the new engine have not yet been released, the intended design will generate 4,400 horsepower while complying with more stringent air-quality regulations to be imposed in 2005. GE said the new engine would use a 12-cylinder air-cooled design to reduce the production of polluting gases and particulates by 40 percent, while improving fuel consumption.

155

GENESIS

S ome of the most unusual modern American diesel-electrics are General Electric's GENESIS types. In the early 1990s, Amtrak sought to replace its fleet of aging 1970s-era diesels, primarily Electro-Motive F40PHs and, to a lesser extent, GE P30CHs. Unwilling to settle for an adaptation of an existing freight locomotive for passenger work as it had with past orders, Amtrak desired a modern, lightweight state-of-the-art locomotive. Both GE and EMD entered the race to design the new type. Amtrak's specification designated the new machine AMD-103, which according to *TRAINS Magazine*, stands for <u>Am</u>trak <u>D</u>iesel, 103 miles per hour maximum speed. General Electric was awarded the contract, and GE and Amtrak worked together in the design of a completely new diesel-electric that incorporated several European concepts. A name was needed for the AMD-103 specification, and GE held an employee contest that produced the GENESIS branding. Today, three different models fall under the GENESIS line.

The GENESIS is unique in the annals of modern locomotives. Unlike other modern American locomotives, it was specifically designed for North American passenger services and, thus is fundamentally different from modern freight locomotives. Among notable differences is the use of an integral monocoque body shell and fabricated trucks instead of a bottom supporting locomotive platform and cast trucks. Both of these designs incorporate technology derived from modern

Opposite: Unlike passenger service locomotive designs of the 1960s and 1970s, which were essentially freight locomotives adapted to passenger service, General Electric's GENESIS was a totally new locomotive, specifically designed for passenger operations. Metro-North P32AC-DM No. 205 is seen here north of Breakneck Ridge, as it races toward Poughkeepsie with a commuter train from New York's Grand Central Terminal. *Brian Solomon*

European practice, rather than traditional North American design. According to an article by Bob Johnston in the September 1993 *TRAINS Magazine*, GENESIS is the first modern North American locomotive to use fabricated trucks in place of conventional cast-steel trucks. This lightweight, high-tractive-effort, bolsterless design looks significantly different from other locomotive trucks.

Amtrak desired a powerful and fuel-efficient machine that was significantly lighter and more compact than anything else available on the market. To meet these requirements, General Electric worked with Krupp—the German firm responsible for DB AG's (German State Railway) high-speed ICE-1 body design—in the construction of a monocoque body to support the locomotive. Derived from the French, the term *monocoque* indicates the body shell is integral to the locomotive structure. In this respect, GENESIS is like the full carbody locomotives built in the 1930s, 1940s, and 1950s, such as Alco-GE's FA/FB and PA/PB models described in Chapter 2. To comply with the most restrictive mainline clearances, the GENESIS is lower and narrower than most North American road locomotives. According to GE specifications, the GENESIS Series 1 is 14 feet, 6 inches tall and 10 feet wide, making it a foot shorter and more than 2 inches narrower than a typical heavy freight diesel. As a result, GENESIS locomotives can operate on virtually all North American mainlines.

Perhaps the most striking quality of GE's GENESIS line is its radical and unorthodox appearance—it just doesn't look like anything else on American rails, past or present. According to articles by Bob Johnston in *TRAINS Magazine* and by David C. Warner in the June 1993 *Passenger Train Journal*, the GENESIS appearance was designed to fulfill

Where EMD's F40PH-2 characterized Amtrak operations in the 1970s and 1980s, GE's GENESIS is the face of the modern Amtrak. On March 25, 1995, a pair of DASH-40BWHs, otherwise known as GENESIS Series I, leads Amtrak's eastbound *Southwest Chief* toward Chicago. These first GENESIS locomotives featured fading stripes at the back of the locomotive; later GENESIS models used a solid stripe all the way back. *Brian Solomon*

Inset: This detailed view shows how the fading stripe at the back of Amtrak's GENESIS Series I locomotives was accomplished with a pattern of printer-like dots. *Brian Solomon*

Amtrak's specific desire for a modern-looking locomotive that was strong enough to withstand repeated grade-crossing collisions, yet economical to build and repair. Amtrak's designer, Cesar Vergara, avoided complex curves and used angular construction with flat surfaces. Vergara, who has enjoyed a prolific career in railroad industrial design, also developed the original GENESIS paint livery, which featured an unusual fading stripe toward the back of the locomotive. This scheme was intended to visually distinguish the locomotive from the cars, but its effect is often lost on observers, as GENESIS locomotives are often operated in multiple. Only the GENESIS Series 1 was treated with the fading stripe; later models feature solid stripes.

Unlike locomotive performance that can be quantified relatively clearly, locomotive aesthetics are purely subjective. In its early years, the GENESIS design shocked many railroad observers and generated much criticism as a result of its forward-looking and nonconventional appearance. In an August 1994 poll, the readers of *Passenger Train Journal* voted GENESIS the "Ugliest-Ever Passenger Diesel." This opinion, however, was not universally held—in the same poll, readers also listed GENESIS as the third "Most Attractive Passenger Diesel." (Electro-Motive's E8/E9 was voted first, followed by the ever-popular Alco-GE PA.) Despite dismay from some railroad enthusiasts, GENESIS has won awards for industrial design, and today Vergara is one of the most respected names in the industry.

GENESIS diesels incorporate a number of modern features, such as a cruise control speed regulation system that is similar in operation to those on modern automobiles. The cruise control only regulates engine output and does not apply braking systems. As with automotive systems, cruise control is automatically disengaged when brakes are applied. A pioneering feature of the locomotive was in the introduction of an electrically controlled "parking brake" in place of the mechanical hand brake traditionally used on most railroad equipment.

GENESIS Models

All three variations of GENESIS diesels use the same basic monocoque shell, and while they appear near identical externally, they feature significant internal differences. The Series 1, rated at 4,000 horsepower, is designated DASH 8-40BP by GE and P40 by Amtrak. The type debuted in

1993 and 44 were built at Erie between 1993 and 1994; they are numbered in the 800 series. Internally, the GENESIS Series 1 locomotives use DASH 8–era technology. The powerplant is a standard variation of GE's 7FDL-16 prime mover, and traction is provided by GE's GMG 195A1 alternator and four GE 752AH8 traction motors. A 74:29 gear ratio is used for a maximum speed of 103 miles per hour, although in actual service the Series 1 would rarely operate faster than 90 miles per hour. A 79-mile-per-hour maximum speed is typical for passenger trains on many American mainlines, unless equipped with advanced signaling systems. An auxiliary alternator, model GTA33A, drawing up to 1,072 horsepower (800 kW) provides three-phase AC for head-end power used for passenger car heating and lighting. A DASH 8-40BP weighs 268,240 pounds fully loaded and delivers 38,500 pounds continuous tractive effort at 33.3

Three Amtrak GEs—a DASH 8-32PB sandwiched between two GENESIS Series 1s—lead the *Southwest Chief* eastbound past vintage semaphores on the Santa Fe at Chapelle, New Mexico, on September 26, 1995. The longtime domain of EMD's F40PH model, this train is now pulled by these GE units. *Tom Kline*

A pair of Amtrak's P42DCs works upgrade at Lilly, Pennsylvania, with the *Three Rivers* in November 1993. The P42DCs look very similar to the DASH 8-40BWHs but feature slightly greater output. These later GENESIS locomotives also carry lower road numbers, beginning with No. 1. *Brian Solomon*

miles per hour. Like other DASH 8 locomotives, GENESIS locomotives use integrated function electronic controls for optimal performance and reliability, and locomotive engineers run the locomotive with desktop controls. GENESIS Series 1 locomotives featured hostler's controls at the back of the locomotive to facilitate slow-speed yard moves, and as a result feature a small window on the back of the engine. Although potentially useful, this feature was dropped on the later GENESIS types.

General Electric adopted Amtrak's designation scheme for later GENESIS types. Today, the most common GENE-SIS is the 4,200-horsepower model P42DC, which began production in 1996. The first in the series is Amtrak No. 1, and the type now continues into the 100 series. The P42DC uses most of the same primary components employed on the DASH 8-40BP, such as the 7FDL-16 engine and conventional DC-traction motors. It incorporates DASH 9 technology

with features such as electronic fuel injection to improve locomotive performance. The P42DC is capable of 110-mile-per-hour operation, and the most recent order of the type was from Canada's VIA for 21 units in 2001. Used to replace older types in intercity services, they are VIA's first GE locomotives.

The third variety of GENESIS locomotives, and by far the most unusual, is the P32AC-DM, which is significantly different from the other GENESIS types. This specialized machine is designed for service on New York City's third-rail electrified lines—routes that once hosted New York Central's GE-built mainline electrics described in Chapter 1. It's known as a *dual-mode* locomotive (thus the DM in the designation), and is the modern-day successor to EMD's FL9, a type designed in the 1950s for the New Haven. Like the FL9, the P32AC-DM is powered by a diesel engine and can draw power from trackside direct

Passing a boat moored in Rock Cove, Amtrak P42DC No. 196 leads the Spokane section of Amtrak's eastbound *Empire Builder* along the Colombia River at Stevenson, Washington, on July 25, 2002. The single unit will have no trouble maintaining the maximum 79-mile-per-hour speed limit with this consist on this flat water-level track. This locomotive features one of the latest Amtrak liveries, which resembles the scheme used on the *Acela Express* high-speed electric trains. *Tom Kline*

current third-rail using retractable third-rail shoes. Instead of the larger, more powerful, 16-cylinder 7FDL used by the other GENESIS locomotives, the P32AC-DM uses a 12-cylinder 7FDL engine that features electronic fuel injection, works at a maximum 1,050 rpm, and is rated at 3,200 horsepower. One of the P32AC-DM's most significant distinctions is that it uses three-phase alternating current traction instead of conventional DC traction. A single

The unmistakable silhouette of a GENESIS locomotive can be seen through the trees as it races along the Hudson River in January 2000. *Brian Solomon*

Canadian passenger rail operator VIA Rail has been the most recent buyer of the GENESIS locomotive. Its contemporary livery is arguably one of the most pleasing on the GE's modern form. VIA Rail 909 is seen here at Coteau, Quebec. This photograph was made July 12, 2002, the same day as Patrick Yough's photo of the New Haven–painted P32AC-DM in New York City. *Tim Doherty*

GMG 199 alternator is used for both traction and auxiliary power. Four inverters supply controlled AC current to four GEB15 AC-traction motors. The locomotive weighs 277,000 pounds fully loaded (based on specifications from the suburban passenger carrier Metro-North) and can deliver 38,500 pounds continuous tractive effort at 33.3 miles per hour. Like the P42DC, the dual-mode P32AC-DM is designed for 110-mile-per-hour operation.

Amtrak and Metro-North both operate fleets of P32AC-DMs. Amtrak's are numbered in the 700 series and primarily used in Empire Corridor services to New York's Penn Station. Metro-North assigns its GENESIS to its routes radiating from New York's Grand Central Terminal. Four of the P32AC-DMs operated by Metro-North were purchased by the Connecticut Department of Transportation and are painted in a modern adaptation of the New Haven Railroad's famous "McGinnis" livery first used on the GE-built EP-5s. Metro-North often assigns dual-mode GENESIS locomotives to former New Haven branchline services to Danbury and Waterbury, Connecticut. The four CDOT units are used in a pool of equipment for these lines.

GENESIS and the Future

The GENESIS has been a great success. The locomotives are more powerful than older types, allowing Amtrak a unit reduction on some long-distance trains. Also, GE's microprocessor-controlled four-cycle diesel has resulted in considerable fuel savings. Since the introduction of the first GENESIS locomotive in 1993, Amtrak has gradually replaced nearly all of the older road diesels in its fleet—the once ubiquitous EMD F40PH has become a curiosity. By 2001, most Amtrak long-distance trains outside the electrified Northeast Corridor were hauled by GENESIS locomotives.

While the existing GENESIS fleet will likely represent the bulk of Amtrak's diesel fleet for some time to come, as of late 2002, the future of GE's GENESIS line was unclear. American passenger diesels represent only a small portion of the total market, and therefore it is more costly per unit to engineer substantial design changes. This is significant, because more restrictive federal emissions standards will make it impossible for American lines to purchase additional GENESIS locomotives in present configurations. Significant investment will be required to make the type compliant with future air-quality standards.

In 2001, the Connecticut Department of Transportation received four GENESIS P32AC-DMs (dual-mode diesel-electric/electrics) as part of a Metro-North order. Metro-North and CDOT operate 31 Genesis locomotives in commuter service, operating on the former New York Central and New Haven lines radiating from Grand Central Terminal. The CDOT units came delivered in an adaptation of the New Haven's 1950s-era "McGinnis" livery, commissioned by the late Joseph Snopek. Compare this locomotive with the EP-5 electrics built by General Electric in the 1950s. Train 2525 is led northbound by No. 229 at the 125th Street Station in Harlem, New York, on July 12, 2002. *Patrick Yough*

THE EVOLUTION SERIES

From the 1960s through the early 1990s, General Electric's locomotive design changes were aimed largely at improving performance and reliability. Since the late 1990s, however, innovation has been driven by EPA mandates to meet ever-tighter emission controls without compromising locomotive performance, reliability, or fuel efficiency. The results have been some of the most significant changes to GE diesel-electric road locomotives in its five decades of American production.

Despite their technological significance, many of these changes are hidden under the engine hoods. Because they haven't always resulted in obvious modifications to locomotive appearance, they may elude casual observation. While North American Safety Cabs greatly altered the shape of modern locomotives in the late 1980s and early 1990s, today's Tier 2–compliant ES44C4, for example, doesn't look dramatically different from a DASH 8-40CW from the early 1990s. Minor visual cues, such as a change in truck design and radiator thickness, tip off the more recent locomotives.

GE was able to adapt its old 7FDL engine to meet EPA Tier 0 and Tier 1 requirements. However, stricter Tier 2 requirements went into effect in 2005 that demanded more innovation. GE has enjoyed a market advantage because of its superior fuel economy since the 1980s, and by the 1990s, the existing FDL engine

Opposite: On July 9, 2013, a trio of new CSX ES44ACs leading an eastward intermodal train exits the west portal of State Line Tunnel near Canaan, New York, on the former Boston & Albany main line. Since the late 1980s, CSX has preferred GE diesels and has ordered both AC and DC variations of GE's Evolution Series locomotive. *Brian Solomon*

Norfolk Southern's ES44AC heritage units pose for a night photograph at the North Carolina Transportation Museum at Spencer Shops in Salisbury, North Carolina, in July 2012. These three General Electric units are painted to represent Lehigh Valley, Monongahela, and Conrail. NS was a DC-traction holdout but in recent years has found the cost advantages of AC traction appealing. *Patrick Yough*

had been developed to such an extent that any attempt to meet the increasingly stringent emissions requirements would have required an undesirable tradeoff, reducing performance and fuel economy. Instead, the company chose to develop the new, more capable GEVO engine with features that allow the increased fuel injection and cylinder firing pressures to meet emissions goals *and* maintain performance. The resulting technology was an evolutionary advancement of the FDL design and integral to the introduction of GE's Evolution Series locomotives.

In 2003 and 2004, GE built 50 preproduction Evolution Series locomotives for Union Pacific, BNSF, and Norfolk Southern to enable GE to gain field experience with new configurations *before* Tier 2 requirements went into effect. Since the Evolution design was well engineered, few difficulties were found and only nominal design changes were required. The preproduction units share a similar appearance with the later production Evolution units. Evolution Series production began in late 2004, and locomotives were built using either DC or AC traction systems, depending on customer preferences and intended application. For the next 10 years, the ES44AC and ES44DC were GE's standard production models.

In a desire to offer a cost-effective substitute for the six-motor ES44DC, in 2009 GE introduced a variation of its AC traction design: the ES44C4. This AC-traction model employs A1A trucks in place of standard C trucks, allowing for a six-axle, four-motor model. The resulting traction performance is similar to a DC-traction Evolution locomotive while providing many of the cost advantages of AC traction without the high cost of a six-motor AC-traction model. The ES44C4 has equivalent horsepower output to the ES44AC but lower tractive effort. As a result, the primary application for the four-motor ES44C4 has been fast, long-distance intermodal services, which require high horsepower but not great slow-speed tractive effort.

For GE, the advantage of the ES44C4 is that it uses the same essential platform as the ES44AC, thus simplifying production, parts supply, and maintenance. Significant to the locomotive's design is its modern A1A truck with an unpowered center axle. When maximum starting tractive effort is required, a mechanism automatically reduces the weight on the center axle to place more weight on powered wheels. While the center axle remains in contact with the rail, the

amount of the locomotive's weight it carries is reduced. As of mid-2013, BNSF was the sole buyer of the ES44C4, acquiring more than 670 units of the model with more on order for 2014.

In 2013, General Electric began exploring a new option for BNSF, Canadian National, Canadian Pacific, and other customers. To comply with pending Tier 4 emissions requirements for 2015, GE created a strategy to build new locomotives and convert existing locomotives to burn a blend of diesel fuel and liquefied natural gas (LNG). The advantage of LNG fuel is twofold. Leading up to the decision, the price of LNG had dropped to prices much cheaper than diesel for the comparative energy it provides. Equally important, burning it doesn't emit large quantities of nitrogen oxides and harmful particulates associated with diesel, thus requiring less complicated (and more reliable and less expensive) equipment to comply with Tier 4. The difficulty with LNG is that it requires investment in specialized fueling infrastructure, including fuel tenders. Initially, GE anticipated that LNG locomotives would operate only in select high-density corridors where it would be cost effective to build new fueling points, such as BNSF's busy former Santa Fe Transcon route. Although BNSF predecessor Burlington

Above: A detailed view of the rear A1A truck on BNSF ES44C4 No. 7108 shows the extra equipment that helps distinguish this unusual model. This truck is key to the ES44C4 design: when maximum starting tractive effort is required, equipment on the truck reduces weight to the unpowered center axle in order to increase adhesive weight on the outside powered wheels. *Brian Solomon*

Opposite: In 2007, GE and Union Pacific hosted a Green Locomotive Technology Tour aimed at educating the public and media on cutting-edge air-emissions technology. UP ES44AC No. 7605 (designated by the railroad as a C45ACCTE) was specially painted for the tour. Here it leads an eastbound train through California's Afton Canyon on March 30, 2007. It wore this special paint for a short time; photos of it at work are fairly rare. *Chris Guss*

169

Northern experimented with LNG years ago, the concept didn't enjoy widespread application at that time. However, based on future emissions requirements, a successful application of LNG-diesel locomotives may represent the most significant change to locomotive technology in decades.

General Electric effectively exited the new passenger-locomotive market when it delivered the last new GENESIS diesels to VIA Rail in 2002. GE found it uneconomical to continue to devote engineering and manufacturing resources for small batches of specialized locomotives. Instead, GE partnered with MotivePower Inc. (MPI) to supply primary components for modern passenger diesels to be assembled by MPI. For GE, this offers a cost-effective means of providing its expertise in the cons truction of small-order specialized locomotives. The first of MPI's GE-component locomotives was an order of up to 40 Tier 3–compliant units built at MPI's Boise, Idaho, factory for Boston's Massachusetts Bay Transportation Authority.

Among the recent changes to General Electric's production is the opening of a modern manufacturing facility in Fort Worth, Texas, in January 2013. GE plans to gradually phase out its Erie, Pennsylvania, locomotive plant, a traditional facility that has built the majority of its locomotives sold in the United States. The Fort Worth plant initially focused on locomotives ordered by BNSF, including ES44C4s.

Freightliner Class 70 No. 70011 leads a laden ballast train near Greenholme in Cumbria, England, on the West Coast Mainline on September 11, 2013. General Electric's PowerHaul series locomotive is designed for operation in Europe, the United Kingdom, and other overseas markets. It features AC traction and a 16-cylinder PH37ACmi twin-turbocharged diesel rated at 3,690 horsepower. The first 30 of the type were built for U.K. freight operator Freightliner.
Colm O'Callaghan

BIBLIOGRAPHY

Books

Alymer-Small, Sidney. *The Art of Railroading, Vol. VIII.* Chicago, 1908.

American Locomotive Co., General Electric Co. *Operating Manual Model RS-3.* Schenectady, N.Y., 1951.

——. *American Railroad Journal—1966.* San Marino, Calif., 1965.

Armstrong, John H. *The Railroad—What It Is, What it Does.* Omaha, Nebr., 1982.

Bruce, Alfred W. *The Steam Locomotive in America.* New York, 1952.

Burch, Edward P. *Electric Traction for Railway Trains.* New York, 1911.

Bush, Donald J. *The Streamlined Decade.* New York, 1975.

Churella, Albert J. *From Steam to Diesel.* Princeton, N.J., 1998.

Dolzall, Gary W. and Stephen F. Dolzall. *Baldwin Diesel Locomotives.* Milwaukee, Wis., 1984.

Drury, George H. *Guide to North American Steam Locomotives.* Waukesha, Wis., 1993

Farrington, S. Kip Jr.. *Railroading from the Head End.* New York, 1943.

——. *Railroads at War.* New York, 1944.

——. *Railroading from the Rear End.* New York, 1946.

Garmany, John B. *Southern Pacific Dieselization.* Edmonds, Wash., 1985.

General Electric. *New Series Diesel-Electric Locomotive, Operating Manual.* Erie, Pa., 1979.

——. *GENESIS SERIES 2 P32AC-DM Operating Manual.* Erie, Pa., 1998.

Harris, Ken. *World Electric Locomotives.* London, 1981.

Haut, F.J.G. *The History of the Electric Locomotive.* London, 1969.

——. *The Pictorial History of Electric Locomotives.* Cranbury, N.J., 1970.

Herrick, Albert, B. *Practical Electric Railway Hand Book.* New York, 1906.

Hinde, D.W., and M. Hinde. *Electric And Diesel-Electric Locomotives.* London, 1948.

Hollingsworth, Brian. *The Illustrated Encyclopedia of North American Locomotives.* N.Y., 1997.

——. *Modern Trains.* London, 1985.

Hollingsworth, Brian, and Arthur Cook. *Modern Locomotives.* London, 1983.

Keilty, Edmund. *Interurbans Without Wires.* Glendale, Calif., 1979.

Kiefer, P.W. *A Practical Evaluation of Railroad Motive Power.* New York, 1948.

Kirkland, John F. *Dawn of the Diesel Age.* Pasadena, Calif., 1994.

——. *The Diesel Builders Vols. I, II, and III.* Glendale, Calif., 1983.

Klein, Maury. *Union Pacific, Vols. I* and *II.* New York, 1989.

Kratville, William, and Harold E. Ranks. *Motive Power of the Union Pacific.* Omaha, Nebr., 1958.

Marre, Louis A. *Diesel Locomotives: The First 50 Years.* Waukesha, Wis., 1995.

Marre, Louis A., and Jerry A. Pinkepank. *The Contemporary Diesel Spotter's Guide.* Milwaukee, Wis., 1985.

Marre, Louis A., and Paul K. Withers. *The Contemporary Diesel Spotter's Guide, Year 2000 Edition.* Halifax, Pa., 2000.

McDonnell, Greg. *U-Boats: General Electric Diesel Locomotives,* Toronto, 1994.

Middleton, William D. *When the Steam Railroads Electrified.* Milwaukee, Wis., 1974.

——. *Grand Central . . . The World's Greatest Railway Terminal.* San Marino, Calif., 1977.

——. *From Bullets to BART.* Chicago, 1989.

——. *Manhattan Gateway: New York's Pennsylvania Station.* Waukesha, Wis., 1996.

Pinkepank, Jerry A. *The Second Diesel Spotter's Guide.* Milwaukee, Wis., 1973.

Ransome-Wallis, P. *World Railway Locomotives.* New York, 1959.

Reagan, H. C., Jr. *Locomotive Mechanism and Engineering.* New York, 1894.

Reckenzaun, Anthony. *Electric Traction on Railways and Tramways.* London, 1892.

Signor, John R. *Tehachapi.* San Marino, Calif., 1983.

——. *Donner Pass: Southern Pacific's Sierra Crossing.* San Marino, Calif., 1985.

Solomon, Brian. *Trains of the Old West.* New York, 1998.

——. *The American Diesel Locomotive.* Osceola, Wis., 2000.

——. *Super Steam Locomotives.* Osceola, Wis., 2000.

——. *The American Steam Locomotive.* Osceola, Wis., 1998.

——. *Locomotive.* Osceola, Wis., 2001.

Stevens, John R. *Pioneers of Electric Railroading.* New York, 1991.

Strack, Don. *Union Pacific 2000—Locomotive Directory.* Halifax, Pa., 2000.

Strapac, Joseph A. *Southern Pacific Motive Power Annual 1971.* Burlingame, Calif., 1971.

Books Continued

——. *Southern Pacific Review 1981.* Huntington Beach, Calif., 1982.

——. *Southern Pacific Review 1953–1985.* Huntington Beach, Calif., 1986.

Swengel, Frank M. *The American Steam Locomotive: Volume 1, Evolution.* Davenport, Iowa, 1967.

Trewman, H.F. *Electrification of Railways.* London, 1920.

Winchester, Clarence. *Railway Wonders of the World, Volumes 1* and *2.* London, 1935.

Withers, Paul K. *Norfolk Southern Locomotive Directory 2001.* Halifax, Pa. 2001

Brochures

Bearce, W.D. *Steam-Electric Locomotive.* Erie, Pa., 1939.

General Electric. *Dash 8 Locomotive Line.* (no date)

——. *GE Locomotives.* (no date)

——. *Super 7 Locomotive Line.* (no date)

——. *Series 7 Diesel-Electric Locomotives.* Erie, Pa., 1980.

——. *Achieving a Leadership Position in Turbocharger Technology.* Erie, Pa., 1982.

——. *A New Generation for Increased Productivity.* Erie, Pa., 1984.

——. *A New Generation for Increased Productivity.* Erie, Pa., 1987.

——. *GE Diesel Engines—Power for Progress.* Erie, Pa., 1988.

——. *GENESIS Series.* 1993.

Periodicals

Baldwin Locomotives. Philadelphia, Pa. (no longer published)

CTC Board. Ferndale, Washington.

Diesel Era. Halifax, Pa.

Diesel Railway Traction, supplement to *Railway Gazette* (UK). (merged into *Railway Gazette*)

Jane's World Railways. London.

Modern Railways. Surrey, U.K.

Official Guide to the Railways. New York.

Pacific RailNews. Waukesha, Wis. (no longer published)

Passenger Train Journal. Waukesha, Wis. (no longer published)

Railroad History, formerly *Railway and Locomotive Historical Society Bulletin.* Boston, Mass.

Railway Age, Chicago and New York.

TRAINS Magazine. Waukesha, Wis.

Vintage Rails. Waukesha, Wis. (no longer published)

EMD
LOCOMOTIVES

Baltimore & Ohio was the first to receive Electro-Motive's new E unit. Powered with a pair of 900-horsepower Winton 201-A engines, the "E" delivered eighteen hundred horsepower. Electro-Motive's Winton-powered E's embraced elegant streamlining with flush headlamps, a gracefully slanting nose, and smooth-pilots. Later production units did not embody the same level of finesse and panache as these custom-designed machines. A nearly new Baltimore & Ohio model EA and EB pose with a passenger train at Chicago in the 1930s. *Otto Perry, Denver Public Library Western History Department*

CHAPTER ONE

THE WINTON ERA

In the early years of the twentieth century, transportation in the United States began a period of profound and dynamic change. Rate regulation, rising labor costs, and an escalation in public financing for building roads resulted in growing competition for railway services, while limiting the railroads' abilities to adjust their rates or lower costs. Initially, branch lines were hit the hardest by these changes. Lightly used lines were, at best, marginally profitable. So a niche industry developed to provide self-propelled internal combustion–powered railcars well-suited for branch line work.

Author Edmund Keilty chronicled this fascinating business in his book *Interurbans Without Wires*. Among the manufacturers building these railcars were companies specializing in electric trolley car manufacturing, such as the Philadelphia-based J. G. Brill Company—a logical business plan as there were many similarities between the two types of equipment. Another was the McKeen Motor Car Company of Omaha, Nebraska, famous for knife-nosed streamlined cars powered with internal combustion engines with a mechanical transmission.

Although McKeen built more than 150 cars of various sizes, its cars were unreliable and short-lived with their inadequate technology. More successful was General Electric, which combined internal combustion engines with an electric

transmission. Although not the first to apply this blend of new technologies, GE developed the internal combustion–electric to new levels of perfection and this technology is the direct predecessor to the diesel-electric locomotive.

A cyclical decline in railcar sales during World War I resulted in both McKeen and GE exiting the railcar business. While McKeen's technology was essentially a dead end, GE's efforts led to further development. GE made a brief, but unsuccessful, independent foray into commercial diesel-electric production during the World War I period. (GE later re-entered the diesel locomotive market, first as an electrical supplier for Ingersoll-Rand and later with established steam locomotive manufacturer Alco and then went out on its own again after 1953.) More important than GE's early diesel business was the traction technology and knowledge pool that emerged as a result of its railcar business. Many of the key engineers who invented and refined technology for commercial diesel-electric locomotive production worked for General Electric during this period, including Hermann Lemp and Richard Dilworth.

Lemp's Control System

A gas-electric car used an internal combustion engine to drive an electrical generator that provided current to traction motors for propulsion. Together, the generator, control system, and traction motors powered the electrical transmission and functioned in a manner comparable to a mechanical gearbox in an automobile. Among the difficulties with early rail motor cars were ineffective and unreliable methods of power transmission. The McKeen cars' failings were largely attributed to that company's use of a mechanical transmission, while the early gas-electric cars suffered because they did not effectively or efficiently match engine output with the generator.

To make for efficient operation of an internal combustion–electric propulsion system, engine output needs to match the load drawn by the generator to power the traction motors. Excess engine output is a waste of energy, while inadequate output may cause the engine to stall. Extreme mismatches between output and load can damage the equipment. Working between 1916 and 1919, Hermann

P32313. L.6145. PLAN. 7172. 7-24-28. P.V.V.

Lemp devised a control system that provided optimal performance by matching engine and traction characteristics and putting them under the direction of a single throttle handle. Unfortunately for GE, the company had effectively abandoned its internal combustion rail business before it could take advantage of Lemp's innovation.

The Electro-Motive Company Is Born

The growth of rural highway competition during the 1920s renewed railroad interest in cost-saving railway motor cars to retain traffic. In the early 1920s, an entrepreneur named Harold L. Hamilton sensed a business opportunity where GE and others had given up. He had experience with railroad technology, understood the industry, and had worked as a successful salesman in the highway truck business. Hamilton's insight gave him confidence that he could develop a successful railcar business by improving railcar designs while actively marketing this technology to the railroads. To this end, Hamilton and his business partner, Paul Turner, formed the Electro-Motive Engineering Corporation on August 31, 1922, soon renamed the Electro-Motive Company. Based in Cleveland, Ohio, the new company hired experts in gas-electric car design, among them GE's Richard Dilworth.

Despite its expertise, Electro-Motive began as an outsider in the railroad supply industry. To gain a market, it adopted atypical sales and construction practices. Traditionally, railway equipment suppliers worked with a particular railroad in equipment design and then constructed equipment using agreed-upon specifications. Electro-Motive's approach was to engineer standard designs, coordinate railcar production, and actively market its product, but it neither owned a factory nor actually built product itself. Instead, all construction was subcontracted to established manufacturers. In his book, *Dawn of the Diesel Age*, author John Kirkland explains that "EMC pursued a policy of having the railroad contract with a car builder of its own choosing." He further states, "Electro-Motive would send a foreman out to the car builder's plant to supervise the installation of equipment, including the components supplied though EMC, using the car builder's labor."

The railcars' engines were supplied by the Winton Engine Company, also of Cleveland, and the electrical components, including Lemp's recently invented control system, were typically supplied by GE.

It was nearly two years from the time of Electro-Motive's inception to delivery of its first car, which author Edmund Keilty lists as Chicago Great Western No. M-300. This 35-ton car measured 59 feet 4 inches long and was powered by a 175-horsepower Winton distillate engine. It was constructed in February 1924 by the St. Louis Car Company—a respected builder of railroad cars and electric trolleys. Electro-Motive's early car construction was also contracted to the Osgood-Bradley Car Company, Pullman Standard Car Manufacturing Company, Standard Steel Car Company, and Bethlehem Steel Corporation.

By designing and refining standard product lines, development costs decreased, significantly reducing the price of individual railcars. Streamlining the development process also helped Electro-Motive deliver a more reliable product, as did the company's very high quality standards and high production quality from its suppliers. Some railcars were built primarily to accommodate passengers. Others combined passenger space with room for mail and

181

The rural branch line passenger railroad was a part of American life that has entirely faded from the scene. At one time, thousands of small communities across the lower 48 states, and in Canada and Mexico, were connected and served by branch line railroads. In addition to passenger service, railroads carried the mail, small packages (including express shipments), and other less-than-carload traffic. Marginally profitable at best, branch lines were the first services to suffer from highway competition. On April 20, 1959, Northern Pacific motorcar No. B-21 makes a station stop at Lisbon, North Dakota. *William D. Middleton*

Northern Pacific was a longtime Electro-Motive customer. Gas-electric B-18 was an Electro-Motive product of 1929. It was a 77-foot 2-inch-long car with a 300-horsepower engine assembled by Standard Steel. It crosses the Great Northern at Breckenridge, Minnesota, while an eastward Great Northern freight led by Electro-Motive F units holds off at the home signals on April 20, 1959. *William D. Middleton*

small freight shipments, since most passenger trains of that period were also conveyors of mail and "less-than-carload" (small) freight shipments from rural locations.

The earliest Electro-Motive cars were designed to run singly and came equipped with a relatively low output of 175 horsepower. In early 1925, Winton introduced a 225-horsepower gasoline engine, followed by a 275-horsepower engine later that year. By 1927, 300- and 400-horsepower engines were available. Some of the more powerful cars used a pair of Winton engines. Keilty cites one of these as the Santa Fe car M-190, which used an articulated design and was powered by a pair of Winton 900-horse-power V-12 distillate engines intended to haul up to five passenger coaches.

Electro-Motive's business started slowly but gained momentum in its first few years. It sold just two railcars in 1924, followed by three dozen in 1926. Yet, by the late 1920s, it was the leading seller of gas-electric railcars. Keilty writes that in 1928, Electro-Motive sold 105 cars—the largest number in one year. "By this time [Electro-Motive founder Harold] Hamilton was selling eight out of every ten gas-electrics purchased by U.S. roads," he adds.

General Motors

Electro-Motive's success as an independent railcar builder was short-lived, though. Two crucial events altered the company's course: the onset of the Great Depression after the stock market crash of 1929 and General Motors' decision to

Electro-Motive's doodle-bug building era lasted only a dozen years. Its last cars were a pair of semi-streamlined units assembled by the St. Louis Car Company for the Seaboard Air Line in April 1936. By the time this car was built, Electro-Motive had entered the diesel age and was on its way to becoming the nation's leading locomotive manufacturer. One car survived Seaboard's 1967 merger with rival Atlantic Coast Line and became Seaboard Coast Line 4900. Doug Eisele collection

purchase Winton in 1930. The stock market crash of 1929 and the economic depression it spurned hit American railroads especially hard. As robust traffic levels of the 1920s dropped off, so did orders for new equipment. Railroads were reluctant to invest in new equipment for their normally busy and profitable main lines, and even less inclined to spend money on railcars for lightly traveled branches. Coincident with the beginning of the Depression were the decisions by automaker General Motors to purchase Winton on June 20, 1930, and to run the company as its Winton Engine Corporation subsidiary. It appears that, at the time of sale, GM was largely interested in Winton's work with diesel engines, built for stationary and marine purposes for more than a dozen years.

Winton had been Electro-Motive's engine supplier, and Electro-Motive was Winton's largest customer. This close relationship between the two companies led GM to also acquire Electro-Motive. So on December 31, 1930, six months after acquiring Winton, GM bought Electro-Motive, renaming it the Electro-Motive Corporation. Interestingly, Electro-Motive had used Winton's distillate spark-ignition engines for railcar propulsion, not its diesels.

Some authors argue that GM had a grand plan for entering the locomotive field and acquiring Winton and Electro-Motive were the logical first steps to developing a diesel-locomotive business. In *Dawn of the Diesel Age*, John Kirkland states, "General Motors purchased Electro-Motive Company with the ultimate objective of converting this company from basically a rail motor car engineering, service, and sales organization into an integrated Diesel [sic] locomotive builder."

Historian Albert Churella offers a distinctly different view in his paper titled *Corporate Culture and Marketing in the American Locomotive Industry: American Locomotive and Electro-Motive Respond to Dieselization.* "GM's decision to purchase Electro-Motive had far more to do with chance than with any prior corporate strategy (there was none) to penetrate the diesel locomotive market. In the late 1920s, GM embarked on a program to develop an automotive diesel engine. GM executives decided to buy a leading diesel engine manufacturer and combine that company's technology with GM's capital and R&D facilities," he says.

Churella also explains that forces within Electro-Motive and keen railroad interest in diesels pushed GM into the diesel locomotive business.

Diesel Developments

At this crucial juncture in 1930, the diesel engine had been around for some 35 years. German inventor Rudolf Diesel introduced his first experimental diesel engine in 1893. Although a commercial failure, it led to his design of a much better engine in 1896, which began commercial production in Germany a year later. The diesel is distinct from spark ignition engines since it uses gas compression for ignition. Diesel's engine was inspired by the theoretical heat cycle derived by French scientist N. L. S. Carnot. Although deviating from the Carnot cycle, Diesel's engine was an extraordinarily efficient design, achieving thermal efficiency roughly four times greater than typical steam engines of the period. (Thermal efficiency is a measure of how well an engine converts fuel to work.)

The first diesel engine to operate in the United States was demonstrated at the Electro-Exhibition in New York City during May and June 1898. Early applications for diesels were primarily stationary powerplants. These engines were typically large, heavy machines using a cast-iron block and four-stroke-cycle design. Diesel locomotives were considered as early as 1906, and the first diesel locomotive was developed in Switzerland during 1909 and

The *Zephyr* is seen at a dedication ceremony in Chicago Union Station in the mid-1930s. Today, this famous articulated train set has been cosmetically preserved at Chicago's Museum of Science and Industry. *Henry R. Griffith, William D. Middleton collection*

1913. This machine used a two-cycle engine directly connected to a driving shaft that was coupled to drive wheels using siderods. Although commercially unsuccessful, the engine was a historic first.

In 1918, General Electric built several diesel-electrics, but all were commercial failures. One, designated No. 4, was delivered to the Jay Street Connecting Railroad on the Brooklyn waterfront and joined an earlier GE gas-electric, No. 3. Two others were built: one for the City of Baltimore and the other for the U.S. Army. None of the diesels performed well.

GE and Ingersoll-Rand joined forces in the early 1920s to build and market slow-speed, low-horsepower diesel-electric switchers. A demonstrator was constructed in 1923, and it embarked on a successful tour of eastern railroads in 1924. Alco joined the consortium and began production of commercial diesel-electric switchers in 1925, the first of

which was sold to the Central Railroad of New Jersey. Today, this historic machine, CNJ 1000, is preserved at the Baltimore & Ohio Railroad Museum in Baltimore, Maryland.

By the early 1930s, several manufacturers offered low-speed switchers in the 300- to 600-horsepower range—locomotives typically powered by very large and heavy diesel engines with cast-iron blocks. The heavy cast-iron block was necessary to withstand the forces of high compression needed for combustion, yet this resulted in a high weight-to-horsepower ratio, typically 60 pounds per horsepower. This arrangement was acceptable for slow-speed switching services, but inadequate for high-horsepower applications where the size of the engine would have been prohibitively heavy. The early GE-IR-Alco 600-horsepower boxcabs required a pair of 300-horsepower IR diesels. Winton's own stationary model W-40 diesel during the World War I period weighed 45 tons and produced just 450 horsepower. It had a 200–pound-per-horse power ratio—much too heavy per horsepower for railway applications.

In the late 1920s and early 1930s, several significant advances in engine technology overcame the limitations imposed by the heavy diesels of the earlier era. Especially important among these advances was the development of high-pressure solid fuel injection pumps and multiple orifice fuel injectors. Solid fuel injection forces pressurized atomized fuel directly into the cylinder, eliminating the high-pressure fuel lines and external fuel delivery apparatus that plagued earlier engine designs. Injectors were among the most expensive components of a diesel engine manufacture, requiring precision machining with very tight tolerances. Advances in metallurgy during the 1920s, combined with new welding techniques, also permitted the construction of much lighter engine blocks, which were capable of withstanding the higher stresses inherent in high-output diesel engines.

In the early 1930s, the U.S. Navy—then one of the largest customers for diesel engines—coalesced various recent technological advances into practical commercial technology by providing incentives to build more effective propulsion for submarines. Among the engine producers benefiting from new technology were Cooper-Bessemer, Fairbanks-Morse, General Motors' Winton Engine, and McIntosh & Seymore. Each of these companies ultimately produced compact, lightweight diesels with a high power-

to-weight ratio well suited for use in submarines and rail-road locomotives.

GM's Charles Kettering was in charge of this research and worked with Winton to develop a lightweight, high-horsepower two-stroke-cycle diesel. An article in the December 1937 issue of *Railway Mechanical Engineer* paraphrased a Kettering lecture describing the design process, which offered this insight on fuel injectors: "The limits on the pump for the very high-pressures at which they must operate are very small indeed. As we say in the shop, 'Our limits are a quarter of a tenth of a thousandth of an inch.' "

At that time, General Motors was still very new to the diesel business. While the economy was soft, Kettering's vision of the future was clear when, in the same December 1937 article he said, "We do have the greatest confidence in the world that the Diesel can be developed into a most important industry—one which will be of great service to the railroads, one which will put more men to work, and one which will expand our ideas of the uses of power beyond anything of which we now know."

In light of Kettering's statement, it seems ironic that General Motors' success in diesel locomotive manufacturing produced one of the greatest labor-saving devices for railroads. Powerful standardized diesel locomotives ultimately closed railroad shops all across the United States and around the world. Diesels allowed fewer employees to do the jobs once performed by many.

Winton 201

Two-cycle internal combustion engines had been around for decades in the early 1930s, but most commercial diesel engines used a four-cycle design at the time—including those manufactured by Winton. Seeking to obtain greater

In 1935, Boston & Maine bought a near duplicate of Burlington's original *Zephyr*. B&M number 6000 was initially assigned to the *Flying Yankee*, which ran from Boston's North Station to Portland and Bangor, Maine, over B&M and Maine Central tracks. In later years, it was assigned to a variety of different trains. Working as *The Mountaineer*, it was photographed surrounded by the old guard at Boston's North Station on July 6, 1940. *Carleton Parker, courtesy of Bob's Photo*

Like Burlington's original *Zephyr*, Boston & Maine 6000 has been preserved and is undergoing restoration. However, unlike *Zephyr*, the B&M train may someday run under its own power. The stainless-steel power car for B&M 6000 was being worked on at the Claremont & Concord shops at Claremont, New Hampshire, on June 6, 1999. *Jim Shaughnessy*

The original restoration plan for bringing Boston & Maine 6000 to working order included restoration of the inline Winton 201-A engine—one of the few remaining examples of this early diesel motive power. The engine is seen in the power car in the Claremont & Concord's shops on June 10, 2003. Since the time of this photo, propulsion plans for the 1935 streamliner have changed and the original Winton will probably not be used. *Jim Shaughnessy*

power without a substantial weight increase, Kettering and his GM design group chose to refine a two-cycle design.

In engines, each piston motion up or down is a piston stroke, and its "cycle" refers to the entire sequence of strokes. A four-stroke-cycle engine requires two complete crankshaft rotations and two up-and-down piston sequences of the pistons within the cylinders to complete a full combustion sequence. The first piston upstroke compresses air in the cylinder, raising its temperature to the combustion point. At the appropriate moment, diesel fuel is mechanically injected into the cylinder and, under pressure, it ignites. (The diesel does not require spark plugs for ignition, although some compression engines may use spark plugs for starting.) The explosion thrusts the piston down in the second cycle, called a power stroke. In the third cycle (second upstroke), the piston forces exhaust gases from the cylinder, and in the fourth cycle fresh air is drawn into the cylinder completing the sequence. A two-stroke-cycle engine accomplishes the full combustion sequence in just one crankshaft rotation.

A two-stroke-cycle engine obtains greater power from the same size engine block as a four-stroke-cycle engine (or

as the case with GM's design, a much smaller two-cycle engine can obtain the same output as a larger four-cycle engine). In simple terms, a two-stroke fires twice as often and half as hard as a four-stroke.

During the early 1930s, Kettering and his design group perfected an engine designated the 201, which, in its original format, used an 8-cylinder inline block with 8x10-inch cylinders operating at 750 rpm. Each cylinder produced 75 horsepower for a total output of 600 horsepower. The engine's power-to-weight ratio was about 20 horsepower per pound, nearly 10 times lighter per horsepower than most previously successful locomotive diesel engines. Intended for marine applications, the first pair of working 201 diesels was publicly displayed at the Century of Progress Exposition at Chicago in 1933. Production engines of this design were known as the 201-A.

Birth of the Streamliners

There's nothing like nationwide publicity and public interest to sell your idea. Until 1934, the diesel engine and diesel locomotive were little known among the public. However,

when dressed up in slick, newly designed trains and paraded around the country, the diesel suddenly emerged in public consciousness.

Nationwide rail ridership had reached a new low by 1933. While mass-produced private automobiles and publicly financed highway projects in the 1920s cut severely into railroad passenger revenues, rail ridership dropped to the lowest levels in decades with the onset of the Great Depression. U.S. railroad managers watched this trend with dismay, but few had any ideas how to reverse the trend. Progress in Germany again directed American innovation. In 1932, manufacturer Wagen und Maschinenbau AG built a two-unit, aerodynamic, streamlined diesel-electric railcar powered by pair of 12-cylinder 410-horsepower Maybach diesel engines. The train's design was the result of extensive wind-tunnel experiments, conducted at the Zeppelin Works in Friedrichshafen. The train garnered worldwide attention in its testing phase, and on May 15, 1933, the *Fliegende Hamburger*—The Flying Hamburger—made headlines as the fastest regularly scheduled train in the world. The diesel-powered passenger train was seen as the future.

This event coincided with the Century of Progress Exposition in Chicago, which brought together all the right people to conceive of American equivalents to the Flying Hamburger. What could be a better business strategy than making trains new and exciting? Why not make them more like their competition—cars and airplanes? They could be sleek, fast, modern, and fashionable.

As a result of the Century of Progress, representatives from General Motors, Pullman, and the Philadelphia-based Budd Company (named for its proprietor Edward Budd) met with key railroad officials. Soon both Pullman and the Budd Company were simultaneously tackling competing streamliner projects. Pullman worked with Union Pacific (UP) and Budd with UP's archrival, the Chicago, Burlington & Quincy (Burlington); General Motors agreed to supply modern engines for both projects.

Propulsion was only part of the strategy. Union Pacific and Burlington were racing to get their trains ready first to capture headlines. In early 1934, Pullman's new three-piece

aluminum streamliner was essentially ready to go, but GM's new 201 diesel engine wasn't. To get its train on the road ahead of Burlington's, Union Pacific settled for a Winton distillate (spark ignition) engine instead of a diesel.

On February 12, 1934, Pullman delivered its new internal combustion–powered, high-speed streamlined articulated passenger train to Union Pacific—a train known as No. M-10000 and named *Streamliner*. It was built from a lightweight tubular carbody and covered by a thin, riveted, aluminum skin. The three cars weighed a total of only 85 tons, roughly that of a single heavyweight passenger car. The cab of the train was perched up above an immense mouth-like grill that resembled an ominous, alien face. There was no mistaking this train at the time of its inauguration: it bore no resemblance to conventional steam trains, nor to its railcar heritage.

Inside the carbody, the 12-cylinder 600-horsepower Winton distillate engine provided power for traction motors. Enough fuel was carried to run 500 to 900 miles, and the train was tested at speeds up to 110 miles per hour. Fuel

costs were calculated at less than one-third that of a comparable steam train—a fact that greatly impressed Union Pacific operating officials. On the train's debut, Union Pacific Chairman Averill Harriman announced that the company planned to acquire two similar streamliners for transcontinental service.

Before entering service, the *Streamliner* embarked on a 12,625-mile publicity tour of the United States. This was not just another train—it was a vision of hope. An estimated two million people came to see it, and dignitaries and public officials across the nation inspected the train, including the newly elected president of the United States, Franklin D. Roosevelt. Having concluded its tour, the M-10000 entered regular service on a 197-mile run between Kansas City, Missouri, and Salina, Kansas, as Union Pacific's *City of Salina*.

Burlington's Zephyr

Burlington's *Zephyr* was a product of Burlington and Budd engineering teams. The train's arrangement was similar to that of UP's *Streamliner*, and Burlington worked with the Massachusetts Institute of Technology to conduct comprehensive wind-tunnel experiments to produce the most efficient aerodynamic profile.

Budd employed its proprietary shot-welded process to construct the stainless-steel frame with fluted stainless-steel sides for the *Zephyr*'s body. The train measured 197 feet long and weighed 100 tons, making it nominally heavier than the aluminum *Streamliner*, but significantly lighter than a typical three-car passenger train and steam locomotive. The *Zephyr* featured a distinctive "shovel nose," which contrasted sharply with Union Pacific's "mouth-like grill" and carried a resemblance to a medieval knight's polished helmet. The train's name was the inspiration of Burlington's Ralph Budd (no relation to Edward Budd), who came up with the moniker based on Zephyrus, the Greek god of the west wind.

The *Zephyr*'s engineer rode at the very front, with an unobstructed view of the tracks through a row of forward-facing windows. This feature provided much better visibility

Burlington's *Zephyr* was powered by one of Winton's first 201-A engines, making it America's first successful diesel-powered high-speed passenger train. The Budd-built *Zephyr*'s striking stainless-steel streamlining sparked national interest in diesel-powered trains and stainless-steel fluted-side passenger cars. Many railroads were inspired by *Zephyr* and, to a lesser extent, Union Pacific's *Streamliner* and later ordered streamlined passenger trains. *Otto Perry, Denver Public Library Western History Department*

compared to a steam locomotive, where the engineer had to look past the length of the boiler. Yet it posed a safety hazard for the crew, since thin sheet metal offered little protection in the event of a collision.

The Budd Company unveiled the *Zephyr* in Philadelphia, Pennsylvania, on April 18, 1934. Like *Streamliner*, the *Zephyr* went on a publicity tour before entering revenue service. Aesthetically, the *Zephyr* was a far more striking train than *Streamliner*. The *Zephyr* looked fast, and its tail-end observation lounge provided an extraordinary view of the tracks and passing scenery.

Numbered CB&Q 9900, the *Zephyr* made American history as the nation's first diesel-streamliner. It was powered by Winton's first production eight-cylinder 201-A diesel engine. In a very short time, it proved to be a spectacular success. Its introduction was more than just a boon for Burlington, as it propelled business opportunities for both

the Budd Company and General Motors. The engine demonstrated the great achievements of General Motor's engineering forces, setting an important precedent for further diesel applications. Perhaps no other single train has been so crucial in changing public perception and influencing business practice.

Streamliner Mania

The successes of the *Streamliner* and *Zephyr* sparked a host of similar trains. Not only did UP and Burlington place repeat orders for diesel streamliners, but other railroads wanted them, too. In 1935, Boston & Maine ordered a near-duplicate of the *Zephyr* from Budd, for service as the *Flying Yankee*, while Illinois Central ordered a train similar to Union Pacific's from Pullman, for service as the *Green Diamond*.

Initially, the streamlined look and speed of these trains captured public imagination rather than the diesel engines.

The promise of fast streamlined services led Milwaukee and Southern Pacific to develop their respective steam-powered *Hiawatha* and *Daylight* trains, while numerous other lines dressed up old steam locomotives with elaborate shrouds in an effort to appear modern.

General Motors Enters the Locomotive Business

The early streamliners were a boon for public relations, but proved limiting in revenue service. The primary flaw with the early streamliners was not the diesel engine but the articulated design. As articulated fixed train sets, the early streamliners were inflexible, making it impossible to adjust consists as patronage ebbed and flowed. If any problem developed with the diesel power car or any other car in the train, the entire consist had to be taken out of service for repair. With a conventional train, a railroad could overcome a failure by simply providing a substitute locomotive or switching out a defective car.

Perhaps the early streamliners' most valuable role was in demonstrating the diesel's capabilities in railroad service to railroad management. The diesel streamliners proved they were the future not just to the railroads, but also to officials at Electro-Motive's parent company. Top GM management was forced to see the great potential market for diesel locomotives. The company responded by backing research and development, marketing, and modern construction facilities for these engines and locomotives.

Probably no other company was better suited to make this investment. In 1935, General Motors was the world's largest industrial company, and it made a firm financial commitment to large-scale diesel locomotive production that year.

With GM's commitment came some fundamental changes in the way Electro-Motive did business. In the past, it had strictly been an engineering and marketing firm that relied on subcontractors to construct its products. Now with GM's help, Electro-Motive would build its own locomotive shops and bring the construction process in house. Its new plant was located at La Grange, Illinois, a few miles west of Chicago—America's most important railroad interchange. Yet while its new facility was being built, Electro-Motive continued to rely on its traditional production methods and contracted its early diesel production to its suppliers.

Baltimore & Ohio's "Capitol Dome" emblem on its pioneer model EA No. 51. The hollow shell of this historic locomotive is preserved at the Baltimore & Ohio Railroad Museum in Baltimore. Sadly, the Winton diesel engines and electrical equipment were removed. *Brian Solomon*

Passenger Boxcabs

The failings of the articulated diesel train set demonstrated that the industry really needed a true passenger diesel locomotive—one that could be operated separately and coupled to any consist using conventional Janey couplers rather than specialized semi-permanent drawbar connections. In this regard, Electro-Motive's product evolved rapidly from providing an engine for custom-designed streamliner power cars to producing a commercial diesel-electric passenger locomotive. By the mid-1930s, it had engineered a diesel-electric powerful enough to haul *any* passenger consist and not just specialized lightweight streamlined trains. This was a big step toward establishing Electro-Motive's reputation in the locomotive business.

Steam locomotive manufacturers custom-engineered locomotives for each of their customers and typically worked with the railroads in the design process. By contrast,

This rare view of Rock Island TAs shows them back to back at Blue Island, Illinois, on November 23, 1956. Notice the unusual tapered carbody at the back of the locomotives, designed to match the car profile of the early streamlined *Rocket* for which the locomotives were built. The lower headlight orifice was not part of the original design but was added later by Rock Island in order to fit the locomotives with oscillating headlights.
Jim Shaughnessy

Electro-Motive needed to sell its product to a skeptical and wary industry. It wanted a working demonstrator to show off its product's capabilities. This practice had worked well for the Alco-GE-IR boxcab switchers a decade earlier.

But not all lines needed convincing. By 1935, both Baltimore & Ohio and longtime Electro-Motive railcar customer Santa Fe were eager for diesel power and ordered road locomotives before the demonstrators were ready to roll. Initially, Electro-Motive produced five boxcab road diesels: two demonstrators and three for customers. All five used the standard B-B wheel arrangement and were powered by dual Winton 201-A V-12 diesels that produced a combined output of 1,800 horsepower.

The demonstrators were Nos. 511 and 512 and were assembled at GE's Erie, Pennsylvania, plant. Each unit weighed 240,000 pounds and was typically used together as a 3,600-horsepower pair. The combination was powerful enough to haul conventional long-distance passenger trains. In *On Time*, author Franklin Reck indicates that the boxcab demonstrators burned 2.7 gallons of diesel per mile when hauling a typical 12- to 14-car passenger train, and based on contemporary coal and oil prices, the boxcabs represented a 40 to 60 percent fuel savings over steam.

Santa Fe's boxcabs, popularly known as "The Twins," shared internal characteristics with the demonstrators, yet featured semi-streamlined external styling. These two are generally considered the first commercially-built high-speed passenger diesel locomotives separate from an articulated train. In May 1936, Santa Fe assigned these boxcabs to its newest luxury train—the *Super Chief*, a weekly, all-heavyweight Pullman sleeper, running between Chicago and Los Angeles. With diesel power, the train was able to make the 2,000-mile run in just 39 hours and 45 minutes—15 hours faster than the best steam-powered run.

With this type of service, the boxcabs clearly demonstrated the advantages of diesel-electric locomotives without the problems associated with fixed articulated trains. While often operated together as a single 3,600-horsepower locomotive, the boxcabs could also be separated and used individually. Baltimore & Ohio received a single 1,800-horsepower boxcab, which it assigned for service on the *Royal Blue*—its premier New York-to-Washington train.

Diesel Switchers

When Electro-Motive began building locomotives, the largest-established market for diesels was not passenger locomotives but yard switchers. Consequentially, this was the

market the company targeted, and initially the bulk of its regular production at the new La Grange plant was for switchers. Electro-Motive offered two standard switcher types: a 600-horsepower locomotive that used an 8-cylinder Winton 201-A and a 900-horsepower locomotive powered by a 12-cylinder Winton 201-A in the "Vee" format. Since Electro-Motive was still relying on traditional suppliers for electrical gear, its early diesel switchers were built with either General Electric or Westinghouse electrical components.

Different locomotive models were offered to accommodate different specifications. The SC was a 600-horsepower model with a cast frame (the SC designation a result of the combination of "S" for six hundred and "C" for cast frame), and the SW, also 600 horsepower, used a welded frame. The 900-horsepower models were designated NC and NW models and followed a similar pattern for classification. Cast-frame switchers were built to satisfy an old-school railroad philosophy that was inherently distrustful of new ideas and unwilling to accept that a fabricated, welded frame could withstand the rigors of heavy service. However, the welded frame switchers had significant advantages. They

Cosmetically and technically kin to the early E units, Rock Island's TAs rode on B-B trucks rather than Blomberg-designed A1As. This comparison at Blue Island, Illinois, shows the differences in styling between the TA (right) and the later FP7 (left). Notice the window on the TA behind the cab door. *Jim Shaughnessy*

were much lighter, cheaper to manufacture, and better suited to mass production. So in the late 1930s, Electro-Motive abandoned the cast frame, although competitor steam builders continued to manufacture diesels with cast frames into the late 1940s.

Electro-Motive quickly captured the diesel switcher market, building 56 locomotives in 1936 and 94 in 1937—the lion's share of diesel locomotive production at that time. Although the switcher had been the first lucrative market for the diesel-electric, the diesel switcher was still a tough sell to railroads resistant to change in the mid-1930s.

Electro-Motive promoted the diesel switcher as a cost-saving machine. The company needed to overcome the railroads' reservations to invest in its expensive diesels instead of similar machines offered by traditional locomotive builders such as Alco. One advertisement in *Railway Mechanical Engineer* boasted that on the Rock Island Electro-Motive diesel switchers were operating at 98 percent availability, and each locomotive was "saving $1,000.00 per month over and above carrying and amortization charges." Highlighting these savings, the advertisement reported that Electro-Motive diesel switchers normally reduced fuel costs by 75 percent and cut maintenance costs by 50 percent. Also diesel switchers resulted in less wear on the tracks and fewer derailments.

Winton Es

The boxcab demonstrators generated great interest in passenger diesels while also serving as valuable test beds for company engineers. They allowed engineers to work out design flaws, improve essential technology, and create a better diesel locomotive to compete with well-established steam technology. These early machines impressed many railway officials, but also had flaws that needed to be addressed before a successful locomotive line could be introduced. The Winton 201 diesel engine itself was problem, and ultimately Electro-Motive engineers chose to design a whole new engine, which is discussed in Chapter 2.

Under the direction of Dick Dilworth, Electro-Motive engineers designed an all-new passenger locomotive to match the performance characteristics of the best Hudson-type steam locomotives, considered the most advanced steam locomotive of its time.

Significant changes were made to the cab arrangement. Cab placement with the streamliners and boxcabs had placed the engineer in front and relatively low to the rail. While good for visibility, it put train crews in a perilous position in the event of collision.

A fatal accident on the Pennsylvania Railroad with one of its P5 boxcab electrics had resulted in a redesign to favor a center cab configuration, as used by its famous GG1. A Burlington shovel-nose *Zephyr* suffered from a similar accident. Taking these events into consideration, Electro-Motive relocated the operator's position and changed the front surface to a reinforced rounded nose, designed to deflect objects that might strike the front of the train. The engineer's cab was moved to an elevated position set back from the front and above the protective nose, providing greater forward visibility while shielding the view of tracks rapidly passing below. The latter modification was to alleviate concerns that crews would become mesmerized or sickened by the moving cross-ties, a psychological phenomenon termed "train nystagmus." The cab relocation resulted in significant rearranging of internal components, including the engine(s) and main generator. The cab and rounded nose modifications were concurrent with a new framed body structure, which served as an integral support structure rather than just external covering.

The aesthetically impressive air intake system used by early streamliners was also eliminated. The large front-mounted grills forced debris, insects, birds, and small animals struck by the train into the engine compartment, making a mess that required constant cleaning. With the new carbody, the air intake vents were located on the sides of the locomotive.

Streamlining was both functionally and aesthetically important. The public expected that the new locomotives would have a modern, sleek appearance. When the new E-unit models debuted in 1937, they fulfilled modern design tastes, taking styling cues from both streamliner power cars and the latest GM automotive designs. All the Winton E units were powered by two 900-horsepower 201-A V-12 engines, giving each locomotive 1,800 horsepower. (The "E" designation is believed to be derived from this rating.)

These units rode on a new style of truck, better distributing the locomotive's weight. Designed by Martin Blomberg, these trucks were a six-wheel design, with the outside axles powered and the center axle unpowered. Each truck was designated "A1A" to reflect the power arrange-

ment, and the A1A-A1A wheel arrangement soon became a standard feature of streamlined passenger locomotives. The Blomberg truck employed a system of outside swing hangers, using both elliptical and helical springs, to provide great stability and speed while enabling the locomotive to negotiate tight curves.

First to order Es were Baltimore & Ohio, Santa Fe, and Union Pacific railroads—customers who were already familiar with Electro-Motive diesels. To B&O, Electro-Motive delivered the very first commercially produced streamlined passenger diesel-electrics: 12 model EA/EBs. The EA cab units were typical of the styling adorned by the Winton Es. They featured a graceful sloping nose with inset headlight and a stylish Electro-Motive–originated paint scheme.

In May 1937, Santa Fe received the first of its 11 E1A/Bs, delivered to haul its new Budd-built streamlined

passenger cars. These employed a similar body styling to the B&O's EAs, but were the first locomotives dressed in the unmistakable flashy red, yellow, black, and silver scheme now known as the Santa Fe warbonnet—the work of Electro-Motive designer Leland A. Knickerbocker. While specifically intended for the stylish streamlined E1s, the warbonnet was adapted to dozens of other locomotive types, and it is among the most recognizable railroad liveries of all time.

For Union Pacific, Electro-Motive built six distinctively styled E2A/Bs. Like later streamliner power cars, this locomotive model featured a bulbous front end and rows of side port-hole windows, but it lacked the distinctive grill.

Not all of the streamlined diesels were Es. Rock Island ordered six exquisitely streamlined passenger diesels that rode on B-B trucks rather than the Blomberg A1As. These were rated at 1,200 horsepower and designated as model

TA. To the novice, these locomotives appear to be a prelude to the F-unit model that emerged a few years later, but technologically they had more in common with the Winton-era E units than the later Fs.

On the tenth anniversary of the E-unit debut, an Electro-Motive advertisement in the May 1947 *Railway Mechanical Engineer* touted Baltimore & Ohio's fleet as a showcase for reliability and service. It read: "Thirteen of the 22 General Motors Diesel [sic] passenger locomotives on the Baltimore & Ohio Railroad have completed more than a million miles each on heavy passenger runs. Three have passed the two-millionth milepost. Total mileage for these time-proved veterans is: 21,587,501 miles."

Old B&O E No. 56 had run 2,043,546 miles since it hit the road in June 1936. It averaged 19,840 miles per month. While this old Winton E had the most miles on its wheels, some of the more recent Es had even more impressive monthly averages. B&O No. 80, built in October 1945, was averaging better than 22,000 miles a month and had a 99.5 percent availability for service. Its story is told in Chapter 2, which covers the 567 era—the diesel locomotive manufacturing boom for Electro-Motive.

Electro-Motive built model E2 diesels in 1938 for Union Pacific, Chicago & North Western, and Southern Pacific's jointly operated *City of San Francisco*. The train pictured here was the second-generation streamliner from 1938 that replaced the original articulated lightweight train of 1936. At the time these locomotives were constructed, Electro-Motive was still producing custom-designed machines. The styling of the E2s was unique to this customer. These used Westinghouse electrical gear rather than the GE electrical equipment used by most early Electro-Motive locomotives. *Fred Matthews collection*

Lifeline OF TOMORROW

RISING magnificently to cope with every disaster and emergency for nearly a century, the American railroads have just re-verified the statement that they are "the lifeline of the nation." Manpower, equipment and multitudinous other problems were met and overcome.

Wartime restrictions curtailed improvements and construction, but not planning. And, that planning takes in trains, tracks, terminals — a gamut of seen and behind-the-scene factors. When welded with new materials, new and improved methods, trains that will far surpass anything previously offered — in luxury and style, comfort and service — will emerge from this planning. We of the Seaboard look forward with confidence to the day we enter this role.

Now that Peace reigns again; the saga of American heroes has been written, the Seaboard, together with the other railroads, will again demonstrate and win the approbation of the public as "the lifeline of the nation" . . . a lifeline that will aid us to better enjoy the better way of life promised for the better world of tomorrow.

Our original locomotive, imported from England in 1836. Since that early date, our parent companies and the present Seaboard system have been providing progressively finer service.

CHAPTER TWO

THE 567 ERA

The Winton 201-As compact size and high power-to-weight ratio made it vastly superior to earlier designs. Yet inherent design inadequacies made it a less than an ideal locomotive engine. From the beginning, the 201-A had been intended for marine applications, a very different environment than the gritty, vibration-immersed, frequent start-and-stop, rapid turnaround conditions on railroads.

Electro-Motive knew it had to do better and sought help from its adoptive parent GM. This redesign effort began as early as 1935, as Albert Churella relates in his paper, *Corporate Culture and Marketing in the American Locomotive Industry: American Locomotive and Electro-Motive Respond to Dieselization*. He states that General Motors decisively "authorized the development of a diesel engine designed specifically for railroad service."

So what was exactly wrong with the 201-A, which had successfully powered America's first diesel-electric passenger trains? After it had been superseded by the 567, the October 1950 issue of *Diesel Railway Traction* detailed the 201-A's operating experience and design concerns. Winton had built the 201-A in three configurations for railroad service: the "straight eight"—an inline, 8-cylinder model typically rated at 600 horsepower working at a maximum 750 rpm; a 12-cylinder

Opposite: Wabash E8A 1007 pulls through the switches at St. Louis Union Station on July 22, 1958. This was one of 457 E8As built by Electro-Motive. The dual-engine Es were standard power for many long-distance passenger trains into the Amtrak era. *Richard Jay Solomon*

"Vee" model; and a 16-cylinder "Vee" model. Although cylinder size was consistent between 201-A models, many components were not interchangeable. And variations in the piston heads, connecting rods, water pumps, and cylinder liners and heads, as well as other equipment, meant that railroads needed separate parts supplies for each model of 201-A. *Diesel Railway Traction* notes that a Santa Fe's general mechanical assistant listed a variety of causes for Winton engine failures, including faulty camshafts, crankshafts, bearings, cylinder liners, pistons and piston rings, and problems with the cooling system.

Burlington's H. H. Urbach, in the July 1939 issue of *Railway Mechanical Engineer*, provided more illuminating inside observations by the men who operated and main-

tained America's first fleets of road diesels. In "Operation of Diesel Locomotives," Urbach quotes Santa Fe's J. P. Morris, general assistant of the mechanical department (possibly the same man cited by *Diesel Railway Traction*), as saying this regarding the Winton engine (which is not mentioned by name or model): "On all two-stroke cycle engines, pistons are removed and liners and connecting-rod bearings are inspected once each year, but in some cases we find it necessary to renew these parts between annual inspections."

At the time of Urbach's article, the 567 engine was new, having been in production for about a year. Morris noted in the piece that Santa Fe railroad executives were hopeful that the 567, with its improved type pistons and additional

The stainless-steel styled E5 was unique to the Burlington. Internally, these employed the same equipment as the E3, E4, and E6 models but were styled in a similar fashion as the Winton-era Budd-built trains and intended to operate with Budd-built lightweight stainless-steel passenger cars. On March 31, 1958, the westward *Morning Zephyr* passes St. Anthony Tower between St. Paul and Minneapolis, Minnesota. *William D. Middleton*

Electro-Motive E5 model plate on Burlington E5 No. 9911A. *Brian Solomon*

piston cooling, would "show up favorably with the four-stroke cycle engine in piston performance."

Despite reports of extraordinary availability and very high average monthly mileage as advertised by Electro-Motive, difficulties with the 201-A engines required considerable maintenance. The streamliners with their ultra-fast schedules required nonstop running and quick turnaround times, making for demanding performance on the part of the equipment. This resulted in high wear on the diesel engine and allowed little time for maintenance compared to steam. Demanding schedules gave Electro-Motive engineers an opportunity to learn how lightweight diesels performed and the types of problems they developed. With some of the streamliners running more than a 1,000 miles a day, they functioned as an accelerated learning lab for railroad diesel research. So as the streamliners raced across the plains and prairies, impressing onlookers and passengers alike, there was an unseen sideshow going on *inside* the locomotives.

To insure that these diesels made it over the road, Electro-Motive engineers often rode every run. They did more than just collect data and check oil pressure; they kept the engines functioning, making substantial repairs to their wards. Piston heads and connecting rods were routinely changed at terminals to compensate for high wear rates. Furthermore, it was not uncommon for engines to develop problems en route, requiring Electro-Motive engineers to make heavy repairs at speed as the train journeyed on its remaining engines. (Following the original *Zephyr*, most of the early transcontinental streamliners employed three to four Winton engines, so shutting down one engine for a few hours did not cause undo delay.) The enclosed carbody was more than an attractive Art Deco design for the public—it kept rain and wind from interfering with the mechanics' repairs.

Today, with the high reliability and low maintenance expected of modern diesels, employing rolling diesel maintainers in order to keep locomotives running seems an extraordinary measure. Yet in the 1930s, the ability to repair locomotives on the move was viewed as an asset when compared with steam, which could not be repaired while moving. Consider the opinion of Chicago & North Western's H. P. Allstrand, principle assistant superintendent of motive power and machinery, as paraphrased by Urbach in his 1939

Right: Canadian Pacific Railway E8A 1800 and a Boston & Maine E7A resting side-by-side in CPR's engine house near Montreal's Windsor Station provide a comparison between variations in GM's bulldog nose. The B&M unit has the older style of number and marker lamps and the rounded pilot. CPR 1800 features flush number boards and the straight pilot with enclosed coupler housing.
Jim Shaughnessy

Opposite: One of two Bangor & Aroostook E7As gets a bath at Northern Maine Junction on March 10, 1955. The E7A carbody could be easily distinguished from the later E8s and E9s by its rectangular side windows and wire-covered side air-intake vents. The later Es had four port-hole windows on each side and stainless-steel grilles over the air-intake vents. More important were technological differences inside the locomotive that made the later Es more reliable and more powerful.
Jim Shaughnessy

article: "The possibility of carrying on repair while the unit is en route . . . permits a greater continuity of service than has ever been possible with reciprocating steam locomotives."

The 567

Electro-Motive's 567 engine was an entirely new design with significantly enhanced performance and reliability compared with earlier Winton diesels. The 567 design was much influenced by experience with the Winton 201-A, and it shared some of the older engine's basic design characteristics, such as a welded lightweight steel crankcase; however, there were many changes between the two designs. The 567's piston bore was 8.5 inches compared with 8 inches on the 201, and the operating speed increased from 750 rpm to 800 rpm. (The designation 567 stems from individual cylinder displacement of 567 cubic inches, a classification system that continued with 645 and 710 engine designs.) The 567 was initially built for railroad applications in 6-, 8-, and 12-cylinder formats. Unlike the Winton designs, the various 567 engine formats did allow for component interchangeability wherever practicable. Cylinder assemblies were designed to allow easy removal and replacement.

A high rate of piston failure was a critical Winton weak point. So on the 567, Electro-Motive changed both the construction and material use for piston heads. In latter years, the Winton had used forged aluminum alloy piston heads on the 201-A, but the 567 used malleable cast-iron piston heads. Likewise, the 567's crankshaft was made from carbon steel rather than the 201-A's nickel-chrome alloy steel. Changes were also made to the main bearing design, which had plagued the 201-A. The blower was completely redesigned using geared drive instead of chain drive.

Better Es

At the end of 1938, Electro-Motive introduced the 567 engine on its new E-unit models. Four models—E3, E4, E5, and E6—were built, and each was powered by a pair of 12-567s. The engines were rated at 1,000 horsepower, giving each E unit 2,000-horsepower output.

Externally, there were few differences between the E3, E4, and E6 models, while the E5 was unique to the Burlington. It was easily identified by a distinctive stainless-steel styling along the lines of the original *Zephyr*, although the body shape was consistent with the other new 567-powered Es. The styling of these mass-produced models was more conservative than the earliest E units.

While the custom-designed 201-A-powered Es were built in small numbers for just a few customers, mass-produced Es were sold to railroads all over the country. Of the four models, the E6 was by far the most common model, with 118 A and B units built.

Moving Tonnage

In its first years as a commercial locomotive manufacturer, Electro-Motive quickly dominated the diesel locomotive market. It sold more switchers than anyone else and basically invented the commercial passenger diesel. Yet switchers and fancy passenger diesels were not the largest segments of the locomotive market. To really make its mark on the industry, Electro-Motive planned to tackle the heavy freight locomotive market, which represented the most profitable railroad traffic and the biggest sector for locomotive sales.

With little fanfare in November 1939, Electro-Motive sent out its 5,400-horsepower, streamlined model FT demonstrator, No. 103, on a nationwide tour. This four-unit business-like machine was the first of Electro-Motive's famous F units. Dressed in a stylish dark green and mustard yellow, the locomotive was a four-unit set—two A-unit cabs bracketing two B-unit boosters.

The FT was similarly styled as the early E units, but had a cleaner, more conservative look. It was the first application of what became known as the bulldog nose—perhaps Electro-Motive's most enduring visage. With a more vertical nose slant, the FT had subtle styling that was functional as well as aesthetical. It was intended for mass-production, so could be constructed and repaired easily. It was designed to operate in four-unit sets with the nose section of the trailing cab coupled to freight cars. This was a situation where a long slanting nose was neither practical nor necessary.

Each unit contained a single 16-cylinder version of the 567 engine—Electro-Motive's latest prime mover. Over the next 25 years, this engine would become one of Electro-

Chicago & North Western E3A 5002 and SD7 1660 seem generations apart sitting side-by-side in Chicago on July 17, 1958. However, the SD7 emerged from La Grange only 14 years after the E, and at the time of this photo, the E unit was only 19 years old. Both models employed the 567 engine design, a pair of 12-cylinder 567s for the E, and a single 16-cylinder 567 on the SD7.
Richard Jay Solomon

Motive's greatest successes, selling tens of thousands worldwide. The FT's 16-567 was rated 1,350 horsepower—more than twice the output of the Winton straight eight.

The FT A units were 48 feet 3 inches long, while B units measured just 48 feet 1 inch. Each unit rode on the newly designed four-wheel Blomberg trucks that incorporated a spring suspension system adapted from that used on the A1A Blomberg truck. The April 1941 issue of *Railway Mechanical Engineer* detailed the new trucks by stating the following:

The four-wheel truck assemblies are interchangeable. Greater stability and improved riding qualities in negotiating curves are obtained by the same method of load suspension as on Electro-Motive six-wheel trucks for passenger locomotives. The alloy cast steel truck frames . . . are supported on each of the four journal boxes by twin-group coiled springs. The swing bolster is supported at each end by spring hangers pivoted from the outside of the

On April 18, 1953, Boston & Maine FT 4215 waits for a clear signal to depart the east end of the Mechanicville, New York, yard. Boston & Maine acquired a fleet of 48 FT units 10 years earlier. Their reddish-brown and gold livery, designed by Electro-Motive, echoed the colors of autumnal New England foliage. *Jim Shaughnessy*

Santa Fe was first to order FTs and operated the largest roster of them—320 A and B units. Unlike most production FT units, Santa Fe's had couplers rather than a fixed drawbar connection between the A and B units. This gave the railroad greater flexibility in how it assigned motive power. On September 16, 1950, an A-B FT set works as a rear-end helper on a westward freight crossing California's Cajon Pass. *William D. Middleton*

truck frame. Each of the two traction motors in each truck is supported by the driving axle to which it is geared and a spring motor nose suspension on the truck transom.

This style of truck was perhaps the FT's most enduring legacy. The basic design remained in regular production on freight locomotives for more than 55 years. Hundreds, if not thousands, of these remain in service as of 2006.

Electrical Transmission

The 16-567 engine powered a D-8 main generator that produced 600 volts direct current to power four model D-7b traction motors, a type derived from a General Electric design. One geared motor was connected to each axle, using reduction gearing with a 62:15 ratio.

Reduction gearing is necessary to compensate for inherent limitations of the motors. Because of centrifugal forces, the maximum rotational speed of motors is limited. If a motor spins too quickly, it will be damaged. Minimum continuous speed is a regulated electrical characteristic of DC motors. The motor can only accept so much current before it is damaged by overheating. On American heavy-haul diesel-electric locomotives, this gearing between the motor and axle is fixed, although it can be changed by exchanging components in a heavy locomotive shop. A

Great Northern FTs at Clyde Yard on December 4, 1960. More than any other locomotive, the FT set the wheels turning to banish steam. By 1960, when this photo was taken, mainline steam operations were relegated to excursion service. *John Gruber*

compromise is necessary to select a gear ratio that best suits intended service. The gear ratio is expressed with two numbers; the first number indicates the number of teeth on the bull (axle) gear, and the second number indicates the number of teeth on the motor pinion gear.

The DC generator on these early diesels used a primitive design, with limited capabilities. Its inability to both provide sufficient current at low speed and sufficient voltage at high speed precluded direct motor connections. Instead, relay circuitry was used to arrange different motor connections to best match generator output with the traction motor draw at different speeds. Changing from one arrangement to another was known as "transition" and served a similar function as does an automobile gearbox.

On the FT, four motor connections were used: series-parallel, series-parallel-shunt, parallel, and parallel-shunt. When working the locomotive, its engineer needed to initiate motor transitions by manually moving a transition lever in the cab. Forward transition was made as the locomotive

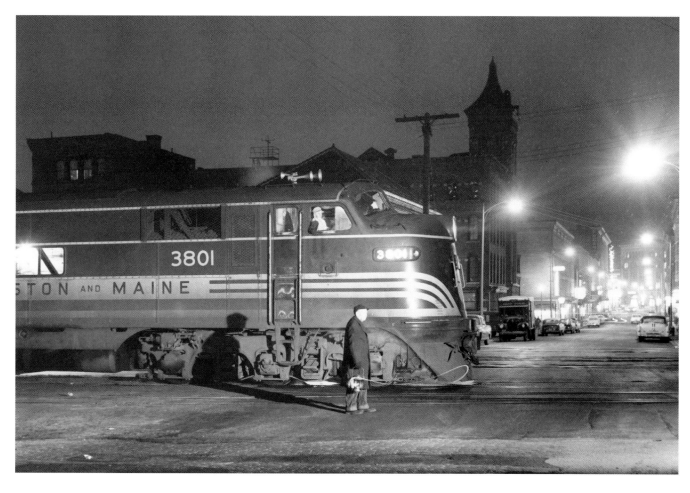

Left: Electro-Motive's E7 was the most popular new passenger locomotive of the postwar era. It was designed for speeds up to 117 miles per hour and featured the neatly streamlined bulldog nose. The E7 was more powerful and more reliable improvement over all previous E-unit designs and sold at a time when railroads were still making a large investment in passenger equipment. On January 17, 1958, Boston & Maine E7A 3801 leads train No. 62 at Troy, New York. *Jim Shaughnessy*

Opposite top: Operation of FTs in two-unit or four-unit sets proved inefficient for some railroads, since 2,700 horsepower was too little power and 5,400 horsepower was too much. Also, operating two unit sets of FTs required turning the units at terminals. After the war, a number of railroads purchased F2A and F3As to facilitate operation of A-B-A sets. An Erie F3A leads two FTs with a heavy eastward freight crossing the famous Starrucca Viaduct near Lanesboro, Pennsylvania, on October 29, 1961. *Jim Shaughnessy*

Opposite bottom: The Missouri-Kansas-Texas' November 1, 1946, public timetable featured F3s. Electro-Motive diesels allowed railroads to put on a modern image, and these streamlined diesels on a crack "red ball" freight, were seen as the way forward. Soon, those dirty old black steam locomotives would be relegated to history. *Richard Jay Solomon collection*

gathered speed and reverse transition was made as it slowed. Later post-World War II F units did away with the need for manually initiated transition by using control circuitry to initiate transition automatically. For a few years after these new F units were introduced, new locomotives were still built with a transition lever on the control stand for situations when older locomotives were operated in multiple.

A-B-B-A

Electro-Motive designed the FT for operation in either 2,700-horsepower A-B pairs or as a full 5,400-horsepower A-B-B-A set, but not as individual units. In the original FT arrangement, the cab and booster units were semi-permanently paired with a fixed drawbar in place of a conventional coupler. In addition, a paired set shared some common electrical equipment, such as batteries, which were located only in the B unit. One reason for this inflexible arrangement was to help avoid labor issues that might arise if each unit was deemed as an individual locomotive that required manning.

The Electro-Motive No. 103 demonstrator with the new 567 engine made its rounds for 11 months, hauling heavy freight and passenger trains while covering nearly 84,000 miles and passing through 35 states. It was tested on 20 Class I carriers. As might be expected, it visited regular customers including B&O, CB&Q, and Santa Fe. It gave an impressive performance and clearly demonstrated the potential of a heavy diesel-electric freight locomotive. The four-unit FT could deliver an impressive 228,000 pounds of starting tractive effort, more than even the most powerful modern steam locomotives.

FT Hits the Grade

Santa Fe was especially keen on dieselization. It was the first to purchase Electro-Motive boxcabs, second to buy its E

continued on page 50

Above: An A-B set of FTs lead a short New York, Ontario & Western freight at Summitville, New York, on March 23, 1957— a few days before the line ceased all operations.
Jim Shaughnessy

Right: Even diesels could not save New York, Ontario & Western. The line was among the weakest American Class I railroads. Bankrupt during World War II, its trusties tried in vain to save the line by investing in cost-saving CTC signaling and new GM diesels. The plan failed and NYO&W was abandoned in 1957. NYO&W's shiny FT and F3 diesels rest in the company's Middletown, New York, shops in March 1957.
Jim Shaughnessy

NYO&W followed up its acquisition of 18 FT units, 9 As, and 9 Bs, with a small order, for F3s. This overhead view of F3A 822 and two FT units at Maybrook, New York, provides a good illustration of some differences between the two models. The dynamic brake vents on the F3 are the two long rectangular areas directly behind the horns. On the FT units, dynamic braking grids and vents were housed in the raised roof areas at the center of the locomotive. *Jim Shaughnessy*

Bangor & Aroostook E7A No. 10 takes a spin on the turntable at Northern Maine Junction in 1955. One of the disadvantages of single-cab, carbody-style diesels was necessity for turning facilities at terminals. Bangor & Aroostook had just two E7s. After BAR exited the passenger business in September 1961, it removed steam generators and regeared its E7s from 57:20 to 62:15 for freight service. Then, in 1967, it traded them back to Electro-Motive. *Jim Shaughnessy*

Santa Fe freight F3s, in the classic A-B-B-A formation, pose for a publicity photograph in California's Cajon Pass on November 23, 1953. A four-unit set of F3s was rated at 6,000 horsepower, 600 more than an original four-unit FT set. Santa Fe had one of the largest fleets of F units and continued buying them through the F9 model. *Santa Fe Railway photograph by Frank E Meitz*

Santa Fe F7s assigned to the *Chief* pose in Cajon Pass. Perhaps the most popular of all American locomotives, the Santa Fe's F units have been reproduced in the tens of thousands by model manufacturers. *Santa Fe Railway photograph by R. Collins Bradley*

units, an early buyer of switchers, and eagerly hoped to eliminate steam operations on desert lines in the Southwest (defraying the high cost of supplying clean boiler water). The first to buy FTs, Santa Fe was dissatisfied with the units' fixed drawbar pairing and insisted its units were equipped with conventional couplers instead.

Santa Fe's first FTs were constructed in late 1940 and entered into service in February 1941. These allowed the railroad to effectively eliminate steam operation between Winslow and Barstow—making this the first long portion of American mainline to boast complete dieselization. This line included the longest unbroken grade in the United States—from the Colorado River crossing at the California-Arizona state line (near Needles, California) to Yampai Summit. Here, Santa Fe found that FTs were more capable of handling freight than even its most modern steam loco-

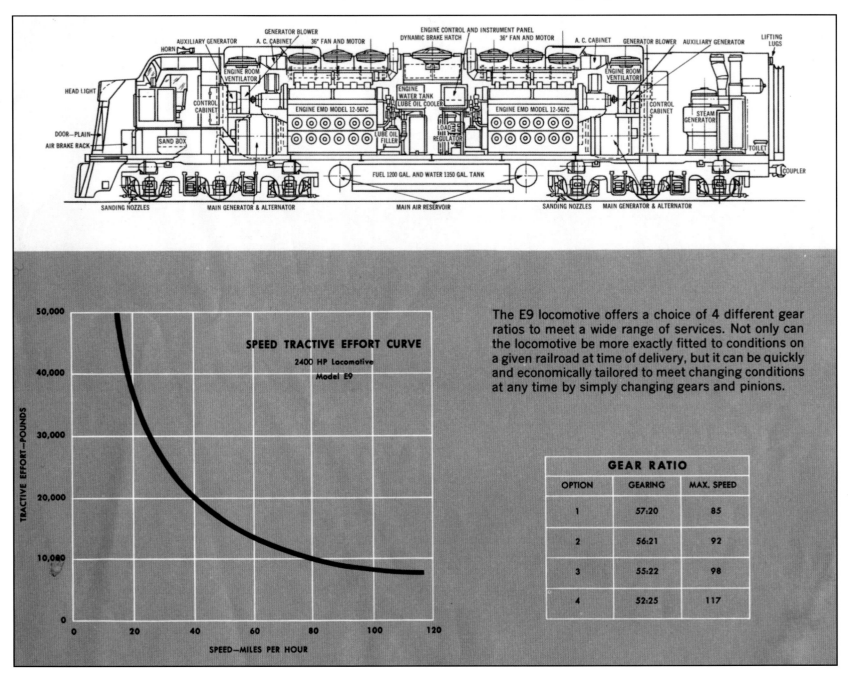

SPEED TRACTIVE EFFORT CURVE

2400 HP Locomotive

Model E9

The E9 locomotive offers a choice of 4 different gear ratios to meet a wide range of services. Not only can the locomotive be more exactly fitted to conditions on a given railroad at time of delivery, but it can be quickly and economically tailored to meet changing conditions at any time by simply changing gears and pinions.

GEAR RATIO		
OPTION	GEARING	MAX. SPEED
1	57:20	85
2	56:21	92
3	55:22	98
4	52:25	117

motives. S. Kip Farrington, in *Railroads at War*, stated that on this run Santa Fe's four-unit FTs routinely hauled 3,500 tons and more without a helper, far great tonnage than the line's best steam power.

The FT provided a cost-effective and powerful alternative to steam. The combination of superior fuel economy, excellent traction, and very high availability made it an instant commercial success. More FTs were sold than all previous Electro-Motive railway units combined. With 320 units, Santa Fe had the most by far, followed by the Great Northern's 96 and Southern Railway and its subsidiaries with 76.

Most FTs were sold as freight locomotives, yet some railroads ordered FTs with steam generators suitable for passenger service. A few lines, including Santa Fe, used these in dual service. Although production was temporarily suspended in 1943 (when Electro-Motive's facilities were allocated for submarine engine production), a total of 555 A units and 541 B units were built between 1939 and 1945. Twenty-three American railroads ordered them.

Dynamic Brakes

An important feature developed for the FT was dynamic braking. Though not a new concept, the application on commercially built diesel-electrics was a first. Some straight electric locomotives had employed regenerative braking similar to dynamic braking, whereby traction-motor current was reversed, making them function as electric generators retarding forward progress. With regenerative braking, the generated electricity was returned to the power grid via the catenary, which helped balance the cost of operation.

Dynamic braking on diesel-electrics wasn't afforded this option, though, so the current generated was distributed to electric resistor grids for conversion into heat, which was dissipated into the atmosphere with blowers. While a less efficient use of energy, dynamic braking was very useful tool for controlling long freight trains. It reduced brake shoe wear and speeded operations by obviating the need to stop to cool overheated brakes or set up air brake retainers—a common practice for controlling heavy air-braked trains descending long grades in the steam era.

Santa Fe's FTs had the first commercial application of dynamic brakes. These were designed to dissipate more

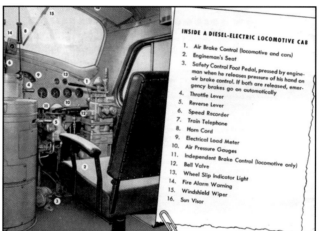

INSIDE A DIESEL-ELECTRIC LOCOMOTIVE CAB

1. Air Brake Control (locomotive and cars)
2. Engineman's Seat
3. Safety Control Foot Pedal, pressed by engineman when he releases pressure of his hand on air brake control. If both are released, emergency brakes go on automatically
4. Throttle Lever
5. Reverse Lever
6. Speed Recorder
7. Train Telephone
8. Horn Cord
9. Electrical Load Meter
10. Air Pressure Gauges
11. Independent Brake Control (locomotive only)
12. Bell Valve
13. Wheel Slip Indicator Light
14. Fire Alarm Warning
15. Windshield Wiper
16. Sun Visor

Above: Canadian National Railway was among the first railroads in the world to experiment with road diesels, but it was slower to embrace commercially produced diesels than lines in the United States. One of just a handful of F3s built for Canadian National, F3A No. 9000, built in 1948, was the railroad's second diesel to carry that number; the first was one of two experimental road diesels built in 1928 to 1929. On October 12, 1956, No. 9000 leads a freight train at Bay View Junction, Ontario. *George C. Corey*

Left: Pennsylvania Railroad's promotional booklet, *Modern Power for Today's Trains*, gave the public a view of a typical Electro-Motive locomotive cab, probably an F3A. The drum-style control stand and automotive-like dashboard gauges were typical of early General Motors diesel cabs. *Richard Jay Solomon collection*

than 4,700 horsepower of energy, but they employed a fairly primitive electrical system and thus were only effective at a narrow speed range. As a result, the dynamic brake was initially viewed as a holding brake. The technology advanced quickly, though. On later locomotives, braking was effective at a broader speed range.

With the introduction of the FT, dynamic braking soon became a standard option on most North America road diesels. Not all railroads took advantage of them, though, as operating locomotives without dynamic brakes cost less.

Baltimore & Ohio Chicago Terminal NW2 9509 switches near Grand Central Station in Chicago on July 21, 1958. This was one of the three NW2s built for B&OCT in 1943, making them a rare example of an Electro-Motive switcher produced during the war. This locomotive was rated at 1,000 horsepower and delivered 62,100 pounds starting tractive effort. The NW2 can be easily distinguished from later switchers by its half-sized front radiator. *Richard Jay Solomon*

A Name Change and War

On January 1, 1941, General Motors reorganized the Electro-Motive Corporation as its Electro-Motive Division. Since then, the initials EMD have become synonymous with diesel-electric locomotives; tens of thousands of EMDs have been built for service around the world. (To avoid confusion in this text, the American diesel-building division has been consistently referred to as Electro-Motive, using the words General Motors, EMC, and EMD only where appropriate for clarification or necessary as a result of quotation.)

By this time, the war overseas had generated an enormous flow of both freight and passenger traffic on American railways. The demand had been anticipated—to some extent. As early as 1937, President Franklin Roosevelt had urged railroads to take measures to prepare for a possible surge of wartime traffic. However, when war broke out in Europe in September 1939, traffic was more intense than anyone envisioned. Never before had so much been expected of American railroads—and no railroad was truly prepared.

These dramatic increases in traffic came after a decade of underinvestment in rail infrastructure and new motive power, and so the surge of traffic placed an enormous strain on railroad capacity. As the war heated up in Europe, the pressure was on. By 1940, lines that had been virtually empty during the Great Depression were choked with traffic. And the demand for motive power further heightened when the United States entered the global conflict in December 1941.

Milwaukee Road No. 80 is a late-build F3A with most of the external features of early F7A units, including large number boards, stainless-steel air-intake vents, and low-profile exhaust fans. The determining features that distinguish F3s from F7s are not external trappings, but internal differences, primarily in the electrical systems. This public relations photo indicates Milwaukee's A-B-B-A set has handled 55 loaded cars weighing 3,575 tons on the 2.3 percent grade in the Washington Cascades between Morton and Divide. *Milwaukee Road photo from the Association of American Railroads, John Gruber collection*

Maine Central E7A 706 leads a short train eastward across the Willey Brook Trestle on the railroad's famous Mountain Division near Crawford Notch, New Hampshire, in May 1953. The E7 was powered by a pair of 12-cylinder 567 engines. This overhead shot provides a view of the rows of four separate engine exhaust stacks for each engine. *Jim Shaughnessy*

Complicating matters, direct American involvement in the war put the need for locomotives in competition for resources with construction of armaments and other military hardware. Soon after the dust on Pearl Harbor settled, the government established the War Production Board (WPB) to govern manufacturing and ration allocation of vital materials. It imposed strict production limitations on locomotives, restricting the number of units built, the types individual railroads could purchase, as well as the types each builder could produce. Not only were material resources in short supply, but the locomotive manufacturers themselves were needed for production of military matériel.

To focus production and limit problems with parts supply, the WPB designated Electro-Motive the primary builder of road diesels, a logical choice it would seem since Electro-Motive had been the largest builder of road diesels prior to the war. While steam builders Alco and Baldwin were allocated construction of diesel switchers, heavy steam locomotives remained their primary output. In addition, a freeze was imposed on implementing any major design changes.

Diesels used crucial materials, such as copper. As a result, WPB denied many railroads requests for new diesels, encouraging lines to buy steam instead, a policy that suited Alco and Baldwin. The need for war machinery during 1942 and 1943 precluded the mass production of diesel locomotives, and Electro-Motive's diesel engines were vitally needed for their original application: in submarines. As a result, production of FTs was temporarily curtailed.

The war had a twofold effect on Electro-Motive's diesel business. It froze locomotive competition, allowing Electro-Motive to refine its product free from market demands. And by placing an enormous strain on motive power fleets, it created a voracious market for new diesels, thus accelerating the decline of the steam locomotive. In the October 26, 1946, edition of *Railway Age*, C. R. Osborn, general manager of the Electro-Motive Division, said this about the wartime impact:

> By the time we resumed full production [after the war], we had 238 passenger units in service for years. They had operated a total of more than 200,000,000 miles of regularly scheduled high-speed service. . . . We [also] had the experience gained from the operation of more than 1,100 of our 1,350-horsepower freight locomotive units

[model FT]. . . . These freight locomotives have handled more than 160 billion ton-miles of freight.

Postwar Diesels

As the war concluded, the WPB relaxed its restrictions. Free from further constraints on design innovations, Electro-Motive implemented changes and introduced new standard models based on its extensive road experience. By combining a variety of changes, these new models resulted in even better locomotives with improved performance and reliability.

Electro-Motive's policy, derived from General Motors' automotive building practice, focused production on standardized models, introducing changes and new features collectively whenever possible, rather than implementing design changes to individual orders. Standardization cut across model lines as well as within them, so primary components were interchangeable between old and new models and between different lines of locomotives whenever practical. This not only simplified parts supply and maintenance, but allowed railroads to implement many component

In the warm glow of the morning afternoon sun, Rock Island E7A No. 633 arrives at Joliet, Illinois, with one of the railroad's famous *Rockets*. As built, Electro-Motive's E7A measured 71 feet 1¼ inches over coupler faces, 13 feet 11 inches to the roof line, and was 10 feet 7 inches wide over outside grab irons. Using a 52:25 gear ratio, E7As were capable of a top speed of 117 miles per hour, although few railroads in the United States had track or signaling that could safely accommodate such speeds. *Richard Jay Solomon*

design improvements on older models without undertaking complex rebuilding. For example, traction motor models were built to similar specifications, allowing new motors to be installed on older units.

New models were intended to address Electro-Motive's customer needs and keep the company competitive in the postwar market. Shrewd marketing skills and mass-production capabilities had guaranteed the popularity of its F-unit line and within a decade, almost every Class I railroad in the United States used them in one capacity or another. So with each new postwar model change, primary components such as the engine, traction motor, main generator, and auxiliary systems were upgraded in these units.

The E7

The first new postwar Electro-Motive model was the E7—built in February 1945. Like the FT, this locomotive used the bulldog nose rather than the steeply slanted nose of the earlier Es. Although it looked different, internally it was very similar to the E6. The E7A measured 71 feet 1.25 inches long, while the E7B was about a foot shorter.

Among the more significant changes was the revised 567 engine, designated 12-567A, which retained the same output but addressed some of the reliability problems that emerged during the hard service of the war years. Improvements to the cooling circuit aimed to reduce water leakage into the crankcase, which could cause premature bearing failures, among other problems.

Worn-out steam locomotives and rising costs, along with easing of traffic volumes, left railroads ravenous for new, more efficient locomotives after the war. Because freight locomotives were among the highest priority in the war effort, WPB restrictions had precluded production of passenger locomotives since 1941, and more than three years had passed since the last E unit left La Grange. With this type of demand, the E7 quickly became Electro-Motive's best-selling passenger locomotive. Louis Marre indicates in his book, *Diesel Locomotive: The First 50 Years*, that in the four-year production run, La Grange churned out 428 E7As and 82 E7Bs.

Although many railroads looked toward dieselization, steam builders remained blindly optimistic in 1945 that modern reciprocating locomotives had a place on American railroads. State-of-the-art 4-8-4 Northern types were among the most powerful and most-efficient passenger steam lines ever built.

Pushing the steam locomotive in a new direction was Pennsylvania Railroad (PRR). During the war, the railroad worked with Baldwin to design the divided-drive Duplex-type Class T1, using a 4-4-4-4 wheel arrangement intended to rival the best of the prewar passenger diesels. Prototypes had fared well in testing, but the war precluded production. Convinced of the T1's superior capabilities, the PRR went ahead and ordered 50 of these fast machines in 1945.

While PRR's extensive duplex fleet was unique, its loyalty to steam was not. New York Central's locomotive genius, Paul Kiefer, also believed that modern steam could provide a competitive motive power solution to off-the-shelf diesel-electrics. Working with Alco, he designed a prototype super 4-8-4 Niagara, intended for both high-speed passenger service and fast-freight service. With the Niagara, New York Central intended to match the output of a three-unit set of Electro-Motive Es.

Without question the Niagara was an extremely powerful locomotive, delivering 62,400 pounds of starting tractive

Burlington's distinctively styled E units were used in both long-distance passenger services and on its intensive Chicago-to-Aurora suburban services. At the Chicago coach yards near Roosevelt Road, an E8A 9946A and an E9A 9985A wait with modern bi-level suburban coaches. The former locomotive was later transferred to Amtrak, becoming No. 340. The latter remained in Chicago–Aurora suburban service through the 1980s as No. 9910. What appear to be vents on either side of the headlight housing is actually styling, painted on the nose to resemble the early shovel-nose *Zephyrs*. *Fred Matthews*

effort and producing a maximum of 6,600 cylinder horsepower at 77 miles per hour (maximum drawbar horsepower was 5,050 at 63 miles per hour). A Niagara could haul an 18-car passenger train at a sustained 80-miles-per-hour without straining. Convinced that this was the way forward, Central placed orders with Alco after the war.

While PRR's T1s, although capable of impressive performance, were fraught with difficulties, Central's Niagara had good reliability and remarkably good performance. But when it came to weighing running costs, both types just couldn't match Electro-Motive's E7. By the late 1940s, the game was over. Neither PRR nor New York Central was still considering steam over E units. After the new Es arrived,

both the T1s and Niagaras had startlingly short careers as premier passenger locomotives. If the two largest passenger carriers could not make the most modern steam pay, there wasn't hope for steam on the smaller railroads (an exception was Norfolk & Western, which continued to build its J-class 4-8-4s until 1950). The E had doomed passenger steam, much in the way the FT had doomed freight steam.

The E7 was not the be all and end all; some railroads were not impressed with it. Although a very good locomotive, it had its share of failings. In *Southern Pacific Historic Diesels: Volume 3*, Joseph A. Strapac points out: "[Southern Pacific] viewed the E7 (with much justification) as a frail device, better suited to the water-level New York Central

than the harsh operating environment of the far West. Far too often, SP's combination of heavy trains and rugged profiles forced dispatchers to assign helpers to E7 consists."

Southern Pacific was no minor player in the market for passenger diesels. It was the third-largest conveyor of railroad passengers during the war. Although it bought 17 E7s, initially operating them in A-B-B sets, it preferred Alco's PA/PB passenger diesels for its long-distance services. In mountain service, the PAs had the advantage, with their rugged GE-752 traction motors and dynamic brakes. SP ultimately had the largest roster of PAs. The E7 did not enjoy widespread popularity in the West. Some railroads, like Santa Fe, also bought PAs, while others looked toward passenger service F units for mountain work. Later E units overcame some the E7's failings.

Better Fs

Freight locomotives represented the largest share of the new locomotive market, and in this area Electro-Motive had a clear advantage. It wasted no time in implementing a host of improvements to its successful F-unit line. To show off these innovations, it built a model F3 demonstrator in 1945. The F3 was powered by another new variation of the 567, the 567B.

Like the 567A, the 567B had addressed cooling circuit inadequacies, among other problems, and it produced 150 more horsepower than the older 16-567. Since each F3 had a 1,500-horsepower engine, a four-unit F3 was rated at 6,000 horsepower.

But supply problems hindered Electro-Motive from beginning F3 production immediately. Instead, it offered a

On the evening of August 31, 1958, at Spokane, Washington, Northern Pacific F7s lead NP train No. 1, the westward *Mainstreeter*, and Spokane, Portland & Seattle F3A No. 800 leads SP&S train No. 3. Many western railroads operating in graded territory preferred Electro-Motive F units over Es in mountain passenger service. Great Northern, Northern Pacific, Rio Grande, Santa Fe, Southern Pacific, SP&S, and Western Pacific all operated fleets of passenger Fs. *Fred Matthews*

Lehigh Valley F7s in the classic A-B-B-A combination lead an eastward freight at Sayre, Pennsylvania, on August 20, 1965. In the distance, an Electro-Motive switcher drills the yard. Sayre was the location of Lehigh Valley's primary locomotive shops and a large yard. *Jim Shaughnessy*

compromise: an interim model designated F2. It was rated at 1,350 horsepower—the same as the FT. The F2 was produced for a just few months in 1946 and was discontinued when the F3 entered mass production. Some railroads, such as Boston & Maine, found that a four-unit set of FTs produced too much power, while two units too little. So they purchased small fleets of F2As to pair with A-B FTs, permitting A-B-A locomotive sets.

With the F3, Electro-Motive worked out a host of service problems and made a much more reliable locomotive. In addition to the 567A engine, the locomotive came equipped with a better main generator. Belt-driven and mechanically-driven internal appliances were replaced with

state-of-the-art appliance systems powered by three-phase AC motors. This upgrade increased reliability and reduced maintenance costs.

One of the selling points of the F3 was service flexibility. The same basic model could be tailored to a variety of road service applications by specifying the gear ratio. In total, the F3 could be ordered with eight different gear ratios. Locomotives built with the 56:21 ratio permitted a maximum speed of 102 miles per hour and delivered 21,000 pounds of maximum continuous tractive effort. This arrangement was designed for high-speed passenger service, but not especially practical for heavy freight applications where a slower top speed was expected and high tractive effort was required. On the other end of spectrum, the 65:12 gear ratio permitted a top speed of just 50 miles per hour, but delivered 42,500 pounds of continuous tractive effort—well suited for slow-speed drag service. Probably the most common gearing was the 62:15 ratio.

The F3 had a relative short production run, ending in February of 1949 with the introduction the F7. In a little more than three years, Electro-Motive built a total of 1,111 F3As and 696 F3Bs, representing the lion's share of La Grange's total output in that period.

New Models for 1949

The American locomotive transition from steam to diesel power reached a watershed in 1949. Steam was dead. With the exception of Norfolk & Western, no American line was ordering new steam power and railroads planned for eventual total dieselization. Electro-Motive was America's number one locomotive manufacturer and looked to keep its place by introducing significant improvements to its whole line. It brought out new models in every major category, each using improved standardized components: better trac-

Southern Pacific FP7 6447 leads train No. 19, the westward *Klamath*, near Dunsmuir, California, in 1961. Mount Shasta looms majestically above the train. Southern Pacific placed the train number in the locomotive number boards, rather than the locomotive number, as was a more common practice. Odd numbered trains were considered westward by timetables, regardless of compass direction. The top headlight was an oscillating light, while the bottom headlight was a fixed twin-sealed beam. *Bob Morris*

tion motors, improved main generators, and more sophisticated fuel injectors.

An article in the May 1949 *Railway Mechanical Engineer* detailed Electro-Motive's new models and the improved technology. The E8 had supplanted the E7 in Electro-Motive's passenger line. The E8 eliminated belt-driven exhaust fans and other appliances, using three-phase AC motor-operated components—equivalent to changes introduced to the F-unit line with the F3 in 1946. Using higher-capacity steam generators, the E8 provided more effective train heating, and a nominal increase in engine output boosted the locomotive horsepower from 2,000 with the E7 to 2,250 with the E8. One disadvantage of the E7—the lack of dynamic brakes—was rectified in the E8, Electro-Motive's first A1A-A1A passenger model so equipped.

Traction was also significantly improved on the E8. The electrical systems of early Electro-Motive diesels were not as well regarded as comparable Alco units, so Electro-Motive's new D-27 traction motor design used recently developed silicon insulation. This insulation, combined with an improved stator design and more effective cooling fans, allowed for greater tractive effort at low speeds.

This meant that locomotives could operate for a longer time while overloaded, giving them better short time ratings (the amount of time a motor could be overloaded without risk of damage). The E8 was rated at 27,000 pounds continuous tractive effort, versus a 21,400-pound rating on the E7.

Further improvements to the D-27 were consistent with the rest of Electro-Motive's design philosophy. This motor was interchangeable with older motors, allowing railroads to take advantage of the new design without needing to re-engineer the locomotives to accommodate them. This practice simplified parts inventory and minimized mechanics' training. A new fuel injector design permitted the use of a cheaper, lower-grade diesel fuel and better dynamic brakes made for easier train handling. The E8 was also more powerful than the E7, delivering 2,250 horsepower, instead of 2,000 horsepower.

Bangor & Aroostook was one of the railroads that bought BL2s new to operate them in road service. Two of the railroad's eight BL2s are seen at Northern Maine Junction on July 12, 1976. This unusual-looking model was derived from the F3 and used the 16-567B engine, D12(A)-D14 main generator, and standard D-17 traction motors, and it rated at 1,500 horsepower. At 57 feet 10½ inches long, a BL2 was slightly more than 7 feet longer than the F3A. Bangor & Aroostook routinely operated its BL2s in combinations with other Electro-Motive 567 diesels. *Jim Shaughnessy*

Electro-Motive sold 421 E8As in the United States and Canada between 1949 and 1955, when it was superseded by the 2,400-horsepower E9. These later E units were among the finest passenger diesels ever built. To this day, engineers sing their praises. "Of all the locomotives I've worked on in my 36 years of railroad experience, the E8s remain my favorite," veteran locomotive engineer George W. Kowanski said in an interview for this book. "They were elegant machines that rode smoothly and were dependable. They had two prime movers instead of just one. You knew with an E8 you would get over the road."

Likewise, the new F7 resembled the F3 in outward appearance, but it embodied component design improvements that made it a more reliable, more productive locomotive. The D-27 traction motor resulted in a 23 percent improvement in continuous tractive effort ratings. Using 62:15 gearing, the F7 was rated at 40,000 pounds of continuous tractive effort, compared with 32,500 pounds for the F3. During F3 production, external changes had been implemented to the carbody. Stainless-steel air-intake grilles replaced the older wire covering, and a new boxy number board was introduced. However, late-build F3s appear virtually identical to early-built F7s. The model differences were purely internal. Shortly after the F7, Electro-

Electro-Motive marketed semi-permanently coupled switchers with cabless B units as low-speed, high-tractive effort transfer locomotives. These were designed for yard work and moving heavy cuts of cars at slow speeds between yards. Transfer locomotives were given the "TR" prefix in their model designation. A number of railroads ordered "cow-calf" sets with one cab unit and one cabless unit. Chesapeake & Ohio alone ordered three-unit transfer sets with two cabless units—a model designated as TR3 and known colloquially as a "herd." C&O 5063 works at Baltimore & Ohio's Connellsville, Pennsylvania, yard on November 7, 1971. *R. R. Richardson photo, Doug Eisele collection*

Often overlooked by photographers seeking more glamorous subjects, Electro-Motive switchers have worked mainlines, branches, yards, and industrial sidings for more than 70 years. In the summer of 1964, Indiana Harbor Belt SW7 8879 hauls a local freight at Porter, Indiana. The SW7 was built as a 1,200-horsepower locomotive powered with a 12-567A diesel. *Richard Jay Solomon*

Above: A Great Western Railway SW1 switches at Windsor, Colorado, in August 1985. The 600-horsepower SW1 was introduced in 1939, before General Motors reorganized the Electro-Motive Corporation as its Electro-Motive Division. The model was built as late as 1953. It used a six-cylinder 567. *Thomas L. Carver*

Right: Boston & Maine SW9 1225 hauls a local freight at Ashuelot, New Hampshire, on the run to Keene in March 1978. Electro-Motive switchers were ideal for branch lines and short local freights where high horsepower was not required. *Jim Shaughnessy*

Motive introduced the FP7, which was 4 feet longer than the F7 to accommodate a larger steam generator and water storage for passenger services.

Branch Line Locomotive

Electro-Motive introduced its NW3 light road-switcher in 1941, shortly after Alco pioneered the road-switcher type with its RS-1. While Electro-Motive built several models of the road-switcher in the early years, they were essentially moderate-output locomotives sold for passenger switching or branch line passenger operation and were not of the general purpose variety. The competition had been keen to innovate in this area, though, offering greater model varieties to cater to a larger market share.

But Electro-Motive was comfortable with its three basic types—E unit, F unit, and switchers—and it was already building as many locomotives as it could. It had little need for new types that might compete with its existing models.

A trio of Boston & Maine GP9s lead an eastward freight east of Mechanicville, New York, in May 1970. Introduced along with other comparable models in 1954, the GP9's road-switcher configuration, combined with the greater reliability offered by the new 16-567C diesel and improved electrical equipment including the D-37 traction motor, made it one of the best-selling locomotives of the period. *Jim Shaughnessy*

Diesels were substantially more expensive than steam. To make the most of a railroad's investment, early dieselization programs focused assignments on the main lines and high-priority trains where they would earn the best return. This left the secondary lines, branches, and less-important services to steam.

To accomplish complete dieselization, a railroad needed to purge steam from the far corners of its system. But the savings from diesel investment was harder to justify for secondary services; multiple streamlined Fs were neither appropriate nor truly effective for such operations. That's where the branch line diesel came in. Electro-Motive tested the road-switcher market with a distinctive-looking, semi-streamlined branch line locomotive in 1948. The demonstrator was designated BL1, while production models were BL2s.

These combined features of an F unit with the convenience of a switcher. They were designed with a bidirec- tional cab view and came equipped with footboards to aid in switching moves. Initially, the BL2s were not intended for multiple-unit operation, but this deficiency was soon rectified and most were ordered with multiple-unit capa- bility. Yet the curious-looking machines did not sell well compared to the Fs, and Electro-Motive discontinued the BL2 just 13 months after production began, having sold 58 of them.

This model was just a prelude to a true road-switcher, which more closely resembled those built by Alco, Bald- win, and F-M.

General Purpose

At the end of 1949, American railroads had nearly 12,000 diesel locomotives in service. The majority of these were either working in mainline freight or passenger services, or

served as yard switchers. As the 1950s dawned, railroads were moving toward total dieselization—a concept promoted by Electro-Motive a decade earlier. Where a few lines such as Gulf Mobile & Ohio had already achieved this, many railroads were still in the process of purging steam from the mainline. Anticipating the need for new diesels on secondary runs and branch lines, Electro-Motive decided the time was right to market its own general purpose road-switcher, one market area where its competition had demonstrated an advantage.

Traditionally, branch lines were operated with castaway mainline power—old steam locomotives long paid for—so railroads were reluctant to make a large investment in new branch line locomotives. To entice sales in branch line diesels, Electro-Motive had to make a locomotive that would pay its own way. This is where the general purpose model came in.

The advantage of the road-switcher type was its great versatility and relatively low cost. Electro-Motive's GP7 had lower production costs than an F7, and it could perform virtually any job on the railroad, by itself or with other locomotives. It could work on the mainline in freight, and, if equipped with a steam generator, in passenger service, too. Its rapid loading characteristics made it well suited for working yard switching; it was equally able to lead a short freight up the branch where it could work light sidings and switch industrial trackage.

By putting several of these diesels together, they could haul a heavy freight on the mainline. If needed, a GP7 could tie on to the back of a heavy freight and serve as a helper. It did all of this and used the same primary components of Electro-Motive's F units: the same engine, the same electrical gear, and the same trucks. It didn't have any specialized

With 16-567C engines roaring, a quartet of Boston & Maine GP9s works eastward with a freight from the yard at Mechanicville, New York, across the Hudson River bridge near Stillwater. The sights and sounds of Electro-Motive 567 diesels were once commonplace all over the United States and around the world. *Jim Shaughnessy*

The GP9 provided a low-cost motive power solution for virtually every application. Here, a single Denver & Rio Grande Western GP9 works on the former three-foot gauge Monarch Branch in the Colorado Rockies on August 24, 1957. The locomotive is hauling a string of limestone cars near a mine at the top of Monarch Pass. *Jim Shaughnessy*

An eastward quartet of new Rio Grande GP9s rolls through dual-gauge trackage at Salida, Colorado. This was where the three-foot-gauge Monarch Branch diverged from Rio Grande's "Royal Gorge Route." The narrow gauge remained steam-operated until the railroad converted it to standard gauge. For a very short time, Rio Grande's GP9s coexisted with dual-gauge operation at Salida. Close inspection of this photo shows a three-foot-gauge Mikado under steam to the left of the switch stands. *Jim Shaughnessy*

Financially strapped New Haven replaced its aging electric fleet and World War II–vintage Alco DL109s with custom-designed, dual-mode diesel-electric/electrics built by Electro-Motive. FL9s were powered by a 16-567 diesel and could draw power from high-voltage, direct current third rail in New York City suburban territory. Sixty of the unique locomotives were built between 1956 and 1960, making them the last of the F units to leave La Grange. A pair of new FL9s cross New Haven Railroad's bridge at Cos Cob, Connecticut, with the Grand Central–bound *Mayflower. Jim Shaughnessy*

To accommodate weight restrictions on the Park Avenue viaduct approach to Grand Central, Electro-Motive used an A1A Flexicoil truck to support the rear of the locomotive and thereby reduce the axle load. As a result, the FL9 was one of only a few locomotives to employ a B-A1A wheel arrangement. Note the retractable third-rail shoe between the first and second axles (below the porthole window). *Jim Shaughnessy*

maintenance needs and was easy to repair. On the down-side, the GP7 wasn't very attractive. To keep production costs down, Electro-Motive opted to build the GP7 as cheaply as possible.

Its easy maintenance, simple design, and overall versatility quickly made the 1,500-horsepower GP into one of Electro-Motive's fastest-selling new locomotives. In its five-year production run, more than 2,700 GP7s were built for North American service.

Where Es had displaced modern Hudsons and North-erns from premier passenger runs—locomotives that were too heavy for branch lines—and Fs displaced a variety of big machines used for freight, the GP7 deposed some of the railroad's oldest steam. Branches had long been the domain of antiques: Moguls, Ten Wheelers, Consolida-tions, light Mikados, and light Pacifics. Most of these old steam locomotives had at least three decades of hard work behind them; some were well into their fifth decade of service. In the 1910s and 1920s, many railroads had invested in gas-electric railcars for branch line work—the original internal combustion– electrics—and these too were sidelined in favor of the road-switcher. It was ironic

that both the oldest steam and the oldest internal combustion–power were replaced in just a few years by the newest type of diesel.

More Facilities

In the first few years after World War II, massive demand for diesels provided Electro-Motive with as many orders as it could fill. It would seem that this was an ideal situation, but it put Electro-Motive in a bit of a quandary. As high as demand was in the mid-1940s, the manufacturer knew that once full dieselization had been completed, the market for new locomotives would become rapidly saturated. Yet when this saturation would occur was difficult to predict. Many pundits thought steam might survive for another 20 years.

Thus, Electro-Motive's problem was that if it sold diesels too slowly, it would effectively give away business to its competition—in fact, many of the orders for Alco, Baldwin, and F-M were directly attributable to Electro-Motive's inability to deliver diesels soon enough. However, if Electro-Motive made massive investment in expanded plant capacity, which wasn't justifiable in the long run, then the

manufacturer would be saddled with facilities for which it had no need. Ultimately, Electro-Motive compromised.

At the end of the war, it leased space from Pullman on the south side of Chicago to assist in the construction of car-body components for Es and Fs. This facility became known as EMD Plant 2. This was a logical expansion, as only 10 years earlier Pullman had constructed many of Electro-Motive's early streamliners. Passenger cars and loco-motive car bodies were similar in construction.

In 1948, Electro-Motive made a more serious expansion when it acquired the Cleveland Diesel plant that had been used for wartime military production. Electro-Motive had now returned to Cleveland, Ohio, where it began its business more than 25 years earlier. The homecoming was short-lived, but for six years EMD Plant 3 was among the most productive locomotive facilities in the United States. This facility was primarily used to assemble switchers, including the new GP7 road-switcher in 1949. The 567 engines and other components were built at La Grange and shipped by rail to Cleveland.

Electro-Motive's initial diesel sales were aimed at domestic railroads, but by the end of the 1940s, Canada had emerged as a large potential market. Early sales to

Canadian roads were accommodated by La Grange, but opening a Canadian facility soon made sense. It could reduce import costs (as a result of duties and shipping) and further expand production capacity. So in 1950, Electro-Motive opened its London, Ontario, plant run as General Motors Diesel Limited.

Not only did London build locomotives for Canadian National, Canadian Pacific, and other Canadian lines, but also for American railroads with significant operations north of the U.S. border, such as New York Central and Wabash. After 1953, London also assembled Electro-Motive diesels for overseas export.

Unlike Plant 3 in Cleveland, London remained significant to Electro-Motive production for many years. Canadian lines were slower to adopt the diesel than their American counterparts, and they bought large numbers of new diesels into the early 1960s, keeping London busy. As will be discussed in Chapter 4, the London plant ultimately became Electro-Motive's primary assembly facility following changes in the 1980s.

The United States was the first large nation to implement total dieselization. But by the 1950s, nations around the world were considering the cost savings afforded by

Left: Union Pacific SW7 1812 works cab-first past Reservation Tower in Tacoma, Washington, in November 1977. Built by Electro-Motive in 1950, this locomotive weighed 234,840 pounds and produced 60,425 pounds of starting tractive effort. *Thomas L. Carver*

Below: A gathering of Conemaugh & Black Lick Railroad's Electro-Motive switchers catches the sun at Johnstown, Pennsylvania, on August 31, 1989. Three SW7s are present—110, 112, and 113—and have been rebuilt with 12-cylinder "645AC" engines. Also present is the Bethlehem Steel Bar Rod and Wire Division SW1 28 that originally was a C&BL unit. *Patrick Yough*

Below: In 1952, Southern Pacific was the first to take advantage of Electro-Motive's six-motor road-switcher, model SD7, which rode on newly designed Flexicoil trucks. Some of SP's SD7s remained active until the mid-1990s, giving them more than 40 years of service. In later years, most SD7s were assigned to yard service, such as this pair seen working California's Roseville Yard at sunset in February 1990. *Brian Solomon*

Above: Louisville & Nashville GP7s 503 and 505 depart Louisville, Kentucky, with an army extra on July 25, 1958. These passenger-service GPs have larger-than-normal fuel and water tanks below the frame, which require the relocation of air reservoirs to the roof. *Richard Jay Solomon*

dieselization. Alco and Baldwin had been early to capitalize on the export diesel market, having long-established themselves as international steam locomotive builders.

As domestic sales began to soften in the mid-1950s, Electro-Motive expanded its business in the world market. The manufacturer built some export locomotives at its plants in North America for shipment overseas, but it also licensed its diesel technology to a host of other builders around the world. By 2006, its locomotives were working in approximately 75 different nations.

Overseas railroads have a variety of different track gauges (the inside distance between the rails), loading gauges (the height and width of railroad equipment determined by line-side restrictions), axle-loading (maximum weight permitted by each axle), and cab and coupler requirements. These are often very different from North American railways. So Electro-Motive engineered a great variety of export models, typically lighter, lower, and narrower than the locomotives built for the United States and Canada.

Although locomotives built for export might look strange to American eyes, they sound familiar. Those 567, 645, and 710 engines can be heard reverberating across plains and valleys, through canyons and valleys, over mountains, and working in towns and cities all over the world.

Southern Pacific operated the largest fleet of SD9s, known on the railroad as "Cadillacs"—a comparison to General Motors' luxury cars known for their cushy ride. Six-motor Flexicoil trucks were designed for high tractive effort and distributing locomotive weight over a greater number of axles, so the comfortable ride was a side effect. SP SD9s were assigned to a cable-laying train on Donner Pass in 1990. *Brian Solomon*

9-Lines

The 9-series locomotives introduced a number of improvements, including the more powerful and more reliable 567C-series diesel engine. The FP9, the passenger F unit, was largely built for the Canadian railroads. By 1957, when this locomotive was built at London, Ontario, the F unit had largely fallen out of favor in the United States. Among the external changes that help distinguish most F9/FP9s from earlier Fs is the flush headlight rim. Canadian National No. 6537 catches the sun at Ottawa Union Station in May 1972.
Jim Shaughnessy

In the early 1950s, the competition boosted road locomotive output from 1,500 horsepower to 1,600 horsepower. Electro-Motive did not react immediately, nor did it need to, because it was raking in orders just about as fast as it could build locomotives. It dominated the domestic market. The manufacturer's phenomenally successful F7, new GP7, and E8 models were outselling everything else.

By 1953, Fairbanks-Morse and Alco were both offering road-switchers that produced between 2,250 horsepower and 2,400 horsepower—significantly more than Electro-Motive's most powerful locomotives. Despite this great power advantage, these high-horsepower locomotives did not enjoy brisk sales. The next year, Electro-Motive introduced its new models, incorporating the latest round of innovations and its new and much-improved 567C engine.

The 567C worked at 835 rpm (compared to earlier engines that worked at 800 rpm) to produce 1,750 horsepower, an increase of 250 horsepower over earlier models. Equally important were further improvements to the cooling circuit that eliminated additional water leaks and resulted in a vastly more reliable engine than either the 567A or 567B. (So much better was the 567C that Electro-Motive made the improved cooling circuit available to older engines, which could be upgraded to a 567AC or 567BC specification.) The 567C crankcase can be easily distinguished from earlier models by its round hand-hole covers instead of those of rectangular design.

The 9 Series locomotive models included the E9, F9, FP9, GP9, and SD9; however, the SW9, introduced a few years earlier, was not part of the series and was actually supplanted by the SW1200—a model that incorporated its horsepower output in its designation.

The Last of the Es and Fs

Although the best of their respective lines, neither the E9 or the F9 sold as well as the models they supplanted. This decrease in sales reflected changes in the nature of American railroading, the rise of the road-switcher, and the cooling of the locomotive market as dieselization approached completion.

After World War II, railroads remained optimistic about their passenger services. A number of lines—including the Pennsylvania Railroad, New York Central, and Southern Pacific—had substantially invested in modern streamlined passenger equipment in an effort to improve long-distance services and retain riders who were drawn back to the lines during the war. The flagship passenger trains were often the first mainline runs to receive diesel power. As a result, many lines had effectively eliminated their passenger steam by 1953, resulting in a comparative small market for new passenger locomotives.

The effort to sustain passenger ridership was in vain. Automotive sales picked up at a furious rate as the postwar economy blossomed, and publicly funded highways made long-distance road travel easier than ever before. Improved airline service further cut into rail ridership. By 1954, the passenger business, and thus the passenger locomotive market, was in steep decline. So while the E9 remained in production until 1964, longer than the combined runs of the E7 and E8, only 100 E9As and 44 E9Bs were built.

Electro-Motive's F unit was the locomotive that had sold American railroads on total dieselization, but its intense reign didn't last very long. Roughly 7,600 F units were built over a 20-year span, but despite a variety of improvements, very few F9s were sold to domestic lines after 1955. While the F9 was the most powerful and most reliable F unit ever built, the type had fallen out of favor compared with Electro-Motive's own general purpose line. The GP9 offered all of the same improvements found on the F9, but it was cheaper, more versatile, and easier to maintain. So much for good looks.

Streamlining, which sold diesels in the early years, was dropped when railroads realized they could buy the advantages of diesels without the fancy dress. This trend toward

utilitarian design had not been Electro-Motive's intent. The F unit had been its primary product line, and Electro-Motive was caught by surprise when its "ugly" road-switcher began outselling the F unit.

There were a variety of strikes against the F unit, including inherent operational limitations imposed by its unidirectional design. Electro-Motive had anticipated that F units would be operated in sets with cabs at either end. Also since virtually all steam locomotives were unidirectional, steam-era terminals were always equipped with turning facilities—either a turntable (usually in conjunction with a roundhouse) or a wye arrangement. But because diesels had greatly reduced the amount of maintenance necessary for locomotives, many railroads eliminated small

maintenance facilities that had been equipped for unidirectional steam units.

Instead, the roads focused on building centrally located maintenance facilities designed to cater to diesel locomotives' heavy maintenance. At away points, smaller diesel facilities needed to provide only fuel, water, and sand, and perhaps a pit to inspect or repair damaged traction motors. Railroads could save a lot of money by eliminating expensive roundhouses and turntables—especially on lightly used lines.

In the late 1940s, the need for cabless B units changed when railroads negotiated with labor that, while firemen were to be retained on diesels, it would not be necessary to station one on each and every diesel unit. This decision

freed railroads to assign locomotives as needed and gave another function to the road-switcher. Originally targeted for branch line service, the road-switcher's economical operation was now applied almost everywhere.

The GP locomotive offered a lot of flexibility. The building-block principle of assigning motive power allowed a railroad to put together as many diesel units as it needed. A railroad did not need not be concerned if the lead locomotive had a cab, since all GPs had cabs (the exceptions were Union Pacific, Pennsylvania Railroad, and, to a limited extent, Santa Fe, which ordered cabless GPs).

Another advantage was that because GPs could be geared for passenger service as easily as for freight, railroads didn't need to worry about investing in specialized passenger locomotives; if their passenger service declined, re-gearing the passenger GPs was easily accomplished. Furthermore, unlike Es, GPs could be assigned to dual traffic on lines that didn't require fast passenger trains. Such was the case on Boston & Maine, which used its GP7s in both freight and passenger service. Furthermore, full-carbody designs were not conducive to switching moves and could pose difficulties in the event of a lead locomotive failure on the road if only a single A unit was employed.

The F9 was the last regular F unit model offered. The passenger FP9 was not popular in the United States, although it captured a small market in Canada and Mexico. In 1956, Electro-Motive designed a specialized dual-mode diesel-electric/electric model FL9 for the New Haven Railroad, and in 1960 New Haven's second order of these FL9s was the last group of Fs built.

While the F was on its way out, the GP9 became one of Electro-Motive's most successful models of all time. In less than six years, Electro-Motive built more than 3,500 GP9s for domestic use. Ultimately, more than 4,000 GP9s were built for North American service.

The GP9 spelled doom for the last remaining steam operations. Norfolk & Western, which had resisted dieselization, ultimately concluded steam was dead when it determined that the performance of the GP9 outweighed any financial advantages of steam power. Norfolk & Western was the last major railroad to use steam on a large scale. It had refined conventional reciprocating steam power to a higher level than any other American railroad, setting standards for performance, availability, and efficiency. As late as 1953, it was still building new steam switchers. But in 1954, it finally began the transition and had 100 percent dieselized operations by 1960.

Special Duty

Fairly early into road-switcher production, Electro-Motive divided its road-switcher line. In 1952, the manufacturer offered a six-axle, six-motor road-switcher that was the same as the GP7 in every other capacity. Viewing the six-motor road-switcher as a "special duty" type, Electro-Motive designated the locomotive as model SD7.

This model showed an important deviation from Electro-Motive's earlier locomotive building policy. Previously, it had essentially ignored the specialized locomotive market and focused on mass-produced models. If a railroad needed higher tractive effort, it could order an F unit with lower gearing.

Placing all adhesive weight on six-powered axles—the C-C wheel arrangement—was hardly a new concept, though. Back in 1930, General Electric pioneered this arrangement with an order for 42 class R-2 electrics for New York Central's West Side freight operations in Manhattan. Each truck had three nose-suspended traction motors, one driving each axle through single reduction gearing.

During the war, Alco adapted a variant of its RS-1 for six-motor operation. But Alco's pioneer application of C-C trucks wasn't entirely successful. The truck design didn't permit easy access to the central traction motor, which made maintenance difficult. After the war, Alco developed an improved three-motor C truck and marketed six-motor diesels after 1946. Likewise, Baldwin had been selling six-motor road-switchers since 1946, including massive center cab twin-diesel transfer locomotives. Lima-Hamilton had briefly sold this latter type in 1950 and 1951 before merging with Baldwin.

Like its four axle-counterpart, the SD7 was powered by a 16-cylinder 567B engine rated at 1,500 horsepower. Measured over coupler faces, the SD7 was 60 feet 9 inches long—nearly 5 feet longer than the GP7. It rode on newly designed six-axle high-adhesion Flexi-Coil trucks, which permitted easy access to the center traction motor, and had distinctive large radiators at the rear of the hood. The SD7 was hardly designed for restrictive service, as it was capable of negotiating 23-degree curves, ascending grades as steep as 5 percent, and hauling a 5,500-ton train on a level track.

Electro-Motive built a SD7 demonstrator—a pioneer that was dressed in bright red paint and sent on tour. Among the SD7's first buyers was Southern Pacific, which soon became Electro-Motive's largest SD7 customer. It acquired 43 of the 188 built. Facing tough grades just about everywhere it ran, Southern Pacific had natural six-motor territory. Among the other SD7 customers were Baltimore & Ohio, Bessemer & Lake Erie, Burlington, Chicago & North Western, Great Northern, Milwaukee Road, Pennsylvania Railroad, and Union Pacific.

With the development of more powerful engines, the special-duty line ultimately prevailed as Electro-Motive's dominant type. By the mid-1960s, six-motor locomotives were outselling four-motor locomotives, and by the mid-1990s, six-motor locomotives were exclusively built for road-freight service. Interestingly, Southern Pacific, the first

Opposite: Boston & Maine NW2 1204 wears a fresh coat of blue paint at the Mechanicville, New York, yard on February 8, 1969. In the early days of Electro-Motive switcher production, some railroads still preferred cast-steel frames instead of the more modern welded frames. Switchers with cast frames used the suffix "C" in their designation, while those with welded frames a used a "W." Initially switchers were built as either 600 horsepower or 900 horsepower, which determined the prefix of their model designation. The NW model was a 900-horsepower welded frame switcher. By 1939, output had been boosted to 1,000 horsepower using the new 12-567 engine, so the new model was designated NW2. B&M 1204 emerged from La Grange on July 3, 1942. *Jim Shaughnessy*

customer to buy Electro-Motive's six-motor freight diesels,
was also the last to buy its four-motor freight units with an
order for GP60s in 1994.

More Power

By the late 1950s, the domestic locomotive market quieted
as railroads achieved total dieselization—largely ahead of
expectation. As the market contracted, the weaker competitors dropped out. Baldwin, which had merged in 1951 with
Lima-Hamilton, was the first to throw in the towel. Fairbanks-Morse was next.

A recession in 1957 dried up traffic and many railroads
were storing motive power. It was a tough time in the locomotive business. Electro-Motive hoped to make sales by

remanufacturing older locomotives, both its own designs as
well as repowering other manufacturers' with its engines.

A few railroads, such as Union Pacific, had been search-
ing for more powerful locomotives. In the early 1950s, Union
Pacific had worked with GE to develop very high-output gas
turbines. In 1955, it also looked to boost output of its Electro-
Motive diesels and retrofitted several GP9s by replacing the
Roots blowers with turbochargers. Electro-Motive had been
reluctant to develop a turbocharged engine, but it followed
UP's experiments with interest. Ultimately, this led Electro-
Motive to finally engineer its own turbocharged models.

Its first commercial turbocharged model was the
2,400-horsepower SD24, introduced in 1958, followed by
the 2,000-horsepower GP20 a year later. Prior to produc-

tion of the GP20, Electro-Motive worked with UP, experimentally installing nine new 567D2 turbocharged engines into UP's GP9s.

At the time of its launch, the SD24 was the most powerful single engine diesel built by Electro-Motive. Powered by the turbocharged 16-567D3, it equaled the output of the dual 12-567Cs that powered the E9 and sounded unlike anything else that emerged from La Grange.

John Bonds Garmany's *Southern Pacific Dieselization* notes that the three-unit demonstrator was painted in Southern Pacific's latest livery—scarlet and gray—and came equipped with the SP lighting package, including oscillating headlights and a red oscillating warning light. The locomotives were appropriately numbered 7200, 7201, and 7202

to fit neatly into SP's roster. Electro-Motive thought that SP would surely purchase the high-horsepower six-motor monsters, but following evaluation, SP snubbed the new model. Instead it looked overseas to German-builder Krauss-Maffei for hydraulic types.

After several years of dabbling with its European toys, SP finally came around to Electro-Motive's high-horsepower, six-motor types, but it never bought the SD24. Other western carriers did, including Burlington, Santa Fe, and Union Pacific. The only eastern railroad to buy them was Southern. A lone unit was also sold to Kennecott Copper. In the short term, Electro-Motive sold SP on its GP20, the hot rod of the GP series.

This Bangor & Aroostook GP7 has been renumbered 1776 and painted in patriotic colors in honor of the American bicentennial. It catches the last light of the winter sun in March 1975 as it works freight NO-43 (Northern Maine Junction to Oakfield) near the company's shops at Derby, Maine. Trailing is F3A No. 46 and a BL2. *Don Marson*

St. Johnsbury & Lamoille County's northward freight works near Bakersfield, Vermont, on the first day of summer, June 21, 1969. Leading are GP9s 200 and 201, units originally built for New York Central as 5960 and 6056, respectively; trailing is an Alco RS-3, also acquired secondhand. Road-switchers are ideal motive power for branch line railroads and many GPs cast off by the Class I carriers have found work with short lines. *Jim Shaughnessy*

Turbocharger Tech

Prior to experiments with turbocharging, all of Electro-Motive's diesels used a positive-displacement Roots blower to scavenge exhaust gases and force fresh air into the cylinders for combustion. The turbocharger was a significant design change for Electro-Motive. Many locomotive historians have deemed Electro-Motive's turbocharged development as a technological milestone and use it as a line of the division between first- and second-generation diesels.

Though new to Electro-Motive, other diesel builders, including Alco and Baldwin, had used turbochargers for years to boost output. In turbo-equipped engines, exhaust gases spin a turbocharger that powers a compressor that forces fresh air into cylinders under pressure. Electro-Motive engineered an unusual type of turbocharger that was driven by a direct gear train off the engine at the lower throttle positions; at the higher throttle positions, when exhaust gases can spin the turbine faster, an overrunning clutch disengaged the gear train and allowed the turbine to freewheel. (This feature is required by the two-stoke design. It acts like a blower at low output and a turbo at high output.) The

result is that the turbo only freewheels when the engine is working at higher rpms.

The maximum rotation of the turbocharged 567 engine remained 835 rpm—same as the 567C with a Roots blower. But the turbocharged engine used a lower compression ratio, 14.5 to 1. While the turbocharged 567 required more maintenance, it offered several distinct advantages: high output, improved fuel economy, and the ability to deliver full output at high altitudes where thinner air impairs combustion.

Higher engine output required equivalent changes to the engine's electrical equipment. Among these changes was a new traction motor design, model D-47. This motor took advantage of an improved insulating material in the form of epoxy resin. Electro-Motive advertised in the April 27, 1959, edition of *Railway Age* that improved insulation, along with better ventilation and power cables, allowed for a more powerful motor with better short time ratings without increasing the motor size.

As with earlier advances, Electro-Motive carefully engineered these changes to insure compatibility with older designs. Railroads didn't need to order new locomotives to take advantage of improved components.

More powerful locomotive models were crucial to Electro-Motive's strategy for generating sales with railroads that had already completed dieselization. The success of the diesel had resulted in operation of longer, heavier freights. The ability to run longer freights led to the need for even more power. While once a rival to the most powerful steam, by the late 1950s an A-B-B-A set of F units was no longer powerful enough to move the heaviest freights.

Electro-Motive hoped to entice railroads to trade in older Fs by offering unit reduction. If fewer diesels could accomplish the same work, the railroads could lower costs by reducing the number of machines they needed. Three 2,400-horsepower SD24s nearly equaled the output of five F7s. Likewise, three GP20s had the same output as a traditional four-unit F3 or F7 set. And at 5,400 horsepower, three GP18s equaled the power of a four-unit FT. Fewer units also meant fewer engines, fewer main generators, fewer traction motors, fewer multiple unit connections, and presumably fewer problems and lower maintenance costs.

The introduction of its turbocharged engine line produced a second primary division in Electro-Motive's road-switcher line. Where it had started with just a four-motor normally aspirated road-switcher, by the late 1950s Electro-Motive was offering four- and six-motor units. These were powered by either a normally aspirated 567 diesel or a turbocharged 567.

In the four-motor category, Electro-Motive had the GP18—essentially a nominally improved version of its very successful GP9—and the new turbocharged GP20. Likewise in the six-motor category, it offered the SD18, an improved SD9, and the high-horsepower SD24. In addition, Electro-Motive anticipated a market for a more moderately powered, normally aspirated locomotive and included in its catalog a third type of four-motor road-switcher—the model RS1325. This road-switcher used a 12-cylinder 567D1 to produce 1,325 horsepower, making it roughly equivalent to the output of the old FT. These used the new two-axle Flexicoil trucks rather than the conventional two-axle Blombergs.

The RS1325 was not embraced in the United States, though, and only two units were built, both for Chicago & Illinois Midland. The comparable GMD1 model—built at the London plant for the Canadian market—sold more

Although designed for passenger service, E units could be used to move tonnage. With the loss of most passenger work, Erie-Lackawanna assigned its old E8s to freight work in later years. Three E8s work a westward freight on the old Erie mainline at Port Jervis in February 1974. *Jim Shaughnessy*

Electro-Motive delivered three GP18s to New York, Susquehanna & Western in 1962. In October 1963, No. 1804 was working a freight in New Jersey. The following four decades were remarkably tumultuous for American railroading, especially lines in the Northeast. Few locomotives operating in 1962 are still serviceable today, and most of the railroads on the map then have changed hands at least once or have even been abandoned. Yet through it all, NYS&W's three GP18s have soldiered on and were still working for the company in 2006, albeit on a much expanded system. *Richard Jay Solomon*

than 100 units. Some of these rode on A1A trucks to reduce axle weight, making them suitable power for light branch lines.

By dividing its line and offering a variety of models, Electro-Motive had changed its postwar production approach of offering just one basic type of road freight unit. To broaden sales, Electro-Motive decided it needed to cater designs to railroads' specific motive power needs.

New Designations

Coincident with these new models was a short-lived attempt at linking model designations with horsepower output. Each of these new model designations reflected the maximum horsepower. The GP18 and SD18 delivered 1,800 horsepower, the GP20 put out 2,000 horsepower, and so forth.

The manufacturer's designations were not universally applied to Electro-Motive's line and this naming system was largely dropped with the next major round of innovation in the early 1960s. One incongruity was with the second order of New Haven FL9s, which were powered by the 1,800-horsepower 16-567D1 engine. In theory, using the new system of designations, these ought to have been classified as

In 1959, Electro-Motive introduced a variety of new road-switcher models. Along with the GP18 and new turbocharged GP20, it also offered the moderately powered RS1325, so designated because its 12-567D1 produced 1,325 horsepower. American railroads expressed almost no interest in the RS1325, and the only two were sold to Chicago & Illinois Midland in 1960, where they've worked in relative obscurity for decades. C&IM No. 30 was photographed at Powerton, Illinois, on May 8, 1980. *George W. Kowanski*

Above: Union Pacific, while known for its uniformity in the modern era because it ordered standard models by the hundreds, once claimed perhaps the most eclectic collection of late-era Electro-Motive 567 diesels. On January 30, 1976, UP GP30 833 leads a pair of SD24Bs and a DD35B along with another unit at Colton Tower in the Los Angeles Basin. The SD24B was unique to UP, and the DD35B was only ordered by UP and SP. As a cabless D-D type, it was unlike anything else to emerge from La Grange. *Brian Jennison*

Below: Chesapeake & Ohio traded 1952-built six-motor Alco RSD-5s to Electro-Motive on an order for SD18s delivered in 1963. These unusual six-motor units incorporated components from the trade, notably the Alco tri-mount trucks and GE 752 traction motors. With less than 50 built, and only five railroads ordering the model new, the SD18 was relatively obscure among the thousands of locomotives built with 567 engines. C&O SD18 7317 leads another of the type at Russell, Kentucky, on March 24, 1973. *R. R. Richardson, Doug Eisele collection*

Among the railroads that took Electro-Motive's offer for trades was Soo Line, which turned back Alco FAs on new GP30s. Electro-Motive recycled the AAR Type B trucks from the Alco cab units. On September 25, 1977, Soo Line GP30 701 and FP7A 502A lead a southward freight at Mundelien, Illinois. Some of the old Soo GP30s continued to ply these rails after 1987, when Wisconsin Central acquired the route from Soo parent Canadian Pacific. *Terry Norton*

model FL18. While domestic locomotives went on to use a designation system not linked to output, Electro-Motive's export lines continued to use a logical horsepower-based designation system for decades.

The Low Short Hood

The advent of the low short hood option coincided with Electro-Motive's changes to its road-switcher line and the dominance of this style of locomotive in the late 1950s. Since the GP7 was introduced in 1949, Electro-Motive built road-switchers with high short hoods. The high short hood served dual functions: it housed auxiliary equipment, including steam generators and water storage for passenger services, and it provided protection for the crew in the event of a collision.

By the late 1950s, with the diminishing need for new passenger locomotives and the growing preference to assign road-switchers on long hauls, priorities had changed. A low short hood offered better forward visibility, which was important for engineers facing forward for the better part of a long run. Yet the first Electro-Motive road-switchers built with low short hoods were designed that way for an entirely dif-

ferent reason. They were a special order of GP9s built for Phelps-Dodge in 1955. This pioneering application of the low short hood on a GP9 was intended to give the crew improved rear visibility over their train of copper-laden ore jenneys.

More significant was Southern Pacific's order for low short hood road-switchers four years later. John Bonds Garmany wrote that SP ordered a low short hood for further evaluation from both Electro-Motive and Alco and was the first Class I railroad to request this option. The style was new, but not the concept; Electro-Motive's BL2 had been designed with a low short hood, too.

With the development of the SD24, the GP18, the GP20, and other new models, the low short hood became a standard option. By the early 1960s, it was the preferred arrangement on new locomotives. Yet a few lines, such as Illinois Central, Norfolk & Western, and Southern, continued to order high short hood locomotives for another two decades.

There had never been a universal standard for which end of a road-switcher was designated the front of the locomotive, so lines that designated the long hood as the front saw little advantage to ordering a low short hood.

New Competition Ups the Ante

While Electro-Motive was dabbling with turbochargers and the last heavy steam was finally put to bed, new competitive forces emerged in the American locomotive market. German locomotive manufacturer Krauss-Maffei (K-M) entered the American market in 1961, selling high-horsepower diesel-hydraulics to Southern Pacific and Denver & Rio Grande Western (D&RGW). Unlike a diesel-electric that uses a generator and traction motors to transmit the engine power to the wheels for forward motion, a diesel-hydraulic uses a hydraulic transmission.

In the case of Southern Pacific's and Denver & Rio Grande Western's imports, each unit had a pair of Maybach V-16 diesel engines driving a Voith hydraulic transmission system and rated by K-M at 4,000 horsepower. (The European system measures brake horsepower, different than conventional American practice. In the United States, the K-Ms carried a 3,450-horsepower rating.) By any measurement, this was significantly more than anything coming out of General Motors. Yet, the hydraulics were not ideal for American operating practice.

High-maintenance requirements neither suited Rio Grande nor SP. D&RGW gave them up first, while SP placed a repeat order with K-M in 1963 for an additional 15 locomotives. But by the mid-1960s, SP had given up on hydraulics too, and American builders, including Electro-Motive, had matched and exceeded the output of the K-Ms using robust diesel-electric technology.

While K-M certainly raised a few eyebrows at La Grange, more serious long-term competition emerged from General Electric—Electro-Motive's one-time electrical supplier and contract builder of some of its earliest diesel-electric locomotives. No stranger to the locomotive business, General Electric had been building electrics since the 1890s and had been one the leading builders of gas-electric railcars prior to World War I. It had pioneered much of the technology used by diesel-electric manufacturers.

In more recent times, General Electric had been a partner with Alco. It ended that relationship abruptly in 1953 and became a heavy diesel builder in its own right. As to why GE didn't just stay with Alco, the second most successful diesel-electric manufacturer in the United States, Albert

A northward BN freight destined for Vancouver, British Columbia, and led by three Burlington Northern GP30s, crosses a trestle over Steamboat Slough of the Snohomish River at Everett, Washington, in April 1980. The GP30's unusual body style makes it easy to distinguish from all other Electro-Motive road-switchers. Between 1961 and 1963, Electro-Motive built 623 of the type before it was superseded by the slightly more powerful GP35. *Thomas L. Carver*

Toledo, Peoria & Western's sole GP30, No. 700, leads freight No. 122 at Mapleton, Illinois, on May 6, 1980. This locomotive was remanufactured in August 1963 from TP&W F3A No. 100, a locomotive that Electro-Motive had built as a demonstrator in 1947. The unusual streamlined rooftop bulge that marks the GP30 was the external affectation of the model's centralized airflow system, which used a pressurized engine compartment. The GP30 was designed in reaction to GE's U25B, which, among other innovations, used a pressurized engine compartment to help seal out particulates and moisture from the locomotive. *George W. Kowanski*

Gulf, Mobile & Ohio operated GP30s and GP35s that rode on AAR Type B trucks from Alcos traded back to Electro-Motive in the early 1960s. GM&O GP35 No. 638 rolls along near Chenoa, Illinois, in 1986. *Steve Smedley*

Churrella writes that General Electric executives "felt their company's reputation was being tarnished by association with ALCo [sic]" in his paper, *Corporate Culture and Marketing in the American Locomotive Industry: American Locomotive and Electro-Motive Respond to Dieselization.* Churrella continues by noting that "these managers also saw an opportunity to displace ALCo as EMD's only competitor in the domestic locomotive market."

GE's entry into the domestic market was preceded by several years of research and development and export sales.

During the late 1950s, despite slack sales by Electro-Motive and Alco, GE rightly surmised that the market for new diesels would be increasing over the next decade and that demand would be for high-output road-switchers. It was not alone in this evaluation, as the September 1957 issue of *Diesel Railway Traction* reported that Electro-Motive's general manager, N. C. Dezendorf, estimated that during the next five years, some 7,750 American diesel-electrics would be due for major rebuilding.

Both Electro-Motive and Alco hoped that many railroads would take the opportunity to trade in diesels in the 1,350- to 1,500-horsepower range for newer, more powerful models. In anticipation of this, General Electric had licensed the Cooper-Bessemer FDL diesel engine design, an intercooled turbocharged four-cycle diesel. Working from this successful design, it expanded the engine to a 16-cylinder model, which powered two experimental 2,400-horsepower units in 1959.

By 1960, GE, confident with its locomotive design, publicly announced its new domestic road locomotive, the famous U25B. The 2,500-horsepower, four-axle, four-motor U25B was the most powerful single-engine diesel-electric on the market at that time. By 1966, GE had sold 476 units.

Initially, the manufacturer didn't waste resources developing a full line of locomotives and focused on the most lucrative part of the business: heavy freight locomotives.

Where in recent years Alco had provided Electro-Motive with nominal competition, essentially picking up the scraps of the declining market, GE posed a real threat to Electro-Motive. It had the know-how and corporate backing to really go after a large market share. Its 752 traction motor was also highly regarded and the company had a good reputation with railroads.

Although Alco remained in the market until the end of the 1960s, GE was now Electro-Motive's main competition, and GE's actions, more than Alco's, dictated Electro-Motive's responses. The push to increase horsepower resulted in a variety of new models from all three builders. While all delivered higher output, reliability and simplicity of design suffered.

Final 567 Diesels

In 1961, on the heels of GE's U25B, Electro-Motive introduced the GP30. It used a 567D3 engine rated at 2,250 horsepower, effectively supplanting the 2,000-horsepower GP20. With this model, efforts at linking horsepower to des-ignation were abandoned. The GP30 featured a unique looking semi-streamlined road-switcher carbody with a rounded cab roof and a distinctive bump over the cab. Internally, it had a variety of changes, including a pressurized engine compartment and a complex AC excitation system for the main generator.

By the early 1960s, improving economic conditions and worn-out postwar diesel models helped improve the market for new locomotives. As indicated in Louis A. Marre's *Diesel Locomotives: The First 50 Years*, Electro-Motive built 948 GP30s (including 40 cabless GP30Bs for Union Pacific) in the model's two-year production run. There was no corresponding six-motor SD30 model built, though.

To better compete with GE's U25B, Electro-Motive introduced the even more powerful GP35 in 1963. It used a 567D3A engine rated at 2,500 horsepower. Electro-Motive had further boosted the output of the 16-567 design by increasing the maximum operating speed to 900 rpm while also improving the piston head design and redesign-

259

Southern Railway's high short hood GP30 2638 leads freight No. 57 at Danville, Virginia. Southern and Norfolk & Western were the two railroads that ordered GP30s with high short hoods and were among a handful of railroads that tended to designate the long hood as forward and continued to order road-switchers with high short hoods for years after most American lines preferred the low short hood. Southern designated some units as bi-directional, although they did not have factory-built dual controls. *Doug Koontz*

Built alongside the GP30s were Electro-Motive's first dual-cab diesels: Model JL8, designed specially for Córas Iompair Éireann (Irish Transport Company). The JL8 was an adaptation of the earlier GL8 single-cab lightweight diesel built for CIE in 1961 (Class 121). The dual-cab units were CIE Class 141s (road Nos. 141–177). Delivered in 1962, they used an eight-cylinder 567CR prime mover rated at 950 horsepower. The Irish track gauge is 5 feet 3 inches, but the loading gauge is more restrictive than in the United States. In January 2005, the class leader, No. 141, leads another JL8 with a laden Sligo to Waterford timber train at Cherryville Junction, County Kildare. *Brian Solomon*

New England's Housatonic Railroad still operates a small fleet of non-rebuilt former Conrail GP35s. On November 5, 2002, Housatonic freight NX-12 rolls past the Mead Paper Plant at Great Barrington, Massachusetts, on former New Haven Railroad trackage. *Tim Doherty*

ing the air filtration system. Thus, the 16-cylinder engine had gone from just 1,350 horsepower as installed in the FT to almost double that through turbocharging, compression ratio changes, and increased operating speed.

Externally, the GP35 took on a new look. The body and cab had a more angular appearance than Electro-Motive's earlier road-switchers. This basic body and cab style remained the standard for the next thirty years, over various four- and six-motor models. The GP35 sold even better than the GP30, totaling more than 1,300 units. And in 1964, Electro-Motive offered a six-motor model SD35, selling more than 360 of these in less than two years.

With six traction motors and significantly greater weight, the SD35 could deliver much higher tractive effort than its four-motor counterpart. An SD35 weighed 390,000 pounds, compared to a GP35's 263,000 pounds, and delivered 97,540 pounds of starting tractive effort to the GP35's 65,750 pounds. Although SD35 sales paled when compared

to the four motors of the period, it was a building block for some of Electro-Motive's best-selling machines. The high-horsepower, high-tractive effort six-motor diesel represented the motive power of the future.

Double Diesels

In the early 1960s, all three American diesel builders also brought out massive double diesels, which used two prime movers and rode on eight axles. John Bonds Garmany writes in *Southern Pacific Dieselization* that Electro-Motive's initial offering was intended to rival the K-Ms. Designated as the RB-3600, it would have ridden on C-C trucks and been powered by a pair of turbocharged 12-567 engines. Southern Pacific didn't order any, nor did any other lines, so the RB-3600 never left the drawing board.

Later, Electro-Motive introduced the even more powerful DD35, a double diesel that was essentially two GP35s in one massive carbody. It was rated at 5,000 horsepower.

The DD35s were built in both cab and booster configurations and rode on four-axle D trucks, giving them a D-D wheel arrangement. The DD35 with cabs (sometimes described as model DD35A) were 88 feet 2 inches long.

The long wheelbase and four-axle trucks limited where these monsters could be used, so the design was by no means universally accepted. Only Southern Pacific and Union Pacific bought them—western lines that had respectively experimented with the very powerful diesel hydraulics and gas turbines. SP had bought three of the DD35Bs, and Union Pacific ordered a mix of As and Bs totaling 42 units. The GP30, GP35, SD35, and DD35 all demonstrated significant power increases over Electro-Motive's older locomotives.

Recycled Parts

Since the mid-1950s, a number of railroads took advantage of Electro-Motive's incentive to trade older locomotives for credit on new models or remanufacturing. Some lines, such as Boston & Maine, traded back World War II–era FTs and BL2s and received new locomotives featuring recycled components. Other lines turned in other builder's models. Where practical, Electro-Motive incorporated components from these locomotives as well. For example, Missouri

Pacific turned back its fleet of Alco FAs for a portion of its GP18 order. Among the components used were the Alco trucks and General Electric 752 traction motors. A number of lines followed the same principle when they ordered new GP30s and GP35s. Chesapeake & Ohio ordered SD18s using six-motor tri-mount trucks recycled from Alco RSD-5s.

Working Forward

Although it maintained superiority during the horsepower race in the 1960s, Electro-Motive took a circuitous path to achieve success. While trying to build diesels to match the output of its competition, it took several years of development before Electro-Motive produced technology deserving of the reliability standards that it established in previous decades.

The higher-output 567 diesels had unreliable reputations. They suffered electrical problems as a result of complex relay control needed to make the AC excitation system work. They were also known for serious wheel slip problems and high rates of traction motor flashover. To solve both problems, a whole new electrical system was needed. Difficulties with the turbocharged 567 engine ultimately resulted in the decision to engineer a new crankcase with greater cylinder displacement.

On December 22, 2001, freshly painted Irish Rail Class 121 No. 127 and a Class 141 lift a sugar beet train up Taylorstown bank near Ballycullane, County Wexford. The 15 GL8s built for Ireland were the first locomotives exported to Europe directly from La Grange. Originally designated Class B121, they were built without multiple-unit connections and fitted with sanding equipment. Use of sand is prohibited in Ireland, and a dozen or so years after the 121s were delivered, the sand was finally removed from the locomotives. Despite their age, the 121s have proved solid and versatile. More than 45 years after they were delivered, two of the class were still hard at work in mainline service. *Brian Solomon*

CHAPTER THREE

THE
645 ERA

By the mid-1960s, Electro-Motive had been at the top of the locomotive business for more than twenty years. Its 1930s-era 567 prime mover was no longer practicable in obtaining the higher output needed to compete with General Electric's offerings. Modern freight operations demanded even greater unit output.

To stay abreast of the market and remain the nation's top locomotive builder, Electro-Motive set out to engineer a new, more powerful diesel engine. While the new 645 engine was really a refinement and enlargement of Electro-Motive's successful 567 engine, it required a departure from the manufacturer's long-held policy of component compatibility between models.

The 567 engine was in production from 1938 to 1965. In the same period, Alco introduced four new engines: the 539, 241, 244, and 251. Electro-Motive's 8-, 12-, and 16-cylinder 567s all used the same basic design, with most components interchangeable between engines with a different number of cylinders (except for engine-specific components, such as the crankshaft). These consistent part supplies contributed to Electro-Motive's sales popularity—railroads didn't need to maintain a separate parts supply for different locomotive models. Consistency from model to model simplified maintenance as well; shop forces skilled in repairing E units found F units, GPs, and switchers familiar.

Opposite: On request from Santa Fe, Electro-Motive developed an SD45-type locomotive with a full-width body. Using a metal cowling, the new model was designated FP45 and carried a high-capacity steam generator for work in passenger service. Designed for dual service, nine were built in 1968 and delivered in the classic warbonnet paint. After Santa Fe turned over its long-distance passenger services to Amtrak on May 1, 1971, its FP45s entered the regular freight pool and were painted accordingly. In 1989, Santa Fe returned the FP45s to the warbonnet scheme for its Superfleet service. Wearing the blue-and-yellow freight scheme, FP45 5998 pauses for a crew change at Emporia, Kansas, on June 18, 1985, while a freight led by a Santa Fe SD45 rolls the opposite direction. *Scott Muskopf*

Erie-Lackawanna embraced Electro-Motive's 20-cylinder diesels. A pair of the 3,600-horsepower machines is poised atop the railroad's most famous structure, the 1848-built Starrucca Viaduct, located in Lanesboro, Pennsylvania. Below the bridge are the tracks of Delaware & Hudson's Penn Division. *Jim Shaughnessy*

However, Electro-Motive crossed a design threshold with the new 645 engine. In order to make a better locomotive, the engine and electrical parts would have to be somewhat different from those before.

The 645 Engine

The 645 was not a completely new design—far from it. The 645's essential engine parameters were basically the same as the 567's. Like the 567, the 645 used a welded V-type cylinder block with two banks of cylinders divided by 45 degrees. Pistons powered a crankshaft common to both banks. As a two-stroke-cycle design, high compression and positive air scavenging gave the 645 a high power-to-weight ratio. It also could be aspirated by a Roots Blower or turbocharger.

The most significant change in the new engine was enlargement of the cylinder bore to 9¼₆ inches, increasing individual cylinder displacement by 78 cubic inches from 567 to 645 cubic inches. The turbocharged engine, designated 645E3, was built for locomotive applications in 8-, 12-, 16-, and 20-cylinder configurations.

Cylinders are numbered in order, from front to back of the right bank and left bank; Cylinder 1 is at the front of the right bank, and Cylinder 16 at the back of the left bank. Water pumps and governor are at the front, while the flywheel is at the rear. Cylinder firing order varies depending on the number of cylinders. Based on information published in Electro-Motive's *Engine Maintenance Manual Model 645E3*, the 16-645E3 uses the following firing order: 1, 8, 9, 16, 3, 6, 11, 14, 4, 5, 12, 13, 2, 7, 10, 15. The 20-645E3 uses this order: 1, 19, 8, 11, 5, 18, 7, 15, 2, 17, 10, 12, 3, 20, 6, 12, 4, 16, 9, 14.

Electro-Motive published data indicates that low idle speed on the 645 was set at either 235 or 255 rpm and normal idle speed was 318 rpm. As with the 567 engine, each throttle position on the 645 increased rpm to match engine output with capabilities of the electrical system. In "run eight" (maximum throttle), the engine worked at 904 rpm.

Electrical Innovations

With increased engine output came corresponding changes to the electrical and air systems. As mentioned in Chapter 2, the electrical arrangement used on late-era 567 locomotives had proved problematic.

In *D-Day on the Western Pacific*, author Virgil Staff put together a detailed description of the technological hurdles overcome as Electro-Motive increased output of its diesels in the 1960s. He also writes of the trials and tribulations facing Electro-Motive and Western Pacific, a moderate-sized railroad at the time. He says that with the GP20, Electro-Motive pushed traditional DC excitation of the main generator to the limit and went in a new direction with GP30:

Electro-Motive then devised a system involving the D14 alternator as the power supply for the main generator excitation. In order to obtain this excitation, EMD had employed a magnetic amplifier system, which was actually a system controlling and converting the three-phase D14 AC power

Early in the 645 era, the SD45 was the biggest seller and the most powerful of the line. The turbocharged 20-cylinder 645 diesel was rated at 3,600 horsepower and produced a deep sound that had the aura of pure power. Here, a pair of SD45 demonstrators work Delaware & Hudson freight BM-3 at Crescent, New York, on September 17, 1967. D&H later bought three SD45 demonstrators, including 4353, which is renumbered as 803. *TRAINS Magazine* reported in the December 1967 issue that through June of that year, Electro-Motive had sold 473 of the new model, compared with 431 of the 16-cylinder SD40. *Jim Shaughnessy*

Following pages: Following tests in 1967, Delaware & Hudson bought three Electro-Motive SD45 demonstrators, numbering them 801 to 803. The big units were oddballs in D&H's fleet, which consisted largely of Alco and GE diesels, and it swapped them to Erie-Lackawanna for three GE U33Cs in 1969. In this July 29, 1968, photograph, D&H SD45 802 is on its way back from Maine Central's Waterville, Maine, paint shop. *Jim Shaughnessy*

into DC power. Power was rectified and controlled at the same time.

With this system, Staff continues:

Horsepower range was so high that the differential between maximum voltage and maximum current narrowed to requiring 16 steps of traction motor field shunting or transition, and there was not sufficient space in the [electrical] cabinet to include all the relay logic to function with straight relays. Consequently, Electro-Motive provided a motor-driven program switch, which operated switches that in turn selected the shunting contactors to be picked up to provide the different percentages of traction motor field shunting.

Staff notes that the complex relay circuitry didn't always function as intended:

Transition conditions on the GP-35 [sic] often caused the wheel slip system to continue unloading because of an imbalance in the motor field shunting and traction motor currents. If the program switch failed to locate in the correct position at the right time, an out-of-phase situation would

A variation of the SD45 was the SDP45, which at 70 feet 8 inches was longer than the conventional SD45 and designed to accommodate a steam generator at the back for passenger services, thus the extended section beyond the radiators. Notice the difference at the rear of the carbody between the E-L SDP45 3654 and SD45 3534. Erie-Lackawanna, Great Northern, and SP bought units with the extended carbody, although E-L's were strictly freight units and not steam-equipped. They were specifically acquired to carry larger fuel tanks to allow longer runs between fueling. *Jim Shaughnessy*

develop in which the transition circuit was "locked up." Commonly the program switch would become "hung-up" between positions so that it would not move either way, and the unit would remain unloaded.

These problems were eventually brought into check, but the root problem appeared to be overly complex and unreliable relay circuitry required for generator excitation and motor transition. One can see why transition was eliminated from Electro-Motive (and GE) locomotive designs in the future.

To effectively harness the increased power of the turbocharged 645, Electro-Motive engineered a superior electrical transmission system. The state-of-the-art AR-10 alternator incorporated a rectifier with four banks of solid-state silicon diode devices to convert AC output to DC for traction. This combination was more efficient and more compact than a comparable DC generator. An additional benefit was that the alternator was not subject to flashovers, a common flaw that plagued DC generators.

Above: The SD45's high output has great cooling demands and as a result requires larger radiator capacity than the SD40. To accommodate the larger radiators, Electro-Motive placed them at angles to the carbody, giving the locomotive a distinctive flared rear-end appearance. While other models— notably Electro-Motive's GP40X and SD45-derivative models such as the SDP45— also used the flared radiator design, it makes the SD45 easily distinguishable from other Electro-Motive six-motor road-switcher types. *Brian Solomon*

Right: On May 11, 1975, Western Maryland SD40 7495 leads a pair of F7Bs and another Electro-Motive unit at Rockwood, Pennsylvania. *Jim Marcus, Doug Eisele collection*

The 20-cylinder 645 was nearly ideal for Southern Pacific, and the railroad made good use of the type. Not only did it have the largest roster of SD45s, but also encouraged Electro-Motive to design the "tunnel" version, of which it was the sole purchaser. Where other railroads gave up on the SD45 by the early 1980s, SP stuck with the type, sending most through its GRIP overhaul program at Sacramento. In March 1990, GRIP-graduated SD45 7510 leads another SD45 and a SD40 eastward at Applegate, California, in the Sierra foothills on the ascent of Donner Pass. *Brian Solomon*

Although more complex, the AC-DC transmission greatly reduced the number of electrical components, decreased maintenance, and produced significantly higher output to traction motors by using diodes to rectify the external control circuitry. Staff elaborates on the new system, using the GP40 as his example, by noting the following:

Unlike the GP-35s, which started out in series-parallel and transferred to parallel, the GP-40s operated in parallel at all times. The early GP-40s had either three or two stages of motor field shunting, but as rectifier development progressed, Electro-Motive was eventually able to eliminate the shunting altogether, and to develop a straight parallel full-field operation at all times. The numerous problems with the transition circuitry in the GP-20s and GP-35s were not present on the GP-40 because they contained no transition functions.

273

Elgin, Joliet & Eastern is a Chicago-area belt railway that serves the steel industry. Here, two of its switchers work near Gary, Indiana, on January 2, 1995. EJ&E 317 is an SW1200, a 1,200-horsepower model powered by a normally aspirated 12-567 engine, while No. 444 is an SW1001, powered with an 8-645 engine rated at 1,000 horsepower. The SW1001 was designed with a lower profile cab than the standard Electro-Motive SW1000 and intended for working industrial areas with low overhead clearance. With a maximum height of 14 feet 3 inches and a curved roof profile, the SW1001 cab closely resembles that employed on older switchers, such as the SW1200. *Brian Solomon*

The FP45 was adapted into the F45 freight diesel, a cowl-type not equipped with the high-capacity steam generator. As a result, it measured a few feet shorter in length. Santa Fe, Great Northern, and GN's successor, Burlington Northern, bought the F45, and in later years, a number of roads picked up F45s secondhand. Wisconsin Central had six, plus an FP45, all from Santa Fe. This interior view of WC 6656 provides a view of the 20-646E3 diesel engine. *Brian Solomon*

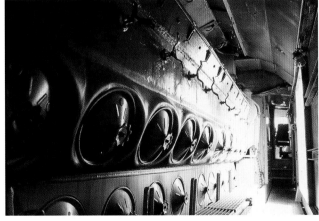

Though much improved, the GP40 was hardly free from flaw. While Staff highlights the early GP40's difficulties, he acknowledges that the model was better regarded than those that preceded it. Also, Western Pacific's examples only covered four-motor models, since it didn't buy six-motor diesels.

Incidentally, the advancement of an AC-DC transmission should not be confused with the significant development of *three-phase* AC traction systems, used on the SD70MAC in the early 1990s and discussed in Chapter 4.

The First 645 Models

Electro-Motive began developmental work on the 645 line in 1964. At the end of 1965, it advertised nine new models—each employing newly refined technology. Each proposed model had essentially the same basic technology, although specifics of platform length, wheel arrangement, method of aspiration, and the number of engine cylinders varied. The first line to order 645 production locomotives was New York Central, with an order for 50 GP40s, in 1965.

Two principal models in the 645 lineup were the four-motor GP40, successor to the GP35, and the six-motor SD40, successor to the SD35. Both the GP40 and SD40 used the turbocharged, 16-cylinder 645E3 engine rated at

3,000 horsepower—a key benchmark for unit reduction. Since the vast majority of postwar F units, GPs, and competitors' units had been built as 1,500-horsepower machines, a 3,000-horsepower unit enabled a two-for-one replacement. Three modern turbocharged 645 engines could now do the same work as six older 567 engines. Rather than assigning six F units to heavy freight, just three SD40s would do the job.

But not all railroads needed or desired 3,000-horsepower machines. The GP40 was designed for high-horsepower applications, such as fast freight or long-haul intermodal runs. New York Central assigned them to its Supervan services. However, the SD40 with its six-wheel trucks didn't appeal to many lines because it caused greater stress to track structure. New England railroads, for example, demonstrated a clear preference for four-motor diesels.

To satisfy these customers, Electro-Motive offered more conventionally designed and more moderately powered locomotives. The 16-cylinder 645E aspirated with Roots blowers was rated at just 2,000 horsepower. It powered the four-motor GP38 and six-motor SD38, representing a more basic advancement of Electro-Motive's GP7 and SD7 road-switcher types. In its original form, the GP38/SD38 also employed a conventional electrical system instead of the AC/DC rectifier electrical system. After 1971, Electro-Motive offered an option with a more advanced AC/DC electrical system on the GP38/SD38, which were designated GP38AC/SD38AC to reflect the difference.

The simplicity and versatility of the GP38 and its related models (the GP38AC and GP38-2) made it very popular. More than 700 GP38/GP38ACs were sold in the United States alone, and the GP38-2, offered after 1972, sold more than 1,800 units. By contrast, the SD38 was a specialized machine aimed at high-tractive effort applications, such as yard transfer work and mineral service. According to figures published in *The Contemporary Diesel Spotter's Guide,*

The guts of the 645 line was the new engine, which was essentially an expansion of the proven 567 design. This view of Southern Pacific SW1500 2552 at the Hardy Street Diesel Shop in Houston, Texas, shows off the normally aspirated 12-645 engine. The locomotive hood rests on the right. SP continued to make a large investment in new switchers in the late 1960s and early 1970s and many of them from all over the system were repaired and overhauled in the Hardy Street shop. Prior to servicing Electro-Motive locomotives, SP built steam engines on this same floor. *Tom Kline*

more than 50 SD38 units were built for service in North America. Only 81 SD38-2s (available after 1972) were built in North America, a small number compared to the thousands of SD40/SD40-2s built during the same period.

Initially, the 645 line offered two switcher models: the SW1000 and the SW1500, both using Roots Blower–aspirated 8- and 12-cylinder 645s, respectively. Although they had a more boxy, utilitarian appearance than earlier Electro-Motive switchers, these two models were essentially the most recent advance in the old 600-horsepower SW1 and 1,000-horsepower SW7 lines.

At 1,500 horsepower, the SW1500 had the same output as the GP7 road switcher. As a result, a number of railroads assigned this model to road-switcher type services, often using them in multiple on road freights or as long-distance locals when not working them in yards. The SW1500 was another strong seller for Electro-Motive, which built more than 800 for domestic applications.

After 1968, a variation on the SW1000, the SW1001 model, was built that featured a low-profile cab to better suit industrial applications. Ultimately, this proved more popular than the SW1000 itself; many were ordered by industrial railways as plant switchers, as well as by commercial railroads.

By the late 1960s, Electro-Motive had added a variety of other models to the 645 line, including mid-ranged models that used the 12-cylinder turbocharged 645E3 engine. It was rated at 2,300 horsepower and sold as a fuel-saving option.

The new GP39 and SD39 models were comparable to the GP38 and SD38 in both output and appearance, but neither type attracted large sales. One of the more interesting variations was the SDL39, a lightweight model with low minimum axle weight built exclusively for service on Milwaukee Road branch lines. Just 10 of these short-frame six-motor locomotives were built, which rank the SDL39 among the most unusual turbocharged 645 locomotives built for a Class I American railroad.

Twenty Cylinders

The top of the 645 line was Electro-Motive's new high-horsepower monster, the SD45. Built on the same platform and employing the same technology as the SD40, the SD45 was powered by the largest of the 645 engines—a turbocharged 20-cylinder 645E3. At maximum throttle, working at 900 rpm, it delivered 3,600 horsepower, 20 percent more than the 16-645E3. Electro-Motive's *SD45 Operator Manual* lists the main generator on the engine as model

AR10B. The approximate weight of the locomotive as built was 368,000 pounds.

From the front, the SD45 looked the same as the rest of the 645 Electro-Motive road locomotives. Yet, it was immediately identifiable by the large angled radiators at the back, which were necessary to provide greater cooling capacity as a result of higher-engine output.

Following extensive testing, SD45 production began in 1966. The model was offered at the same time as the SD40 and SD38, providing railroads a choice of six-motor locomotive models. New, the SD45 cost approximately $290,000,

depending on the specific options and the size of the order. High-tractive effort and high-horsepower were the key features for power and fast freight. Three gear ratios were available: 62:15 for a top speed of 71 miles per hour and minimum continuous speed of 11.3 miles per hour; 61:16

New England Central GP38s work K&L Feeds at Franklin, Connecticut, on Halloween Day 1997. New England Central assumed operations on the old Central Vermont Railway in February 1995. Originally a member of the RailTex short-line family, it later became part of the RailAmerica family. Electro-Motive's GP38 was powered by a normally aspirated 16-645E engine rated at 2,000 horsepower. This basic model was suited for heavy service on secondary lines where high horsepower is unnecessary. Forty years after the model was introduced, hundreds were still in service all over North America, many on regional lines such as New England Central. *Brian Solomon*

for 77 miles per hour maximum and 12.2 miles per hour minimum; and 60:17 for 83 miles per hour maximum and 13.2 minimum.

The SD45 proved very popular with western lines, where moving long, fast freight over great distances and prolonged grades is the rule. Great Northern bought the first SD45, which carried the slogan "Hustle Muscle" on its side. The Southern Pacific, Santa Fe, and later Burlington Northern (inheriting some from predecessors Burlington, Great Northern, and Northern Pacific) amassed large fleets of the powerful machines. The SD45s were no means exclusive to the West, though, as, Chicago & North Western, Erie Lackawanna, Frisco, Norfolk & Western, Pennsylvania, and Southern Railway were among the lines that made good use of the SD45's high-horsepower capabilities.

Although a very good locomotive, the SD45 suffered mechanical ailments that tainted its reputation in its early years. Its massive crankshaft was prone to breaking—a flaw attributed to unwanted stresses for a crankshaft with its firing order and length. In later years, the difficulties with the crankshaft seemed to be overcome. Some railroads, such as Santa Fe, successfully worked SD45s in heavy road service for more than 30 years. Other problems in the SD45 included leaky radiators and inequitable weight distribution—a condition

that could result in harmonic bouncing. In extreme circumstances, SD45 bouncing was known to break rails.

In the long run, the most serious objection to the SD45 was its significantly higher fuel consumption. In the mid-1960s, the cost of fuel was low enough to negate worries of the model's fuel-thirsty tendencies. But in the early 1970s, as the price of fuel rose sharply, greater consumption became a more serious concern. In those years, Electro-Motive's 16-cylinder models, including the SD40/SD40-2, drew the bulk of sales. Between 1965 and 1972, some 1,260 SD45s were produced, making it the most common rail application of the 20-645E3 prime mover. The SD45 was not alone in the application of the big 645 as several derivative models were developed and sold.

Santa Fe was among the last American railroads to operate high-quality, long-distance passenger services. Through the 1960s, Santa Fe, as a matter of company pride, continued to invest in passenger services despite declines in ridership and revenue. In the mid-1960s, Electro-Motive met Santa Fe's request for a shrouded diesel by adapting the SD45 with external cowling that covered the machinery. Distinct from the E and F units where the carbody was part of the locomotive structure, a cowl-type locomotive's shrouds provide nonintegral covering. The new model, designated FP45—"F" for "full width carbody" and "P" to indicate that it carried a steam generator—was designed to work both premier freight and passenger services. Nine FP45s were built in 1968 for Santa Fe. Although not elegantly streamlined like the Fs and Es of the 567 era, the FP45 had a clean overall appearance and was painted in Santa Fe's traditional red, yellow, and silver warbonnet livery.

The cowl shrouding served both practical and aesthetic functions. Its streamlining resulted in lower wind resistance—important when moving at high speeds. Santa Fe routinely operated its passenger trains at 90 miles per hour. The shrouds also protected crew members who walked from locomotive to locomotive when traveling at speed. Although best remembered for their long service on Santa Fe, Milwaukee Road also placed an order for five FP45s.

The success of the FP45 led Santa Fe and Great Northern (and later GN's successor Burlington Northern) to order 20-cylinder F45s solely for freight service. These looked very similar and shared most components with the passenger

Unique to Chicago suburban services were 15 F40Cs built in 1974. These used a full-width carbody and featured corrugated stainless-steel side panels. Powered by a 16-645E3, these were very similar to Amtrak's SDP40Fs, but designed to provide head-end power rather than steam heat. They had 30-year careers working Chicago's commuter trains, primarily on Milwaukee Road routes out of Union Station. *Brian Solomon*

Among the more unusual locomotives powered by the 645 engine was the SDL39 built for Milwaukee Road. Intended for service on branch lines with unusually light axle-loading, this model spread approximately 250,000 pounds over six axles, less than the weight of a typical four-axle unit. *The Contemporary Diesel Spotter's Guide* explains that to reduce weight Electro-Motive used short frame, lightweight trucks, and a 12-cylinder turbocharged engine. While the 10 units, built in two batches in 1969 and 1972, were unique to American railroading, Electro-Motive employed much of the same weight-saving equipment for an order of broad-gauge, double-cab, six-motor JT22CWs built for Ireland's Córas Iompair Éireann in 1976. *Steve Smedley*

FP45, but lacked the large steam generator and thus rode on a slightly shorter frame.

Another specialized 20-cylinder model was developed for premier SD45 owner Southern Pacific. In the early 1970s, Southern Pacific (SP) was among the most successful and most progressive freight railroads in the United States. Its operations were characterized by many miles of difficult mountain grades, which demanded high-horsepower and high-tractive effort. While Electro-Motive 645 locomotives had exhibited excellent performance in graded territory, SP found that performance suffered when climbing in "run eight" (maximum throttle) through long tunnels and snow sheds on its mountain lines in the California Sierra and Oregon Cascades. But the placement of the air-intake vents on top of the long hood contributed to engine overheating in SP's rigorous operating conditions where, in long tunnels at high-altitude, hot exhaust gases were sucked back into the locomotive. The problem was most acute when Electro-Motive was testing the experimental 4,200-horsepower SD45X on SP tracks. So a new six-motor diesel design was engineered with air intakes relocated to midpoint above the rear truck. This modification improved power output in the Sierra tunnels by as much as 20 percent.

This new design was first applied to 20-cylinder models and was designated SD45T-2. It was a 3,600-horsepower type that also incorporated Dash-2 improvements (discussed later on). The "T" in the new designation indicated the "tunnel" airflow arrangement, and the locomotives became known colloquially as tunnel motors.

The *Contemporary Diesel Spotter's Guide* Year 2000 Edition notes that Electro-Motive built 247 SD45T-2s between 1972 and 1975. And between 1974 and 1980, Electro-Motive adapted the tunnel motor design using the 16-645E3 on 310 SD40T-2s for both SP and Denver & Rio

On December 31, 2003, five Union Railroad MP15DCs—Nos. 17, 19, 26, 15, and 14—move a train of coke and coke byproducts from the U.S. Steel Clairton Coke Works to the Union Railroad–CSX interchange at Bessemer, Pennsylvania. *Patrick Yough*

Grande Western. SP's tunnel motors remained standard power on its mountain lines for more than two decades and were operated all across its western system—from New Orleans to Portland, Oregon.

On the Edge of Oblivion

After decades of decline, the railroads' glory days as the premier and dominant form of transport were just a memory by the 1970s. By this time, the federally sponsored interstate highway program was well underway, the latest system of subsidized roads to contribute to the further erosion of railroad traffic. The shift from rail to road and the decline of heavy industry had deprived many railroads of their most lucrative traffic. Contributing to the railroad industry's woes were strict government regulations that imposed an inflexible rate structure and inflexible and obsolete labor arrangements. These labor agreements caused railroads to sustain a level of employment greater than needed to support their traffic.

The situation in the East was the most acute. The merger between the Pennsylvania and New York Central railroads in 1968 produced disastrous results. By June 1970, Penn-Central descended into financial chaos, becoming the world's largest bankruptcy at that time. Railroads across the region followed PC on the path to doom. Ultimately, this situation forced government action, resulting in creation of federal-sponsored Conrail in 1976. Designed to put the eastern railroads back on track, Conrail continued to hemorrhage money through the end of the decade.

In the Midwest, the situation was not much better. Milwaukee Road and Rock Island were in deep trouble. Milwaukee ultimately reorganized, cutting many routes in the early 1980s, including its famous Pacific Extension. Rock Island was liquidated and its key routes were sold to other railroads and large portions were abandoned outright.

While some railroads, notably those in the South and West, remained strong, the threat of coal-slurry pipelines contributed to worries that the entire industry might descend into insolvency. A pall of doom prevailed, as weed-grown mainlines, disused branches and industrial spurs, and decaying yards seemed to forecast the end of railroading. It

Weyerhaeuser is one of the world's largest timber companies and has operated a number of small railways over the years to move its products. On July 12, 1991, a Weyerhaeuser SW1500 and SW7 300 work in multiple with three other switchers and a GP9 hauling a freight across this curved timber trestle at Rocky Point, Washington. Some railroads routinely operated switcher models in multiple with freights on lightweight lines. An SW1500 weighs roughly 10 tons less than a GP40 (depending on specific locomotive options). In addition, switchers have a shorter wheelbase, allowing them to work tight industrial trackage. *Don Marson*

In the 1970s, Canadian National began ordering diesels with the Canadian safety cab that featured a full-width nose and a four-piece windshield. Unique to CN was the SD40-2W, a variation of the SD40-2 built by General Motors Diesel Limited at London, Ontario. Internally, these locomotives are the same as SD40-2s, using the 16-645E3 diesel rated at 3,000 horsepower. In August 1978, CN 5264 leads a freight at Geikie near Jasper, Alberta. In the 1970s, CN was still operating trains by class, and thus new locomotives were delivered with class lamps seen to the sides of the cab number boards. *Thomas L. Carver*

was a time of desperation, leading to merger and retrenchment, but also ultimately to deregulation, improved labor arrangements, and a more efficient network.

General Motors was the world's leading automotive manufacturer, but also a foremost producer of railroad locomotives. Efficiencies afforded by Electro-Motive diesels had helped the railroads to compete with highway transport more effectively. Had the railroads remained wedded to steam and the inefficiencies of steam-era operation, survival of the industry would have been doubtful. During these difficult times for American railroads, Electro-Motive refined locomotive design to new levels while building and selling what many consider its best locomotives of all time. In the 1970s, new Electro-Motive diesels were one of the few bright spots in an industry on the edge of oblivion.

Dash-2

In 1972, Electro-Motive introduced its new Dash-2 line. It successfully implemented electrical system changes, along with a host of other improvements, to make Electro-Motive's already successful 645 series diesels even better. Consistent with earlier design refinements, Dash-2 grouped a host of small improvements under one label. Since the 1950s, model changes tended to reflect increased output, but Dash-2 improvements neither altered output nor resulted in substantive external changes. Instead, Dash-2 reflected improved reliability.

The Dash-2 line employed an entirely revamped electrical system. Modular solid-state electronics replaced relay circuitry for the electrical controls, dramatically reducing the number of electrical components. With fewer components, dependability increased and maintenance became easier. As a result, the new SD40-2, GP40-2, and GP38-2

Canadian National's GP40-2Ls routinely operated into the United States on its Central Vermont subsidiary. On December 5, 1992, CN 9501 leads northward CV freight No. 323 at Brattleboro, Vermont, in a snow squall. Today, Guilford Rail System regularly operates former CN GP40-2Ls on its EDWJ (East Deerfield, Massachusetts, to White River Junction) freight over this line. *Brian Solomon*

A view from the Canadian safety cab of Canadian National GP40-2L (sometimes designated GP40-2W) No. 9522 at Hamilton, Ontario. Entrance to the cab is via a central door in the nose of the locomotive. This type of cab led to the development of the North American safety cab, adopted by most railroads in the United States after 1989. *Brian Solomon*

models sold extraordinarily well. They were among builders' most successful machines and remain highly regarded to this day for their ruggedness, power, and reliability.

To avoid confusion, new model designations were devised by inserting a "-2" after existing model designations; in this way Electro-Motive preserved its basic nomenclature while highlighting a host of improvements to its line. To the casual observer these designations may seem like a minor change, but they were a major coupe from a marketing perspective.

SD40-2

Some Dash-2 models had more changes than others. The SD40-2, for example, had a frame roughly 3 feet longer than the SD40, measuring 68 feet 10 inches over the pulling faces (as per Electro-Motive specifications published in its SD40-2 operators' manual). The longer frame

increased the distance between the truck centers to 43 feet 6 inches between bolsters, and it was evident in longer running board sections at the front and back of the locomotive.

The SD40-2 also employed a more advanced truck design—the HTC (sometimes listed as HT-C for high traction with "C" designating three-powered axles)—in place of the three-motor Flexicoil truck. Although the two trucks looked similar, the HTC featured an improved motor arrangement, better dampening, and other changes that contributed to a more effective weight transfer and superior wheel/rail adhesion. The presence of a dampener, which has the appearance of an automotive shock absorber, on the second axle quickly distinguishes the HTC truck from its predecessor.

An article by Sean Graham-White, "Power for the Future" in *Extra 2200 South* Issue 110, indicates that the SD40-2 calculated tractive effort based on 21 percent continuous adhesion, whereas the SD40 had just 18 percent continuous adhesion. In ideal traction conditions, the SD40-2 was rated at 27 percent adhesion. Improved adhesion allows a locomotive to apply power to the rail more effectively, increasing pulling power and reducing the chance of stalling on a grade.

The technological success of the SD40-2 made it the standard American freight locomotive in the 1970s and 1980s; nearly 4,000 were built for service in North America. The SD40-2 was purchased in large numbers, replacing older, less-reliable, and poorer-performing locomotives. Many railroads traded in early GE road diesels and Alco models—some of which were only a decade old—for new SD40-2s. By the early 1980s, the SD40-2 had become a ubiquitous symbol of heavy freight railroading.

Over the years, praise for the SD40-2 has been loud and emphatic. Railroaders love its great reliability, rapid loading characteristics, solid pulling power, and good riding qualities. If you ask experienced locomotive engineers about their favorite machines, the SD40-2 is always a top contender.

Woe Be the Passenger

At the end of World War II, American railroads' blissful optimism about the future of long-distance passenger services led to a buying frenzy of lightweight passenger cars and fast, powerful streamlined diesels—of which the most successful were Electro-Motive's E units. These locomotives had been designed from the wheels up for passenger service. The looked and acted the part and were excellent machines.

Nearly 25 years later, it appeared the end was near for the American passenger train. Neither railroads or builders wanted to invest in a specialized passenger locomotive design. Where the early streamliners, beginning with UP's *Streamliner* and Burlington's *Zephyr*, had been the symbols of hope and rejuvenation for long-distance passenger services, later passenger consists were neither accompanied by public fanfare nor expected to bring about change.

Yet the long-distance passenger train didn't die alto-gether. Amtrak was hastily formed by Congress in 1971 to provide intercity passenger services, while maintaining a national network of intercity trains. While a practical plan for financing Amtrak operations seems to have been ignored, participating railroads were required to donate equipment or cash to Amtrak in the beginning. As a result, Amtrak inherited a ragtag fleet of Es and FPs, along with self-propelled Budd rail-diesel cars (RDCs), GG1 electrics, and passenger cars, some of which were more than 30 years old.

The handful of relatively new passenger locomotives were largely reclaimed for freight work—although some made regular appearances on company business trains. There were a few exceptions. Since Amtrak was not intended to operate short-haul suburban services, these routes remained in the hands of the railroads. For example, Southern Pacific retained its San Francisco—San Jose Commute services, and so it re-assigned recently-built SDP45s, bought for its *Daylights*, *Sunset*, and *Overland*.

Slovenian Railways Class 664-111 leads the daily Ljubljana, Slovenia–to–Budapest, Hungary, intercity train No. 247, the *Citadella*, east of Pragersko, Slovenia, on August 19, 2005. This model G26HCW-2 was built under license by Duro Dakovic and originally designed for freight service, although some are now used for both freight and passenger service in Slovenia and Croatia, formerly components of Yugoslavia. It is powered by a normally aspirated 16-643E engine. The majority of Slovenia's mainlines are electrified with 3,000-volt direct current overhead, but a few strategic lines remain diesel-hauled. *Brian Solomon*

Delaware & Hudson GP38 7314 has its hood removed while it is worked on at the company's Colonie, New York, shops. The locomotive's 16-645E engine is clearly visible. On its left side are the Roots blowers used to aspirate the diesel. The Roots blower is a positive-displacement device and one of the primary features that distinguishes the normally aspirated Electro-Motive engines from the turbocharged models. Below the Roots blowers is the main generator, which on 645 models is really an alternator. *Jim Shaughnessy*

(Sometimes on weekends, the railroad also worked these locomotives on short freight runs.)

A few railroads bought new 645 diesels for suburban passenger service. Central Railroad of New Jersey (CNJ) ordered 13 GP40s with steam generators, designated GP40P (presumably 'GPP40' would have had negative connotations). These have survived in suburban service for decades, although in later years the locomotives were rebuilt and steam generators were replaced with head-end power (HEP) electric equipment. In 1974, for its Commute services, SP bought three GP40P-2s, similar to CNJ's units, which augmented the SDP45s and replaced aging Fairbanks-Morse Trainmasters.

Eight GP40TCs were built in Canada in 1966 for Ontario's GO Transit suburban network, which served greater Toronto. Although few in number, these were some of the first locomotives equipped with head-end power (HEP). There are two approaches to HEP: either power is generated by the locomotive's prime mover (the main diesel engine used for traction) or by an auxiliary diesel engine. GO Transit's GP40TCs used the latter method, with unusually long frames providing space at the rear of a long hood for an auxiliary 12-cylinder diesel and 500kW alternator. The GP40TCs are among Electro-Motive's most unusual models, and despite limited application, the entire fleet was purchased by Amtrak in 1990. As of 2006, some remain in service as standby power for passenger trains and work train service.

Amtrak's inherited Fs and E units were little more than a stop gap; it desperately needed new diesel locomotives to operate its national passenger network. To keep its costs down, Amtrak and Electro-Motive adapted freight locomotive designs to develop Amtrak's first new diesel locomotives. Cowl-type SDP40Fs were delivered by Electro-Motive in 1973 and 1974. Like Santa Fe's FP45s, these were six-axle, six-motor locomotives that used a covered cowl design.

Powered by the 16-645E3 diesel engine, rated at 3,000 horsepower and geared for 103 miles per hour, the SDP40F was an adaptation of the successful SD40-2 freight locomotive. It had several significant differences, though. It was 72 feet 4 inches long, 3 feet 6 inches longer than the standard SD40-2. Fully loaded, the SDP40F was significantly heavier as well. And since Amtrak still used steam heat, the SDP40F was also fitted with a pair of Vapor OK-4625 steam generators. Water to supply steam was stored in below-frame tanks (divided to accommodate diesel fuel and water—at 2,850 and 2,150 gallons, respectively) and in round 1,350-gallon tanks located inside the engine compartment in front of the steam generators.

Unlike the E unit it was designed to supplant, the SDP40F had a troubled history, which resulted in an unusually short career in passenger service. The model was involved in 17 suspect derailments, resulting in some railroads imposing strict speed restrictions on its operation. Although detailed investigations in the mid-1970s attempted to determine the causes of the SDP40F derailments, Amtrak basically gave up on the model when the more successful four-motor F40PH was proven a more reliable type.

On January 26, 1974, three Boston & Maine GP38-2s lead a westward freight across the Hudson River Bridge near Mechanicville, New York. Boston & Maine preferred four-motor diesels, and from the mid-1950s it had bought Electro-Motive diesels exclusively. Its 12 GP38-2s, Nos. 201 to 212, were delivered in 1973. For the American bicentennial, No. 212 was renumbered 200 and painted in a patriotic livery reflecting the aesthetic tastes of the period. *Jim Shaughnessy*

Rather than fix the troubled SDP40Fs, Amtrak took the politically astute path and traded most of them back to Electro-Motive as credit towards HEP-equipped F40PHs. In the last half of the 1970s, Amtrak made a diligent effort to replace or convert steam heat with HEP, which was more effective and significantly more reliable. A few SDP40Fs worked as long-distance trains until 1981, by which time the steam-heated equipment had been largely replaced. In 1984, Amtrak traded its 18 remaining SDP40Fs to Santa Fe in exchange for switchers.

F40PH

In 1976, Electro-Motive adapted the F40PH model for Amtrak from the successful GP40-2 3,000-horsepower freight locomotive. The manufacturer incorporated a cowl covering and made significant alterations to the electrical system to accommodate a HEP generator and related elec-

trical appliances. The modified F40PHs were powered by variations of the 16-cylinder 645E3 engine (also used in the SDP40F). Most models used a 57:20 gear ratio for a top speed of 103 miles per hour, while Nos. 329 to 360 were built with 56:21 gearing for a top speed of 110 miles per hour.

Whereas GO Transit's GP40TCs produced HEP using an auxiliary engine and generator, Amtrak's F40PH generated HEP from the prime mover. This design change resulted in an unusual electrical system and fundamental differences in control of the engine. Amtrak's 1983 *F40PH/P30CH Operating Manual* explains that the F40PH's HEP generator had three operating settings that were selected by the engineer: normal, standby, and isolate. In the normal position, the 645 engine operated at a maximum speed of 893 rpm—even when the locomotive was stationary—in order to run the three-phase HEP generator at constant speed. In the standby position, engine speed was

Left: If one photo were to encapsulate 1970s mid-America passenger railroading, this would be it. On October 18, 1975, St. Louis Union Station's enormous, decaying, and grossly underutilized steam-era train shed looms over Amtrak's *National Limited* (New York–Kansas City) led by a new SDP40F and an inherited E9B. Electro-Motive's SDP40F was adapted for Amtrak in 1974 from the SD40-2 freight locomotive. Intended for high-speed service with outdated steam-heated equipment, they were equipped with large steam generators. Later, the model was associated with several high-profile derailments that limited their usefulness to Amtrak, itself embroiled in a complex, ongoing funding struggle. *George W. Kowanski*

Below: Boston & Maine's last new locomotives were 18 GP40-2s delivered in 1977. On a clear February afternoon in 1978, three of the new units are ready to depart Mechanicville Yard with an eastward freight. An improvement on the GP40 introduced in 1965, the GP40-2 can be distinguished from its older counterpart by its small oval sighting window below the radiator vents at the back of the locomotive. *Jim Shaughnessy*

Electro-Motive delivered 45 new GP38-2s to Southern Pacific in 1980. These were assigned to local freights and work trains, while some units were specially equipped for snow service on Donner Pass and the Oregon Cascades and assigned to flangers in season. Ice breakers on the roof could be raised and fixed in place to remove icicles that formed in snow sheds and tunnels in the mountains. In addition, special circular windows with a rotating blade were used to keep ice and snow from obstructing the crew's view, and protective grates were placed over the central cab windows for added safety. *Brian Solomon*

reduced to 720 rpm (much faster than the ordinary idle speed), necessary for HEP at a lower rate.

Since HEP requires constant high engine speed, the throttle that normally matches engine output with the needs of the generator had different functions than on ordinary diesel-electrics. On the F40PH, the throttle did not control the speed of the engine; instead it adjusted excitation of the main generator as required to supply current to traction motors.

In early 1976, Amtrak ordered the F40PH for short-haul corridor services using new HEP-equipped, Budd-built Amfleet cars. Later, when it gave up on the SDP40F, Amtrak's F40PH became its standard workhorse diesel, assigned to long-distance services all over the country (outside of exclusively electrified zones in the Northeast).

Between 1976 and 1987, Amtrak ordered a total of 210 F40PHs new from Electro-Motive. The initial batch was numbered 200 to 229 and was painted with red, white, and blue stripes to honor the American bicentennial. Some later locomotives were designated F40PHRs, reflecting trades on SDP40Fs.

The success of the F40PHs led a number of other passenger train operators to buy them. By the mid-1970s, most suburban services were being run by local and state agencies rather than traditional railroad companies. Chicago's Regional Transportation Authority, predecessor to the current Metra, was the first non-Amtrak F40PH buyer. It already operated the 1974-built F40C, a six-motor cowl-type passenger locomotive very similar to Amtrak's SDP40F, but equipped for HEP and featuring corrugated stainless-steel side paneling.

Ultimately, Metra ordered three variations of the F40PH, including the F40PH-2 and the uniquely designed F40PHM-2 that featured a distinctive cab profile. During production of Metra's F40PHM-2s, Electro-Motive shifted all of its locomotive assembly to its London, Ontario, plant. Electro-Motive's La Grange, Illinois, plant ended regular locomotive assembly following completion of the last Metra F40PHM-2 in December 1992.

Massachusetts Bay Transportation Authority was another F40PH user. In 1987 and 1988, it ordered a variation of the type that used an auxiliary engine and generator for HEP. This model was designated F40PH-2C and, like the other F40PH models, it was a B-B type, riding on

Looking like jack-o-lanterns on Halloween, Bessemer & Lake Erie six-motor Electro-Motive diesels grind through the yard at Albion, Pennsylvania, on the evening of October 31, 1996, with a train from the Norfolk Southern (the former Nickel Plate Road) connection at Girard. Leading is an SD38, followed by a vintage SD9 and an SD38AC. The SD38 was a 2,000-horsepower, six-motor machine intended for slow-speed, high-tractive effort applications, such as the movement of mineral trains. *Brian Solomon*

Canadian Pacific SD40-2s lead coal empties near Invermere, British Columbia, in September 1980. CP was an early proponent of radio-controlled remote helpers, and the lead SD40-2 here has a slightly longer nose section to accommodate radio equipment. *Thomas L. Carver*

Blomberg trucks. It used a 64-foot 3-inch frame, 8 feet 1 inch longer than a standard F40PH, in order to accommodate the HEP equipment.

Electro-Motive's *F40PH-2C Operator's Manual* details the HEP equipment as the following: a Cummins-VTA28G1 turbocharged diesel, working at maximum speed of 1800 rpm, powers a Marathon Magna One three-phase AC generator delivering 480 volts AC at 60Hz. MBTA's F40PH-2Cs used 57:20 gearing for a maximum of 90 miles per hour (imposed by preset overspeed protection).

There are several advantages to generating HEP with auxiliary equipment. First, it is more fuel efficient, as it doesn't require the prime mover to be working at maximum rpm just to generate power. It also reduces wear on the prime mover, usually the most expensive individual component of a locomotive. In addition, generating HEP with auxiliary equipment leaves more power available for traction. Finally, there is an element of redundancy with this setup. If the prime mover fails, the locomotive can continue to

Above: In October 1986, Conrail GP40-2 3393 races eastward through Fairport, New York, along the former New York Central Water Level Route. High-horsepower, four-motor locomotives like the GP40-2 were well suited to Conrail's fast intermodal services. *Brian Solomon*

Right: With their dynamic brakes wailing, a quartet of Southern Pacific Tunnel Motors descends the east slope of Donner Pass near Andover, California, on March 31, 1990. Electro-Motive developed the SD45T-2 in 1972 for Southern Pacific. It used a revised airflow to better accommodate high-altitude operations through long tunnels and snow sheds. A second type of tunnel motor was adapted from the SD40-2 in 1974, designated SD40T-2, a model acquired by both SP and Rio Grande. *Brian Solomon*

Left: In 1996, Union Pacific merged with Southern Pacific, inheriting both SP's and Rio Grande's Tunnel Motor fleets. In February 2000, Union Pacific 4805, a machine built as an SP SD45T-2, races through Funks Grove, Illinois, a long way from the high-altitude tunnel territory for which it was designed. *Steve Smedley*

Below: For many years Electro-Motive's F40PH was synonymous with Amtrak's long-distance services. On December 18, 1994, on its way from Joliet to Chicago's Union Station over the old Alton Route, Amtrak F40PH-2 389 crosses the non-interlocked level crossing at Brighton Park. *Brian Solomon*

High horsepower and rapid acceleration made the F40PH and its variants ideal for suburban passenger trains that need to maintain tight schedules with frequent station stops. Chicago Metra—known as Regional Transit Authority until 1986—operates one of the most intensive diesel-powered passenger services in the world. A lineup of locomotives at Metra's Fox Lake, Illinois, terminal shows a mix of F40PHs and six-motor F40Cs. Notice the differences between the nose and cab styles of F40C No. 613 and the four-motor F40PHs to either side of it. *Chris Guss*

provide heat and light to the train. Likewise, if the HEP generator fails, the train can still make it over the road.

Super Series

With further increases in petroleum prices in the mid-1970s, fuel economy was more an issue than ever before. It was in this area that General Electric had a decided advantage, as its four-stroke-cycle 7FDL engine burned less fuel to produce the same power as Electro-Motive's 645. As a result, Electo-Motive looked to upgrade its Dash-2 models for better performance and fuel economy. The result was the more powerful 16-645F3 diesel, initially rated at 3,500 horsepower, 500 horsepower more than the 16-645E3. The locomotive included an improved wheel slip control system called Super Series, refined to provide the improved adhesion needed to make practical the application of so much power.

According to the *Contemporary Diesel Spotter's Guide*, the first applications of the new 645F engine were on 23 experimental GP40Xs, built for Santa Fe, Southern Pacific, Southern Railway, and Union Pacific in 1977 and 1978. Specifications for the GP40X, as published by Electro-Motive in the 1977 *GP40X Operator's Manual*, indicate these were 1 foot longer than the standard production GP40-2s, measuring 60 feet 2 inches over pulling faces. They featured large angled radiators along the lines of the SD45 and GP40P.

Southern Pacific's and Union Pacific's trial units were fitted with an experimental new HTB truck (high–adhesion "B", sometimes identified as the HT-B) in place of the traditional four-axle Blomberg. Those units equipped with the HTB truck were nominally taller than those with Blombergs: 14 feet 8¾ inches versus 14 feet 7½ inches. Approximate weight was 264,000 pounds.

In 2004, Canada's VIA Rail dressed six of its F40PHs in advertising liveries. No. 6401, photographed at Montreal on October 24, 2004, promoted the film *Spider-Man 2*. *Brian Solomon*

The SD45-2, built from 1972 to 1974, was produced in relatively small numbers compared to either the SD45 or the SD40-2. The only lines to order them were Clinchfield, Erie-Lackawanna, Santa Fe, and Seaboard Coast Line. E-L's 13 models came with extra-capacity 5,000-gallon fuel tanks, 15 percent larger than normal. After the creation of Conrail in 1976, the 13 E-L locomotives were assigned to helper service at Cresson, Pennsylvania, where they worked for most of their careers. On the morning of July 30, 1987, a pair of these big units drift downgrade at the Bennington Curve near Gallitzin, Pennsylvania. *Brian Solomon*

Chicago Metra ordered a variation of the F40PH that featured a windshield profile flush with the front of the locomotive. Designated F40PHM-2, these 30 locomotives, built in 1991 and 1992, are known colloquially as Winnebagos because of their resemblance to the popular brand of motor home. With the Sears Tower in the background, Metra F40PHM-2 departs Union Station on June 22, 2004, with an Aurora-bound suburban train. *Brian Solomon*

With a full moon rising, Conrail SW1500 9529—built for Penn Central—works the yard at West Springfield, Massachusetts, in October 1984. *Brian Solomon*

Electro-Motive supplanted its SW1500 with the "multipurpose" MP15 model in 1974. Riding on Blomberg trucks, the MP15s were more flexible than traditional switchers. The MP15 type was ultimately built in three variations, each with its own model designation. The basic version, designated MP15 (later MP15DC), used a traditional electrical system, while the MP15AC employed a more advanced rectifier electrical system similar to 645 road units. Beginning in 1984, a fuel-saving MP15T variation was introduced that substituted the normally aspirated 12-645 with a turbocharged 8-645. At Rock Springs, Wisconsin, Chicago & North Western MP15 1316 catches a wink of autumn sun on an otherwise cloudy October day in1995. *Brian Solomon*

297

The operating speed of the 16-645F engine had increased. Normal idle was 314 rpm, and full speed at "run eight" was 954 rpm—50 rpm faster than the 645E3. An experimental main generator (alternator) was used, model AR10X2-D14, which produced a maximum 1,265 volts direct current (rectified from AC output) at 4,680 amps (continuous output). Four D87X traction motors were used. The locomotives had two fuel tank options: either the basic tank with 3,000-gallon capacity or the special tank with 3,500-gallon capacity.

In 1978, Electro-Motive tested an experimental SD40 model equipped with the new Super Series wheel slip. The next year, the manufacturer built four experimental SD40Xs for Kansas City Southern using the 16-645F, which like the GP40X was rated at 3,500 horsepower.

Among the changes developed for the SD40X was relocated dynamic brake equipment. Instead of dynamic brak-ing grids located at the top center of the long hood in exter-nally bulging "blisters," the new brake equipment was situ-ated inside the long hood, directly behind the cab. Frame length was the same as the SD40-2's. A little more than a year later, another six very similar experimental units, des-ignated SD50S, were built for Norfolk & Western.

GP50

In 1981, Electro-Motive began regular production of GP50 and SD50 models, which were based on experience with the various experimental models. These used production 16-645F engines. Like the GP40X and SD40X, these units were initially rated at 3,500 horsepower (although later pro-duction models were rated at 3,600 horsepower).

In addition to the new engine, the GP50 and SD50 models employed the latest generation of electrical compo-nents, including model D87 series traction motors. Electro-

Canadian Pacific SD40-2F 9023 is photographed at East Deerfield Yard in September 2000. These were the last of the SD40-2 types, an order of 25 built in 1988 (9000–9024), several years after the 710 engine was in regular production. *Brian Solomon*

Canadian National SD50F No. 5400, the class unit, leads a westward freight west of Coteau, Quebec, on October 22, 2004. Sixty units of this model were built by GMD for CN between 1985 and 1987. The cowl type was powered by a 16-645F3B engine rated at 3,600 horsepower. Geared for speeds of 65 miles per hour, they were numbered 5400 to 5459.
Brian Solomon

Electro-Motive's GP15-1 was a moderately rated road switcher that used a revised airflow pattern similar to that employed by the SD451-2 and SD40T-2. Many GP15-1s were built from recycled components. The closeup shows the GP15-1's rear engineer-side air-intake vent.
Brian Solomon

Motive had implemented changes in the armature design that reduced eddy currents in the armature coils, thus reducing the amount of heat produced by the motor. This improvement—combined with greater field coils surface, polymide film insulation, and improved motor blower efficiency—helped keep the D87 series motors cooler when operating at maximum loads. They then could do more work than comparable older motors.

Mechanical changes to the gears and the bearings that couple the motors to the axles were designed to accommodate higher torque and horsepower output. According to Electro-Motive publications, these modifications increased the D87 motor continuous ratings by 11 percent.

Another innovation standard with GP50 and SD50 included the Super Series wheel slip control, developed by using licensed technology from Swedish firm Allmänna Svenska Elektriska Aktiebolag (ASEA) and applied to the experimental units in the late 1970s. Electro-Motive describes this advance as a "wheel creep control system" and explains in the *Locomotive Service Manual GP50* that "the term wheel 'slip' is not adequate to express an allowed slip condition. In this manual, *controlled* wheel speed above locomotive ground speed is called wheel creep and is usually expressed as a percentage above ground speed."

The manual describes operation of the wheel slip controls as thus:

> Conventional wheel control systems are limiting systems—when wheel slip reaches a specific low value, the applied power is reduced to completely eliminate slipping. The Super Series wheel creep control system applies precisely the amount of power that results in the wheel creep percentage providing maximum tractive effort.
>
> Wheel creep occurs when the friction level required to support the tractive effort at the wheel

In the late 1970s, Conrail sent inherited GP7s and GP9s to Electro-Motive for remanufacture into 1,500-horsepower GP15-1s. No. 1664 was out-shopped eight years prior to when this photo was taken on December 31, 1987, at Framingham, Massachusetts. Conrail routinely assigned its GP15-1s to local freights around its system. This one was leading symbol freight MBSE (Middleboro, Massachusetts, to Selkirk, New York). *Brian Solomon*

Clyde Engineering has been Electro-Motive's Australian licensee since the late 1940s. While no American railroad ever operated an Electro-Motive carbody unit with a C-C (six-motor) wheel arrangement—American E units used an A1A-A1A wheel arrangement—a variety of six-motor carbody types were built for Australian lines by Clyde. This model AT26C-2M, No. CLP8, is one such locomotive. It was built with a 16-645E engine and is painted for Genesee & Wyoming Incorporated's Australian Southern Railroad subsidiary. G&WI is an American-based company with several subsidiaries in the freight railroad business in a number of countries, including Australia. *Don Marson*

Red Nacional de Ferrocarriles Españoles (RENFE), the Spanish national railway, has operated Electro-Motive diesels for decades. This double-cab diesel-electric is a RENFE Class 333, General Motors Model J26CW-AC, built under license by MACOSA in the mid-1970s. It is powered by a 16-654E3 and, similar to Denmark's Class MZ, it is built by GM licensee NOHAB. This RENFE Class 333 was photographed hauling an empty mineral train near Masias, Spain, on September 26, 2001. At 5 feet 6 inches wide, RENFE has the broadest track gauge in Europe. *Brian Solomon*

exceeds the available friction at the wheel-rail interface. As with previous EMD control systems, main generator output is controlled by applying the companion alternator output to the main generator field through silicon controlled rectifier [SCR]. The SCR is turned on by a signal from [the] sensor module.

From this point on, the Super Series wheel creep system diverges from the conventional approach to wheel control. In previous systems, wheel slip was sensed and corrected in terms of traction motor current. The Super Series system enables wheel creep by precisely monitoring and controlling the applied traction motor voltage.

Among the equipment incorporated in the wheel creep system was a locomotive-mounted Doppler radar gun to measure track speed. The radar transceiver was mounted at the front of the locomotive beneath the coupler pocket. The radar signal frequency varied with the locomotive speed. An onboard computer analyzed data, and actual speed was compared with motor speed and the difference used to compute the amount of wheel slip correction. The Super Series wheel slip system permitted 33 percent adhesion in ideal conditions and 24 percent adhesion in poor conditions.

Interestingly, the radar system employed on Super Series produced similar frequencies to those used by police speed enforcement radar on highways. In fact, the train's radar system has been known to trip radar detectors in automobiles.

The service manual indicates that the locomotive's 16-645F3B engine had a normal idle speed of 200 rpm (based on 3,600-horsepower output) and a maximum speed of 954 rpm. To accommodate greater output, the GP50 used an AR15 alternator. Two main generator options were available: the

Three Rio Grande SD50s lead a unit coal train at Tabernash, Colorado, on March 23, 1986. Rio Grande had just 17 SD50s. Built in 1984, these were the railroad's last new six-motor diesels. The SD50 was powered by the 16-645F and equipped with Super Series wheel slip designed to enhance performance at slower speeds. Although Rio Grande's were rated at 3,500 horsepower, later SD50s (those built after October 1984) were rated at 3,600 horsepower. Measuring 71 feet 2 inches long, the SD50 was noticeably longer than both SD40 and SD45. *Scott Muskopf*

Three CSX SD50s lead a fly-ash train at M&K Junction, West Virginia, on October 13, 1994. *Brian Solomon*

As the sun rises on CSX's Mountain Subdivision (the old Baltimore & Ohio West End) in October 1994, SD50s roar eastward with a loaded coal train near Oakland, Maryland. *Brian Solomon*

basic AR15, which produced 1,385 DC maximum voltage, and the AR15 with "high locomotive speed capability," which produced 1,450 DC maximum voltage. In either situation, the AR15 had a maximum draw of 4,680 amperes.

The model had three fuel tank options: 3,000 gallons, 3,400 gallons, and 3,600 gallons. Electro-Motive's GP50, like its predecessor the GP40-2, was designed for fast freight service, typically priority intermodal runs. It was offered with either the Blomberg or the HTB truck. But the HTB never caught on.

The GP50 also was offered with four gear ratios and either standard 40-inch or 42-inch wheels. With the gear ratio and wheel differences, the locomotive could reach eight different maximum speeds, from 70 to 92 miles per hour. With the most common 70:17 ratio and 40-inch wheels, 70 miles per hour was the top recommended speed. Since freights weren't operated faster than 70 miles per hour in the United States, there was little need for GP50s with faster gearing.

The GP50 was the same length as the GP40—259 feet 2 inches long—and with the Blomberg trucks, it was 15 feet 6½ inches tall and 10 feet 3 inches wide.

For economy applications, where mid-range output was more appropriate, Electro-Motive offered the new GP49. Like the GP39 and GP39-2, it used a 12-cylinder turbocharged 645 diesel to produce more moderate horsepower. This model was derived from the experimental GP39X—of which six were built in 1980 for Southern Railway, a railroad with a tendency to experiment with unusual four-motor models. The GP49 was powered by a 12-645F3B engine operating at a maximum 950 rpm. The engine produced 2,800 horsepower—nearly the output of the standard GP40-2. As in the GP50, the AR15/D18 alternator and D87 traction motors were used.

Electro-Motive's external specifications on the GP39 were essentially the same as the GP50, and the GP49 could be obtained with 70:17, 69:18, or 67:19 gearing, for top speeds of 70, 76, or 82 miles per hour, respectively. While the GP40-2 had been a very popular model, the GP49 attracted only nominal interest and produced no large orders. Alaska Railroad ordered nine units with low short hoods that featured the optional L-shaped windshield on the engineer's side. The unusual model seemed to be exclusive to the 49th state, except *The Contemporary Diesel Spotter's Guide* notes that Southern's experimental GP39X units

with high short hoods were later boosted from their original 2,600-horsepower capabilities to 2,800 horsepower levels, and thus re-designated GP49s.

Six Motor 16-645F3: SD50

By the early 1980s, the six-motor road switcher was the most popular locomotive type for road freight service in North America. While a few railroads continued to order four-motor models, large road switchers made up the bulk of sales. As a result, Electro-Motive introduced the six-motor SD50 as an improvement on its popular SD40-2. It offered greater output and significantly better fuel consumptions. Unfortunately,

In May 1989, Norfolk Southern GP50 7068 departs Buffalo with a RoadRailer intermodal train that will head westward on the old Nickel Plate Road mainline. *Brian Solomon*

Southern Railway was the only eastern carrier to acquire the experimental GP40X (its three units were numbered 7000 to 7001). The high-horsepower GP40X used a modern wheel-slip system derived from that developed by ASEA for the Rc electrics. The GP40X's flared radiators appeared most prominent on Southern Railway, which tended to operate them long hood first. *Doug Koontz*

this model neither sold as well as the SD40-2, nor demonstrated the same high level of reliability that the SD40-2 did.

During SD50 production, Electro-Motive boosted output from 3,500 to 3,600 horsepower on the model. SD50s with 3,600-horsepower output used an AR11A main generator (alternator) with maximum current draw of 7,020 amps and either a D14 or D18 companion alternator for auxiliaries (depending on options). The SD50 could be ordered with either a 3,400- or a 4,000-gallon tank fuel tank. The HTC truck was standard equipment, and four gear ratios were offered, along with either standard 40-inch or 42-inch

wheels. The 70:17 gearing and 40-inch wheels allowed a maximum speed of 70 miles per hour.

The SD50 was impressive because of its length. At 71 feet 2 inches long, it was significantly longer than the SD40, SD45, and SD40-2 models. It was also slightly taller than the GP50, at 15 feet 7⅛ inches above the rail. The weight of the locomotive varied with options, with the heaviest weighing 390,000 pounds. Improved wheel slip and electrical improvements allowed for the SD50 to deliver substantially higher tractive effort than the SD45/SD45-2, which were similarly rated at 3,600 horsepower. According to Chicago & North

Western's SD60 manual, its SD45s could develop between 69,000 and 82,000 pounds of tractive effort at maximum throttle, compared with 93,600 and 115,000 pounds with the SD50. Short-time over ratings were also better with SD50.

Despite improved performance characteristics and better fuel economy, unanticipated difficulties with the 16-645F engine and other problems brought the reliability of GP50 and SD50 locomotives into question. History has proven that both the 16-645F diesel engine and Super Series wheel creep control system were not as reliable or successful as the Dash-2 model systems they replaced.

Some observers believe the 16-645F was simply one step beyond what the 645 design could support. In an interview in the May 2005 issue of *TRAINS Magazine*, former Electro-Motive engineer Jack Wheelihan explains that by working 50 rpm faster than the 645E design, the 645F engine produced different and unanticipated levels of vibration that caused serious damage to the whole locomotive.

Ultimately, Electro-Motive decided to refine yet another new engine, the 710, which corrected problems inherent in the 16-645F. While 16-645F engines remain standard in 2006, these are often de-rated, or rebuilt into 16-645Es.

A freshly rehabbed 12-645E3 diesel engine—the choice powerplant for Electro-Motive's GP39, SD39, and numerous export models. This turbocharged engine has been used as a fuel saver, generating 2,300 horsepower with just 12 cylinders, compared with 2,000 horsepower from a 16-645E aspirated with a Roots blower. *Brian Solomon*

Electrics

Enormous investment in railway electrification in Europe coincided with intensive research and development in electric locomotive technology by European locomotive manufacturers, electrical supply companies, and government research laboratories in the postwar period. Although much of this electric railroad technology was pioneered in the United States, the lack of research and a domestic market for this type of motive power resulted in European and Japanese builders developing successful advanced, modern electric locomotive designs.

However, the dramatic rise of fuel costs in the early 1970s led several American freight railroads to consider electrification as an alternative to diesel-electric operation. Anticipating a market for heavy freight electrics, Electro-Motive built two experimental prototypes in 1975 and 1976. These used electrical equipment licensed from Swedish manufacturer ASEA.

The Model GM6 was constructed first, and it used a six-motor arrangement riding on HTC trucks. It was rated at 6,000 horsepower and numbered 1975, the year it was con-

structed. The GM10, numbered 1976, was also a six-motor model, but rode on three pair of "B" trucks in a B-B-B arrangement. While unusual in the United States (Pennsylvania Railroad operated some experimental electrics with this arrangement in the 1950s), B-B-B electrics were common in Italy, Spain, Japan, and Yugoslavia, among other places. This locomotive was rated at 10,000 horsepower. Both were designed for operation from 11 kV 25Hz overhead catenary on Conrail's former PRR electrified lines. Conrail was the only remaining heavy mainline freight electrification in the United States at that time.

Ultimately, freight railroads decided to stick with diesels. Even Conrail—with its sizeable fleets of former Pennsylvania Railroad E44s and a handful of former New Haven EP4s (Conrail E33), both built by GE—eventually discontinued electric freight operations. This decision came largely as a result of logistics relating to Amtrak's ownership of the Northeast Corridor. While the electric locomotive freight market did not pan out as anticipated, Electro-Motive's partnership with ASEA did put it in a good position to assemble electrics for passenger applications.

Following an unsatisfactory experience with modern GE electrics, Amtrak looked to Europe for more effective high-speed electric motive power in the mid-1970s. Before deciding what type to purchase, it imported a French six-motor electric and a Swedish State Railways (Staten Järn-väger) Rc4, the latest in the Rc series line (built by ASEA) for Northeast Corridor testing. Based on this purchase, Amtrak found the compact high-horsepower Rc best suited its requirements.

The Swedish Rc, developed in the 1960s, was the first commercial locomotive to employ semiconductors, called thyristors. These replaced conventional electro-mechanical or pneumatic motor controls. Thyristors provide step-less traction motor regulation, permitting maximum motor output without wheel slip. This design provides more efficient electrical energy use and increases tractive effort.

Amtrak ordered a derivative Rc-type, designated AEM-7. It was built by Electro-Motive under license at La Grange. The AEM-7 shared a resemblance with the Swedish proto-types, but used a tougher body shell, which was necessary to comply with stricter American safety requirements. It was also much more powerful because it is designed to run much faster than comparable Rcs in Sweden, where the maximum speed was only 84 miles per hour in the late 1970s. Amtrak routinely assigned AEM-7s in *Metroliner* service where they would reach speeds of 125 miles per

Left: Amtrak imported a Swedish Rc-4 electric for Northeast Corridor testing during 1976 and 1977. Built by ASEA and lettered for Amtrak, the compact machine demonstrated the capabilities of thyristor motor control. Amtrak used this as the basis for its successful AEM-7 design and Electro-Motive was licensed to build the type. A secondary result of the experiments was Electro-Motive's licensing of an ASEA advanced wheel-slip-prevention system that it modified for application on its high-horsepower diesel-electrics, beginning with the experimental GP40X. On March 16, 1977, Amtrak X995 leads train No. 175 across the Susquehann River at Harve de Grace, Maryland. This locomotive was later returned to Sweden where it was used for many years.
George W. Kowanski

Opposite: Rising petroleum prices in the mid-1970s caused by the OPEC oil embargo led Electro-Motive to build two experimental electrics in 1975 and 1976 on speculation that American freight railroads might electrify key mainlines. At the time, Southern Pacific and Burlington Northern were among lines considering electrification as an option. Electrical equipment was licensed from the Swedish company, ASEA. This locomotive, model GM6 (1976), numbered for the year it was built, was rated at 6,000 horsepower and used a C-C wheel arrangement. A similar-looking machine using B-B-B wheel arrangement was Model GM10, numbered 1976. Neither model entered production, as American lines ultimately stuck with the diesel.
Thomas L. Carver

hour. (American track accommodates significantly greater axle weight than in Europe, and modern North American locomotives have tended be larger and heavier than European designs.)

Initially, Electro-Motive built 47 AEM-7s, which were mostly delivered to Amtrak in the early 1980s. These were used on the Northeast Corridor, permitting Amtrak to retire the last of its former Pennsylvania Railroad GG-1 fleet and to reassign other equipment. Amtrak ordered additional AEM-7s to replace locomotives damaged in accidents.

The AEM-7 was relatively short—measuring just 51 feet 5¾ inches long, 14 feet 6 inches tall, and 10 feet wide. Yet, its small appearance didn't mean it was a light hauler.

As built, the AEM-7 weighed 199,500 pounds, delivered 51,500 pounds of starting tractive effort, and produced up to 7,000 horsepower. While it was fast and powerful, Amtrak limited a single AEM-7 to hauling just 8 to 10 Amfleet cars because of its limited HEP capacity. It was unable to reliably provide heat and electricity to longer consists. To overcome this HEP problem, Amtrak double-headed long trains.

As with the F40PH, Amtrak paved the way for modern electrics. Soon some of the commuter agencies established to relieve Conrail of its suburban passenger operations ordered AEM-7s for passenger services. Among these were seven AEM-7s built under license by Electro-Motive for push-pull service on the Philadelphia-based South Eastern

Pennsylvania Transportation Authority (SEPTA) lines and four more for the Maryland Rail Commuter Service (MARC). Additional Rc-derivative types were licensed by builders other than Electro-Motive.

Beginning in 1983, General Motors Diesel (GMD) in London, Ontario, built seven model GF6Cs (six-motor electrics with a C-C wheel arrangement) for British Columbia's recently built and electrified 129-kilometer Tumbler Ridge coal line. These entered regular service in 1984 and were conceptually similar to their 1975 prototype. The *1988–1989 Jane's World Railways* reported that, except for

the traction motors, the majority of the electric equipment on the new GF6Cs was supplied directly by ASEA. The locomotives' trucks were Electro-Motive's proven HTC model, such as those used on the SD40-2.

The GF6C was built as a single-ended machine with full-width carbody. It used a widenose cab with three-piece windshield and typically worked in pairs, hauling 98-car unit coal trains. The GF6Cs drew current from high-voltage overhead catenary energized at 50kV AC at 60Hz. The locomotive was rated at 6,000 horsepower, with a maximum speed of 56 miles per hour (90 kilometers per hour).

Left: In 1985, U.K. aggregate mover Foster Yeoman ordered a small fleet of Electro-Motive-built six-motor diesels, designated Class 59, to haul its stone trains. These dual-cab, bi-directional diesels were based on the successful EMD SD40-2 and powered by a 16-cylinder 645E3C engine. The success of the Class 59 led another aggregate company to make a similar purchase in the mid-1990s and ultimately led to the development of the Class 66, the best-selling modern diesel-locomotive in the United Kingdom. On July 21, 2000, English, Welsh & Scottish 59205 leads a stone train at Wandsworth Road in London. In the background is the disused Battersea Park Generating Station. *Brian Solomon*

Opposite: Electro-Motive built the AEM-7 electrics for Amtrak under license from ASEA. Amtrak's new AEM-7, derived from the Swedish-designed Rc-4, hauls train No. 94 *The Colonial*, east under the old New Haven Railroad catenary at Stamford, Connecticut, on March 28, 1982. In the early years of the twentieth century, New Haven pioneered high-voltage mainline electrification. While American companies did much of the original work developing overhead electric railroad technology, the trend toward dieselization refocused the American locomotive market. Today, high-output electric locomotives use European designs. *George W. Kowanski*

CHAPTER FOUR

THE 710 ERA

For 18 years, Electro-Motive's 645 engine was the heart of some of the manufacturer's most successful diesel-electrics of all time. Yet, it had not proved reliable when boosted to meet the higher-horsepower demands of the Super Series. The introduction of the GP50 and SD50 further revealed serious inadequacies with the 645F.

These engine problems manifested at a bad time for Electro-Motive. The company was facing stronger competition from General Electric. For years, Electro-Motive had been number one in diesel sales, but in 1983 it fell behind General Electric. Although Electro-Motive temporarily regained the top position, GE was again in the lead by the mid-1980s.

The reasons behind this transformation were complex and related to GE's decision to finance and engineer a much better locomotive. Even before its sales figures demanded change, Electro-Motive recognized the need to develop a new, more powerful engine with higher reliability and better fuel consumption. Over a four-year span beginning in 1984, and at a cost of roughly $138 million, Electro-Motive planned the production of this new, more powerful engine, designated the 710. It was built experimentally from 1984 and entered regular production in 1987.

Opposite: Electro-Motive three-unit GP60 demonstrators EMD 5, EMD 6, and EMD 7 lead a Burlington Northern freight over Bozeman Pass at Muir, Montana, on June 15, 1986. *D. L. Zeutschel, Brian Jennison collection*

Where the 645 block, with its larger cylinder bore, was an advancement of the 567, the 710 block was an adaptation of the 645 engine that lengthened the piston stroke from 10 inches to 11 inches. Thus, each cylinder had a 710-cubic-inch displacement versus the 645-cubic-inch displacement on the earlier engine. Despite increased stroke, the 710 engine was only nominally larger than the 645. This engineering consideration was important because the more powerful engine had to fit inside the locomotive body.

In conjunction with greater cylinder displacement, Electro-Motive designed an improved fuel injector and a new turbocharger for the 710. The fuel injector was tailored for new combustion requirements mandated by lengthened piston stroke and related changes to cylinder scavenging. The new crankcase design and turbocharger both were signified by the "G" suffix in the engine designation.

The G-series turbocharger retained the operating characteristics of Electro-Motive's original turbocharger, which was introduced with the 16-567D engines. It was powered by a gear train at lower rpm, relying on an overrunning clutch to freewheel from exhaust gas output at higher throttle positions. To reduce top engine operating temperatures and thus improve component reliability, overall efficiency,

and fuel economy, Electro-Motive redesigned the gas-flow pattern and turbocharger exhaust to lower resistance.

A host of nominal improvements combined to boost output, reduce maintenance, and increase reliability. The compression ratio was increased from 14.5:1 on the 645F to 16:1 on the 710 engine. In General Motors' promotional literature introducing the 60 series, the manufacturer also noted that the 710 engine had a new cylinder head design. This alteration was necessary because of combustion changes that resulted from the lower engine operating temperature. Where the 16-645F engine produced a maximum output of just 3,600 horsepower, the 16-710G was rated at 3,800 horsepower.

60 Series

In 1984, Electro-Motive introduced its new line of 60 series diesels, powered by the 710 engine. Of these, the six-motor SD60 drew the most interest. Externally, the SD60 closely resembled the SD50. But with a new prime mover, a computer-controlled electrical system, and a 3,800-horsepower rating, the SD60 was a much better machine.

Chicago & North Western's locomotive manual estimates that the SD60 was only 3 percent more fuel efficient

Norfolk Southern GP59 4621 leads a westward double-stack container train down 19th Street in Erie, Pennsylvania, in October 1994. The former Nickel Plate Road mainline negotiated several blocks of street trackage in Erie. *Brian Solomon*

The last Electro-Motive four-motor freight diesels were a batch of GP60s delivered to Southern Pacific in 1994. On February 11, 1994, a new SP 9789 gleams in the afternoon sun at Wendel, California, after leading a train over the Modoc line from Klamath Falls, Oregon. These late-era units were characterized by extended-range dynamic brakes, a feature identifiable by the large squared-off cooling grids near the roof on the sides of the long hood. *Brian Solomon*

Right: On March 3, 1999, a westward Union Pacific stack train led by SD60M 6147 passes vintage Union Switch & Signal Style B lower-quadrant semaphores on the former Southern Pacific Tucumcari Line at Coyote, New Mexico. The first modern safety cabs delivered to a U.S. railroad were UP's SD60Ms featuring the three-piece windshield. *Mark Leppert*

Below: Two models unique to Santa Fe were the GP60M and cabless GP60B, both of which are seen here hauling an eastward intermodal train through Abo Canyon, New Mexico, on January 19, 1994. *Brian Solomon*

Left: A Conrail SD60M works eastward at CP 83 in Palmer, Massachusetts, on January 11, 1998. *Brian Solomon*

Below: Electro-Motive's F59PHI was the preferred locomotive for new California-sponsored Amtrak services. An Amtrak *Capitols* train makes a station stop at the new Berkeley Station on July 16, 1995. The streamlined cab and corrugated side panels are reminiscent of Burlington's E5s. Like the E5, these F59PHIs were bought to match the cars they haul—Amtrak's specially designed "California Cars." *Brian Solomon*

than the SD50, but, more importantly, a pair of SD60s hauling a standard unit coal train was up to 18 percent more fuel efficient than three SD40-2s in the same service.

The development of a microprocessor control system was an important 60 series innovation. This corresponded to General Electric's application of microprocessor control on its Dash-8 line at about the same time. Using micro-circuits in place of relays and modular solid-state electronics simplified Electro-Motive's electrical system and reduced the number of components by more than 20 percent.

In 1985, Electro-Motive introduced the four-motor GP60, a high-horsepower four-axle model. It was equipped with the 16-710G engine, rated at 3,800 horsepower, and was designed for fast intermodal work. In the modern era, the market for such locomotives was relatively small. Norfolk Southern, Southern Pacific, and Santa Fe accounted for most of the production run, which spanned nearly nine years.

Consistent with predecessor Southern Railway's penchant for unusual high-output four-motor units, Norfolk Southern acquired a small fleet of 3,000-horsepower GP59s, which utilized a fuel-efficient 12-cylinder 710G engine. These locomotives closely resembled the more powerful GP60 and were also intended for high-horsepower applications.

Production Shift

As Electro-Motive geared up for full 60 series production, it made significant changes in its manufacturing process—the biggest being shifting its locomotive assembly for domestic sales from La Grange, Illinois, to the London,

added, "Emblematic of DD's problems at the time were CP Rail's 25 SD40-2Fs . . . [which] should have been the apex of SD40-2 production, but their troubles surfaced before the units left the plant." Furthermore, he noted, "Inaugural runs of the 9000s were marred by engine problems, traction motor failures, and other defects."

The problems continued into the 1990s. Models suffering from poor reputations for build quality included Santa Fe's SD75Ms, built in 1995, and Irish Rail (201 Class) model JT42HCW, delivered during 1994 and 1995.

For decades, Electro-Motive products had set the industry standard for diesel-electric locomotives. All other builders had been judged by Electro-Motive's products. So it was a disappointment when these new locomotives didn't measure up. But eventually Electro-Motive brought problems into check. In recent times, there have been fewer complaints since the early years of the transition.

Today, the bulk of final locomotive assembly is undertaken at London, with La Grange playing just a support role. In addition, some locomotive assembly is done at other facilities, including Norfolk Southern's former Conrail shops in Altoona, Pennsylvania, and at Super Steel in Schenectady, New York.

Widenose Cabs

The dynamics of railroad transport have changed over the years. Prior to 1989, most road-switcher type locomotives in the United States used what could be described as a conventional cab. Essentially, it was a derivation of the cab that had been used since the introduction of the GP7 in 1949. While many railroads made the transition from high short hood locomotives to low short hoods in the late 1950s and early 1960s, the arrangement of the cab hadn't changed much.

In the early 1970s, Canadian National began ordering road switchers with a widenose cab. It was derived from a cab style used on the American cowl types designed in the late 1960s, as well as Union Pacific's unique DDA40X. Described as the "safety cab" or "Canadian cab," this cab featured a row of four front-facing windshields. Although applied to GP40-2 and SD40-2 models, the Canadian cab was not exclusive to General Motors diesels and was also used by Montreal Locomotive Works and GE. Although largely confined to Canadian operators for years, this was the direct predecessor to the modern North American safety cab.

Ontario–based Diesel Division (DD). This shift started in 1987 and was complete in 1992, when the last locomotives were assembled at La Grange—ending a tradition of more than a half-century.

The transition did not go as smoothly as hoped. In addition to capacity problems, many locomotives built at London were not built to the high standards expected of Electro-Motive products. "La Grange proved to be a tough act to follow," wrote Greg McDonnell in the October 1990 issue of *TRAINS Magazine*. Examining one order, he

Left: In 1998, North Carolina Department of Transportation bought two new EMD F59PHI locomotives for the intrastate *Piedmont* passenger train operated by Amtrak between Raleigh and Charlotte. The unusual paint livery designed by NCDOT's Ellen Holding is an adaptation of the state flag. *Brian Solomon*

Opposite top: On November 9, 2003, with a westward *Capitols* service in tow, Amtrak F59PHI 2013 rolls into the former Southern Pacific station at Davis, California, on its run between Sacramento and San Jose, California. The F59PHIs are primarily used on West Coast passenger services. *Brian Solomon*

Opposite bottom: This interior view of the engine room of North Carolina Department of Transportation F59PHI No. 1797 shows the 12-710G3B-EC engine. *Brian Solomon*

In the United States, the sudden move to the widenose cab was a direct response to changing labor practices. In road freight service the traditional five- and six-person crew that ran 100 miles had by the mid-1980s evolved to a two- or three-person crew working 250 miles or more. The implementation of radio technology, computers, modern dispatching and signaling, and improved automatic airbrake systems allowed this labor reduction without substantially compromising crew safety. There were other changes, too. With longer crew districts, as well as the move toward unit trains and intermodal runs, road crews were less likely to switch while en route. Often the traditional road switcher was really serving as just a road locomotive.

Santa Fe was among the first railroads to implement the use of widenose cabs. Steve Schmollinger wrote in "Cab of the Future," an article featured in the December 1990 issue of *TRAINS Magazine*, that in the late 1980s, Santa Fe borrowed a Canadian National SD50F—a model featuring the Canadian cab—and asked crews to evaluate it. Then Santa Fe worked with both General Motors and General Electric in designing the North American safety cab. This was a modern widenose that included sound proofing to reduce engine noise, desktop controls to give the engineer a forward-facing position, and greater frontal structural safety to protect crews in the event of a collision.

While Santa Fe was interested in using it on its fast Chicago-to-California intermodal trains, Union Pacific was actually the first railroad in the United States to receive a modern widenose cab. This cab came on a variation of the six-axle SD60, designated SD60M, and it entered service during the early part of 1989—20 years after UP's famous DDA40X Centennials, which featured the 1960s-version of a widenose cab. The first UP SD60Ms featured a three-piece windshield, essentially the same cab style used on Canadian Pacific's SD40F-2 (which entered production in late 1988) and the recently introduced F59 commuter rail locomotive.

In 1990, Electro-Motive built 63 North American safety cab GP60Ms for Santa Fe. The high-horsepower four-axles were unique to Santa Fe's line. No other line bought 710 engine four-motor locomotives with safety cabs for freight service. The GP60Ms were also delivered in the line's colorful warbonnet paint. The next year, Santa Fe supplemented its GP60/60M fleet with another unique model, the cabless GP60B. The railroad ordered 23 of these units.

In contrast to Santa Fe's specialized machines, six-motor locomotives with safety cabs emerged as the standard model in the early 1990s. A widenose variation was the SD60I, which used Electro-Motive's WhisperCab™. (The WhisperCab also became known as the isolated cab because it isolated the cab from underframe superstructure and was represented in the model designation by a letter 'I'.) Locomotives equipped with this cab can be identified by the visible separation in the metal between the cab and locomotive nose.

EMD SD70

In late 1992, Electro-Motive unveiled a three-unit SD70M demonstrator set with a new company color scheme: metallic maroon and silver. While the mechanical differences between the SD50 and SD60 represented a distinct advance in locomotive technology, the SD70M reflected only nominal improvements over the 60 series. In the January 1993 issue of *TRAINS Magazine*, Paul D. Schneider highlighted three of these distinct improvements: engine output was raised from 3,800 horsepower on the 16-710G3 to 4,000 horsepower on the 16-cylinder 710G3B; the new D90TR traction motor increased tractive effort (the SD70M delivered 109,000 pounds continuous tractive effort); and the SD70M employed a more advanced microprocessor control system.

Perhaps the most visible change on the SD70M was Electro-Motive's new self-steering—or "radial"—truck model, the HCTR (high-tractive, C-type truck radial). This truck permitted movement of the center axle, facilitating more efficient movement through curves and thus reducing friction between wheel and rail. By reducing friction, both wheel and rail wear were diminished and adhesion and tractive effort were improved. Although SD70M was the first production locomotive to use a self-steering truck, Electro-Motive had been experimenting with self-steering trucks since the early 1980s.

By the mid-1990s, most American railroads were ordering widenose safety cabs. Illinois Central and Norfolk Southern both ordered SD70s with conventional cabs. Conrail's last locomotive orders were dictated by Norfolk Southern and CSX, lines that had agreed to divide the Conrail network. While NS preferred DC traction and conventional cabs, CSX wanted AC traction and safety cabs. So Conrail was the only railroad to simultaneously order

SD70s and SD70MACs—both delivered in variations of the Conrail paint scheme months before NS and CSX assumed the respective portions of the Conrail operation.

In an unusual scenario, Union Pacific shunned the new innovations of recent models and ordered 1,000 retro SD70Ms in 1999. These models represented a back-to-basics approach. Instead of modern desktop electronics, these SD70Ms featured conventional analog engineer's controls and mechanical fuel injection. Over the years, UP's SD70Ms earned a reputation for their dependability. Late-model SD70Ms were powered with emissions-compliant 16-710G3CT-1 engine.

The SD75M, ordered by Santa Fe for its Superfleet intermodal services in 1995, was a variation on the SD70 using all the same essential equipment. It delivered slightly higher output—4,300 horsepower versus 4,000 horse-power—largely using software modifications. A few locomotives were experimentally rated at 4,500 horsepower. Early on, the model developed a reputation for poor reliability, but in recent years the SD75M's performance has been on par with locomotives of the same age.

Canadian National ordered a nearly identical type to Santa Fe's SD75s—designated the SD75I because of their WhisperCabs—with deliveries beginning in 1996.

Externally, the SD75 models are virtually the same as SD70M models.

Three-Phase AC Traction

By the late 1980s, Electro-Motive had lost its long-held position as America's premier locomotive manufacturer to General Electric. For decades, Electro-Motive had comfortably been the leading builder of mass-produced high-quality locomotives. While it made periodic improvements to its line, major innovations were largely pioneered by its competitors. But the tables had turned now; in the past, Electro-Motive had allowed others test the market, now it needed to innovate to secure a larger market share.

To do that, it developed a commercially viable diesel electric with three-phase alternating current traction. While developmental work for AC traction technology had been

Above: Electro-Motive built four SD60MAC prototypes in 1991 and 1992. These experimental locomotives incorporated new three-phase alternating traction technology and other innovations—such as the new HTCR self-steering, high-adhesion truck—with the successful SD60M design. In 1992, Burlington Northern performed extensive tests with the SD60MACs in Powder River coal service. Traditionally, railroads test one another's new equipment prior to purchasing units for themselves, or builders such as Electro-Motive borrow or lease new engines for testing on railroads. Here, three BN SD60MACs haul Kansas City Southern train No. 97 through southern Missouri. *Chris Guss*

Below: New Burlington Northern SD70MACs lead an empty unit train near Edgemont, South Dakota, on May 26, 1995. Electro Motive's SD70MAC was the first mass-produced diesel-electric locomotive in the American market to employ a modern, three-phase alternating current traction. *Brian Solomon*

Opposite: Four days after leaving the plant at London, Ontario, factory-fresh Electro-Motive SD70Ms head west on Union Pacific near Fremont, Nebraska, in October 2002. Union Pacific bucked the trend toward high-tech locomotives when it placed an order for 1,000 SD70Ms in the year 2000. Unlike recent high-tech models, UP went back to basics, specifying locomotives that used a more traditional design, including traditional mechanical fuel injection and analog control in place of sophisticated computerized desktop controls. Yet, modern locomotives must comply with ever-stricter air-quality standards, and later-production SD70Ms use an angled high-capacity radiator design to help lower gas emissions. *Brian Solomon*

ongoing for decades, its use in heavy-haul applications was among the most significant advances in locomotive technology since the advent of the commercial diesel-electric.

While new to the American diesel market, three-phase AC traction was not a new idea. Locomotive manufacturers had built powerful electric locomotives using three-phase AC traction systems since the early part of the twentieth century. While AC motors are very robust, require little maintenance, and exhibit excellent traction characteristics, their operating speed is directly related to the frequency of the current, which limit their practical application for general service.

Advances in microprocessor and semiconductor technology in the 1960s and 1970s made three-phase AC traction practical for locomotive applications, first on straight electrics, then later on diesel-electrics. Especially significant

The F69PHAC was powered by a 12-710G3 engine and used an alternator/rectifier to supply direct current to twin banks of Freon-cooled static inverters. According to 1989–1990 *Jane's World Railways*, these inverters delivered 800kW at 480V at 60Hz to four AC traction motors wired in parallel. The F69PHACs were delivered in 1989 and used as test beds for further development.

In 1991 and 1992, Electro-Motive advanced its AC design with construction of four SD60MAC prototypes that were based on its successful SD60M design but equipped with the Siemens AC traction technology. These incorporated other innovations, such as the new HTCR self-steering, high-adhesion truck. In addition to a nationwide tour, these were tested extensively on Burlington Northern in heavy coal service.

The development of AC technology was just the latest chapter in the long historical relationship between Electro-Motive and the Burlington in pioneering new technology. Burlington Northern was the successor to the old Chicago, Burlington & Quincy of *Zephyr* fame. BN was formed in 1970 as a merger of Chicago, Burlington & Quincy; Great Northern; Northern Pacific; and Spokane, Portland & Seattle—four railroads with close historical and business ties. Recall from Chapter 1 that, in the 1920s, Burlington had been one of the largest customers of Electro-Motive rail cars, and in the early 1930s, it had pushed for the first railroad application of the 201-A diesel to power its new streamlined *Zephyr*. Burlington was among the first large customers for Electro-Motive's diesels, buying a series of streamlined diesel power cars, a fleet of early E units, and later FT freight diesels. In recent times, BN had been one of Electro-Motive's best customers for its successful SD40-2, buying hundreds for service around its system. Burlington Northern was the perfect customer for Electro-Motive to work with in the refinement of its AC traction diesels, and the arrangement proved mutually beneficial.

Burlington Northern was a special case; in the 1970s it had made a massive investment to develop coal traffic in Wyoming's Powder River basin where coal is relatively close to the surface and easy to mine. Low sulfur content and increasingly strict air-quality legislation made Powder River coal especially valuable. BN bucked the trend by building the first major new railroad route in decades; its Orin Line connected with existing lines and reached into the heart of

One innovation applied to the SD70MAC not directly related to its propulsion system is the HTCR radial truck. This self-steering truck is designed to reduce friction between the driving wheels and the rails, minimizing wear to both surfaces. Electro-Motive applied an experimental four-axle radial truck to a Burlington Northern SDP45 in 1984. *Tom Kline*

was the development of high-amperage gate turn-off thyristors (GTO). These are used in inverters—to convert direct current into a modulated variety of three-phase AC output. Modulating the frequency of the AC current allows for convenient speed control of the AC motors, thus overcoming this previous limitation for traction purposes.

Electro-Motive's research into AC traction technology began in the 1970s. Then in the late 1980s, it teamed up with the German electrical company Siemens AG to build experimental AC locomotive prototypes. In the late 1970s, German engineers had refined AC traction for the use on the Deutsche Bahn (German Railway) Class 120 electric locomotive, and then later they applied the same technology to the German InterCity Express (ICE) high-speed electric passenger trains.

Siemens was not alone in its development of AC traction. In the mid-1980s, the technology was also developed by other manufacturers for both French and Japanese high-speed electric trains, as well as for diesels in service in Scandinavia.

Prototypes

After working out an agreement with Siemens in 1987, Electro-Motive accepted an Amtrak order for a pair of four-axle model F69PHAC experimental passenger locomotives.

When delivered in 1995, the SD80MACs were unlike any other locomotive on the Conrail system. Massive radiators, radial trucks, and a newly designed blue-and-white paint scheme immediately set them apart from everything else on the roster. While the 5,000-horsepower SD80MAC was only purchased new by Conrail, the fleet was divided between CSX and Norfolk Southern in 1999. The SD80MAC was the only locomotive powered by a 20-cylinder 710 engine. *Brian Solomon*

the Powder River to tap new mines. By the early 1990s, BN's investment had paid off handsomely: 30 percent of its traffic was coal and the traffic was still growing.

The high volume of heavy traffic encouraged BN to find more efficient ways to move it. In the 1970s, it considered electrification, but high implementation costs had discouraged investment, so it instead settled on a large fleet of Electro-Motive SD40-2s and GE C30-7s. By the early 1990s, these machines had passed their prime and BN was again looking for a more efficient motive power solution. It was for this service that the promise of three-phase AC traction proved attractive. Three-phase AC offered much greater

electric locomotives with AC-DC transmissions since the 1960s. There was one significant change, though: the addition of high voltage inverters to convert DC power to a modulated form of AC for traction.

On the surface, this arrangement seems unnecessarily complicated, but it is the most efficient combination for modern high-horsepower diesel locomotives. The diesel engine produces single-phase AC power by turning the alternator. The direct output from the alternator is generated at a constant frequency and is unsuitable for traction because motor control would be impractical. Instead, single-phase AC is rectified to DC, and the current is then passed through inverters to create three-phase AC output to the traction motors. Inverters modulate the frequency of output to control the speed of the motors.

The SD70MAC's greatest strength is starting and lower speeds when it makes best use of high-tractive effort. An SD40-2 produces 87,150 pounds of continuous tractive effort, while an SD70MAC can develop up to 137,000 pounds. Unlike conventional DC motors that are greatly limited at low speeds by the short time ratings to prevent overheating, three-phase AC motors can operate at full power at slow speed indefinitely without risk of motor damage. This feature allows an SD70MAC to maintain very high-tractive effort much longer than DC locomotives.

Electro-Motive had come a long way since its 103 demonstrator, which had awed steam-men back in 1940. That four-unit FT, which produced 228,000 pounds of starting tractive effort, compared with 175,500 pounds for the SD70MAC. Perhaps a more telling comparison is between a single SD70MAC and a three-unit FT (such as the variety used by Lackawanna with 65:15 gearing for in helper service on its mountain grades in eastern Pennsylvania). The FT combination used three 16-567 engines to produce 4,050 horsepower, powering 12 D7 traction motors to deliver approximately 171,000 pounds starting tractive effort, approximately the same as one SD70MAC powered by single 16-710G3C engine powering six three-phase AC traction motors. The FT used more engines, more motors, required more much more fuel, and produced far greater harmful emissions than the SD70MAC. Not only that, but the FT's motors would have melted if it maintained high-tractive force for any length of time, where the SD70MAC could keep right on pulling.

Top: Conrail's 30 SD80MACs were equipped with radial trucks and 1TB2830 three-phase AC induction motors. *Brian Solomon*

Above: To help employees distinguish new SD80MACs, Conrail painted them in a new livery with this stylized wave on the side to symbolically represent the three-phase AC traction system. Later, Conrail received 15 SD70MACs that were ordered by CSX and similarly painted. *Brian Solomon*

tractive effort and so allowed for substantial unit reduction. Through superior adhesion, three 4,000-horsepower AC traction units could effectively equal the work of five 3,000-horsepower SD40-2s or C30-7s. Another cost savings was achieved with the motors themselves; AC traction motors require less maintenance and have a longer service life than comparable DC motors.

SD70MAC

Based on the success of the SD60MAC, BN placed a large order for Electro-Motive SD70MACs. This was the first mass-produced commercial AC traction diesel-electric model. It used the same basic power generation arrangement that had been employed by most American diesel-

One of the keys to SD70MAC (and other modern AC traction locomotives) delivering very high-tractive effort is greater adhesion afforded by superior motor control and advanced wheel slip systems. Where Electro-Motive calculates tractive effort for the SD40-2 based on 21 percent factor of adhesion, for SD70MAC it uses between 33 and 38 percent adhesion (depending on rail conditions).

In addition to greater tractive effort, AC traction motors provide several additional advantages over DC motors. They have much more effective dynamic braking and enjoy a much longer service life—both of which lower operational costs. However, the savings comes with a heavy price tag. In the mid-1990s, a SD70MAC cost about 25 percent per unit more than a comparable Electro-Motive DC traction locomotive. As a result, most railroads decided that AC traction was too costly for universal application, and it has been primarily applied to heavy-haul services where locomotives are working hard in slow-speed service, such as BN's coal services.

In a May 1994 interview in *TRAINS Magazine*, Burlington Northern Chairman Gerald Grinstein said that

Canadian Pacific received 61 upgradeable six-motor locomotives from General Motors in 1998, designated as SD90/43MACs. These were essentially SD70MACs with the 16-710G engine rated at 4,300 horsepower, but used the larger carbody with high-capacity radiators designed to accommodate GM's new 6,000-horsepower model 265H engine. In 1999, Canadian Pacific received four of the 6,000-horsepower locomotives and was the only railroad outside Union Pacific to sample the type. Conrail's SD80MACs use the same carbody but were powered with a 20-cylinder 710 diesel. *Chris Guss*

In 1995, 6,000-horsepower engines were not yet available for production, so Union Pacific agreed to take upgradeable models designed for the 6,000-horsepower engine but delivered with 16-710G engines rated at just 4,300 horsepower. A pair of these locomotives pounds upgrade at Boca, California, on June 29, 1997. Reliability of the 6,000-horsepower locomotives did not meet expectations, and most of Union Pacific's locomotives were never converted. Later orders were for more locomotives with engines in the 4,000- to 4,400-horsepower range. *Brian Jennison*

Above: In the tradition of New Haven Railroad's dual-mode FL9s are Long Island Rail Road's modern DE30AC-DMs. Electro-Motive built 23 of these specialized hybrid machines for LIRR in 1999. Capable of operating as a normal diesel or drawing current from high-voltage direct current third rail, the DE30AC-DM is a 3,000-horsepower locomotive designed for New York–area suburban service and features a low-profiled body to accommodate restrictive clearances. On March 12, 2003, LIRR No. 510 catches the glint of the setting sun as it approaches Jamaica, Queens, with a double-deck suburban train. *Brian Solomon*

Right: Long Island Rail Road DE30AC-DM 505 pauses at Jamaica, Queens. These locomotives were ordered in 1995 as part of a deal for 46 new passenger diesels. In addition to the dual-mode versions, LIRR also acquired 23 DE30AC locomotives that are strictly diesel-electrics (Nos. 400–422). *Brian Solomon*

"[The SD70MAC] may very well represent the most dramatic step forward since diesel replaced steam." With such a bold assertion, one may expect that the SD70MAC had a radical new appearance to go with its boosted technology. Quite to the contrary. It didn't look significantly different from any other modern Electro-Motive diesel. In fact, other than judging by the paint, or checking the roster sequence, a rail observer would have to look pretty closely to distinguish an SD70MAC from its DC counterpart, the SD70M.

Initially, BN ordered 350 SD70MACs, the first of which were delivered in December 1993. At a public revue in Fort Worth, Texas, on January 10, 1994, top representatives of Burlington Northern, Electro-Motive, and Siemens AG symbolized the relationship that had built this mighty machine. And right next to the new SD70MAC was a preserved E5 with Budd-built streamlined *Zephyr* train set— showcasing Burlington's long ties with Electro-Motive.

The success of the SD70MAC led Burlington Northern Santa Fe to order many of these models, yet BNSF continued to order DC traction locomotives for general freight and intermodal services. Although initially the model was unique to BN (and then BNSF), CSX ordered SD70MACs in the later 1990s.

In 2004, the SD70MAC was phased out in favor of the new SD70ACe.

Different Philosophies

Electro-Motive pioneered AC traction for the North American market, but General Electric was not far behind. GE's AC traction system, while similar to Electro-Motive's in principle, has several significant differences.

The two primary variations between GE's system and Electro-Motive's are with the inverters. General Electric's later entry into the AC locomotive market encouraged it to innovate in order to secure a market advantage. The Electro-Motive/Siemens AC control system uses two inverters, one for each truck—one inverter to control three motors. General Electric's system uses six inverters, assigning one inverter to each traction motor. This allows for individual axle control, permitting higher tractive effort and affording greater reliability. An SD70MAC locomotive would have to reduce power to three axles to prevent wheel slip, while a GE AC4400CW can regulate power to each axle and total locomotive total output is less affected. GE's system also allows for greater variance in wheel diameter, offering a maintenance advantage. Where a single inverter failure on an SD70MAC can cut locomotive output by as much as 50 percent, a single inverter failure results in just a 12 percent cut on a GE. (However, in most situations, a single inverter failure on a GE will not result in an appreciable change in horsepower because the remaining inverters can make up the output difference.) Another design distinction between Electro-Motive and GE inverters is the method of cooling: Electro-Motive uses a chemical cooling system to disperse the intense heat generated by the inverters, while General Electric uses an air cooling system.

Twenty Cylinders Revisited

In 1995, on the heels of Burlington Northern's pioneering order for SD70MACs, Conrail ordered a small fleet of AC traction locomotives from Electro-Motive. These used much of the same technology as the SD70MACs did, but with a larger engine. Instead of the common 16-710G3 engine—typically used on modern Electro-Motive locomotives—the SD80MAC employed a 20-cylinder 710G3. This was the first railroad application of the big engine, which had previously been employed in marine applications. It produced 20 percent more power than the 16-710G3, allowing for a single-engine 5,000-horsepower locomotive.

At the time it offered the SD80MAC, Electro-Motive was in the process of engineering its entirely new H engine, intended to produce 6,000 horsepower. But where the H engine was in its early developmental stages, the 20-710G3 was available immediately and viewed as essentially a proven design. With this engine, Conrail had the most powerful locomotive on the market.

Initially, Electro-Motive produced just 28 SD80MACs for Conrail, plus a pair of demonstrator units (which Conrail later acquired). The model measured 80 feet 2 inches long and weighed approximately 430,000 pounds fully serviceable. A single SD80MAC could deliver 185,000 pounds of starting tractive effort. Through the use of advanced wheel slip control, a pair of SD80MACs rated at 10,000 horsepower could replace four older 3,000-horsepower DC traction locomotives in similar service. While the two SD80MACs produced less horsepower, they delivered equivalent tractive effort. Among the other equipment on the SD80MAC were HTCR II radial trucks with 45-inch wheels, the modern WhisperCab (to reduce vibration and noise inside the cab), and enormous angled radiators at the rear of the locomotive needed for cool the massive 20-710G3.

No other railroads bought the unusual model. It wasn't until 1999, when Conrail's fleet was divided between CSX and Norfolk Southern, that any other road had a SD80MAC. The model has not been viewed favorably and

has been compared to the SD50: both proved to be interim designs aimed at achieving higher output, but without the higher reliability of lower output models.

Electro-Motive SD90MAC

Among engineering goals for modern alternating current traction was development of single-engine 6,000-horsepower locomotive that could enable railroads to replace 3,000-horsepower locomotives on a one-for-two basis, offering the unit replacement strategy that had been successfully applied in 1960s, when a single SD40 was used to replace postwar F units (and the like locomotives).

Building a single unit with a very high horsepower rating was not a new concept. General Electric had built high-output gas-electric turbines for Union Pacific in the 1950s, and the various double-diesel models in the 1960s offered high-single unit output.

Using modern three-phase AC traction technology and a state-of-the-art diesel engine design, Electro-Motive's SD90MAC-H was intended to be a very powerful and fuel-efficient motive power solution for modern freight railroads. General Electric simultaneous developed its AC6000CW in the mid-1990s.

The SD90MAC-H used much of the same equipment as Electro-Motive's 5,000-horsepower SD80MAC, including the 80-foot 2-inch platform HTCR II trucks, the Whisper-Cab, and large radiators at the rear of the locomotive. The SD90MAC-H's defining feature was the pioneer application of the H Engine—model GM16V265 (sometimes listed as 265H).

From a technological standpoint, this engine was significantly different from all previous Electro-Motive engine designs. All of its engines since the Winton 201-A had used a two-stroke-cycle design, but the H engine is a four cycle design. Other noteworthy characteristics included dual turbochargers, electronic fuel injection, and a cast ductile–iron crankcase (Electro-Motive's two-stroke engines use welded steel construction).

Electro-Motive abandoned its traditional practice of using English measurements for designating the volume cylinder displacement and used a metric-based designation instead. Its specifications indicate that the engine produces 6,300 brake horsepower working at 1,000 rpm (6,000 horsepower for traction). It has 16 cylinders with 265x300-

millimeter (10.4x11.4-inch) bore and stroke. Each cylinder has roughly a 1,010-cubic-inch displacement, so in the company's old terminology, the H engine would have been designated 16-1010. Instead, it is known as the 265H.

Before the H engine was ready for regular production, Union Pacific—the primary customer for the new SD90MAC locomotive—placed a large order for motive power. UP was interested in the prospects of a single unit high-horsepower diesel, but UP's rapid traffic growth, combined with its recent acquisition of both Chicago & North Western and Southern Pacific, demanded new locomotives as quickly as they could be delivered. UP wanted powerful

locomotives but didn't have the time to wait for the Electro-Motive to refine the H engine.

To satisfy both UP's immediate and future motive power needs, Electro-Motive and General Electric both offered upgradeable locomotive models in the mid-1990s. These were built with a conventional engine, but capable of accepting new 6,000-horsepower engines at a later date. Electro-Motive's upgradeable SD90MAC came with the older 16-710G3B engine rated at just 4,300 horsepower—making it equivalent to the SD70MAC.

Since their introduction, the upgradeable locomotive's designation has proven to be confusing. In the Electro-

On October 7, 1997, Conrail SD80MACs roaring away in "run eight" lift a very heavy westward freight over Washington Hill on the former Boston & Albany line at Becket, Massachusetts. Where traditional DC traction motors would be damaged if overloaded for prolonged periods, modern AC traction allows locomotives to work at maximum throttle at very slow speeds indefinitely without risk of motor damage. *Brian Solomon*

Motive parlance, the variable horsepower model was simply designated SD90MAC, while the true 6,000-horsepower locomotive was designated SD90MAC-H (the "H" signifying the big engine). This distinction wasn't good enough for Union Pacific and other industry sources. The upgradeable locomotives have been designated as SD9043MACs, SD90/43MACs, or SD9043ACs—where the "43" reflects the 4,300-horsepower rating.

Union Pacific and Canadian Pacific were the primary North American users of the convertible SD90MAC and the SD90MAC-H, but not the only ones. A fleet of 40 SD90MACs, with the 16-710G3B engine, was ordered by CIT Group/Capital Finance to serve as a lease fleet.

As it turned out, the 6,000-horsepower SD90MAC-H was an unusual locomotive. Electro-Motive specifications indicate the model can deliver 200,000 pounds of starting tractive effort and 170,000 pounds of continuous tractive effort, figures that made it the most powerful locomotive on the American market. But its comparative unreliability made its usefulness limiting.

In order to effectively replace two 3,000-horsepower units with one 6,000-horsepower unit, the more powerful locomotive needs to have extraordinary dependability. If one of four 3,000-horsepower locomotives failed on the road, a train could limp along with the three remaining locomotives representing 75 percent assigned horsepower. Yet if one of two 6,000-horsepower locomotives failed, a train had to get by with just half the assigned horsepower. This significant difference in power could result in a costly delay to time-sensitive shipments—an especially important consideration because the 6,000-horsepower locomotives were intended to haul the highest priority trains.

Based upon the large numbers of 4,000-horsepower and 4,400-horsepower locomotives ordered in the mid-1990s, the market for very high-horsepower AC locomotives proved much smaller than originally anticipated by the builders. Even Union Pacific, initially enthusiastic about 6,000-horsepower SD90MAC-Hs, reconsidered and returned to ordering conventionally powered 4,000- to 4,400-horsepower models. Union Pacific has since returned the big locomotives to the lease holder.

Despite the obvious disappointment when American railroads abandoned the 6,000-horsepower locomotive, Electro-Motive continued to work on the engine. In

December 2005, David Lustig reported in *TRAINS Magazine* that through repeated testing Electro-Motive engineers had worked out most the engine's early problems. In September 2005, Electro-Motive found a customer willing to take on the H engine when it signed an agreement with China to jointly construct 300 locomotives of a design based on the 6,000-horsepower SD90MAC-H, the first of which was expected in 2007.

Electro-Motive F59PHI

In recent decades, exhaust emissions have become a growing concern in the United States. More and more, local and federal environmental standards have demanded emissions-compliant locomotives as well as automobiles.

California was among the first big markets to demand emissions-compliant locomotives. In the 1990s, a commitment by California to fund a network of statewide Amtrak

services resulted in it ordering a distinctive fleet of passenger locomotives. California worked with General Motors' Electro-Motive Division to develop a contemporary equivalent to the successful F40PH locomotive. To meet California's requirements, Electro-Motive adapted its F59PH suburban rail services locomotive into a powerful, modern-looking streamlined diesel-electric that complied with strict California emission requirements. Designated F59PHI, it was the builder's first streamlined diesel in a generation designed specifically for the American market. It used primary components of the 59 series, including the 12-cylinder 710G3 diesel, an AR15 alternator, and D87B series traction motors. The engine uses electronic fuel injection and has a 3,200-horsepower rating.

As built, the F59PHI measures 58 feet 2 inches long, 15 feet 11.5 inches tall, and 10 feet 6 inches wide. It weighs 270,000 pounds. The California models were designed with a 56:21 gear ratio, allowing them to operate at a top speed of 110 miles per hour. Among the crew comfort features is the isolated WhisperCab. The locomotives are designed to provide HEP using an auxiliary engine and alternator. The locomotive is shrouded in a cowl, which serves to improve appearance but has an aerodynamic design to reduce wind resistance. The bulbous nose is constructed from fiberglass composite, which, combined with thick steel plates, provides better crew protection than the traditional streamlined bulldog nose used on Electro-Motive's famous E and F units. Subsequent to California's initial acquisition, a number of other passenger service operators ordered the F59PHI for suburban and intermediate length runs.

Much of the same equipment used in the F59PHI was adapted for Irish Rail's Class 201 (Electro-Motive model

JT42HCW), a dual-service, six-motor, double-cab diesel built for 5-foot 3-inch gauge tracks. A similar locomotive is export Model JT42CWR, known as the Class 66, built in large numbers for standard gauge freight services in the United Kingdom and on the European Continent.

SD70ACe and SD70M-2

New stricter emissions requirements for locomotives went into effect on January 1, 2005, leading both Electro-Motive and General Electric to engineer substantial changes to their respective locomotive designs. To compete with GE's new Evolution-Series, Electro-Motive developed two new models: the SD70ACe and SD70M-2 (sometimes referred to as the SD70DCe). These were respective advancements of the three-phase AC traction SD70MAC and DC traction SD70M, which had been the mainstay of Electro-Motive's heavy freight locomotive production for the better part of a decade.

In late 2003, Electro-Motive introduced a prototype SD70ACe with four demonstrator units, numbered GM70 to GM73. David Lustig reported in the July 2004 issue of *TRAINS Magazine* that, following testing at the American Association of Railroad's Transportation Technology Center in Pueblo, Colorado, these demonstrators began making the rounds of American railroads. In addition, Electro-Motive built 20 preproduction units painted for host railroads.

The SD70ACe was powered by the EPA Tier 2–compliant 16-710G3C-T2 engine, rated at 4,300 horsepower. It delivers 191,000 pounds of starting tractive effort and 157,000 pounds of continuous tractive effort. It was designed so that three SD70ACes will equal the performance of three SD40-2s that in tractive effort applications. The locomotive weighs 408,000 pounds and measures 15 feet 11 inches tall and 74 feet 3 inches long. Among its other standard features are Electro-Motive's HTCR radial trucks.

In an article in the February 2004 issue of *TRAINS Magazine*, Electro-Motive engineers Stephen Bareis and Curt Swenson described some of the SD70ACe's technological advancements, which were designed to reduce maintenance and increase locomotive availability. Specifically, Electro-Motive aimed to double the time between required service from intervals of 92 days to 184 days. To do this, the number of inverter components was reduced. Electronic control cards were reduced from 50 to just 2. On the

Above: On Halloween 2005, one of CSX's latest Electro-Motive diesels, SD70ACe 4839, leads train V486-29 at Trammel, Virginia, just north of the summit of the former Clinchfield Elkhorn Extension between Elkhorn City, Kentucky, and Dante, Virginia. The SD70ACe is Electro-Motive's most modern AC traction locomotive. Externally, it appears very similar to the DC-traction SD70M-2, but uses IGBT three-phase AC traction equipment that gives 157,000 pounds of continuous tractive effort. *T. S. Hoover*

Opposite: In 2005, Union Pacific had several of its newest SD70ACe diesels painted in heritage schemes to commemorate some of the railroads merged into its vast western system during the 1980s. Locomotive No. 1982 was dressed in this stylized adaptation of Missouri Pacific's scheme (the Missouri Pacific merged with UP in 1982). The locomotive leads UP's executive passenger train at Spring Junction at Spring, Texas, on August 12, 2005. *Tom Kline*

710 engine, peak firing pressure was reduced by 15 percent, which lowers the stress and fatigue on rod and engine bearings, connecting rods, and pistons. To comply with Tier 2 requirements, Electro-Motive reengineered the combustion chamber, fine-tuned turbocharger operation, and increased the amount of turbocharger aftercooling. Other improvements were designed for ease of maintenance, including better interior access to components that require regular service and a defined separation of piping from the electrical system.

Another change with the SD70ACe was a new standard cab style. It was a variation of a cab style used experimentally on some Union Pacific SD90MAC-Hs a few years earlier. Externally, this cab was more angular and less-refined looking than the standard M-style widenose cab, which had been used on most Electro-Motive six-motor diesels since about 1990. The front nose–door style was changed to simplify the parts supply, substantially altering the nose profile. Because the desktop control arrangement used the late 1980s had proven less than satisfactory to many locomotive engineers, Electro-Motive decided to improve the controls for better operator ergonomics and visibility. Yet with the focus on cost savings and interior ergonomics, the cab's external aesthetics were spartan, resembling military hard-

ware and lacking the refinement and simplicity of earlier Electro-Motive cabs.

About a year after introducing the SD70ACe, Electro-Motive brought out the SD70M-2 to replace its solid-selling SD70M. Externally, the SD70M-2 looks very similar to its AC traction counterpart and shares many common components—including the engine, frame, cab, and enormous angular radiators. The primary difference is that it uses a DC traction system and was the first model to use Electro-Motive's new D100 traction motor.

According to the December 2004 issue of *TRAINS Magazine*, the D100 improved on the D90 by incorporating better commutation and pickup characteristics. Horsepower output is the same as the SD70ACe, but because the SD70M uses DC traction motors, tractive effort is substantially less. It delivers 163,000 pounds of starting tractive effort and 113,100 pounds of continuous tractive effort. By

Below Although Irish Rail's 201 Class diesel-electric has an entirely different appearance from the F59PHI, the locomotive uses the same essential equipment and works in similar services. Built at London, Ontario, in 1994 and 1995, these cowl locomotives are Model JT42HCWs, rated at 3,200 horsepower. Unlike the F59PHIs, they are dual-traffic machines, working both freight and passenger services. The 34 201 Class are Irish Rail/Northern Ireland Railway's newest, heaviest, and most powerful locomotives, routinely whisking passenger trains between Dublin and Cork at speeds up to 100 miles per hour. Like most Irish locomotives, they have cabs at both ends. *Brian Solomon*

Above: Amtrak F59HI leads a *San Diegan* service at Fullerton, California, in 2000. The F59PHI's bulbous nose is a fiberglass composite with thick steel plates below it helping to protect the crew. This protective combination offers greater strength than the 1940s-era streamlined bulldog nose on the E and F units. *Richard Jay Solomon*

Among the locomotives Union Pacific has dressed in special commemorative paint schemes is this new SD70ACe, pictured here rolling through Mumford, Texas, on November 20, 2005. Dedicated in honor of George H. W. Bush, the 41st President of the United States, it was numbered 4141 and painted to resemble the livery on the plane normally assigned to *Air Force One*, the presidential aircraft. This was part of celebrations for the opening of the George Bush Presidential Library on the campus of Texas A&M in College Station, Texas. *Tom Kline*

Locomotive 4305 is a new SD70ACe that was built for Montana Rail Link and sent to Railway Equipment Leasing Company's (RELCO) new Albia, Iowa, facility for testing. After tests were complete, MRL's units were sent to Coast Engine and Equipment (Ceeco) in Tacoma, Washington, for painting. This view of the rear fireman's side of the locomotive shows the extra-capacity radiators. The area at the very back of the locomotive houses dynamic-braking grids and cooling fans. *Chris Guss*

design, it is capable of replacing four SD40-2s in tractive-effort applications.

End of an Era

After months of intense speculation, General Motors' announced on January 12, 2005, that it was selling its Electro-Motive Division to a consortium of Greenbriar Equity, LLC and Berkshire Partners, LLC. Times had changed—GM had been suffering financially and Electro-Motive, once a GM showcase subsidiary, was no longer part of GM's primary business. Electro-Motive also was no longer America's foremost locomotive builder, a position it proudly held for almost four decades.

In the 1980s, General Electric surpassed Electro-Motive and had remained decidedly on top of the domestic locomotive market. During the mid-1990s, GE consistently outsold Electro-Motive by two-to-one or better. Although Electro-Motive pioneered three-phase AC traction for the North American market, GE quickly perfected its own system and was soon outselling Electro-Motive in this area as well.

The numbers improved for Electro-Motive with the new millennia and its domestic totals were closer to GE's. Its export market remained strong. Among its successes had been the JT42CWR, better known as the Class 66. In just a few years, the Class 66 has become the standard freight locomotive in Britain and is now cleared for service in a number of countries in Europe.

The sale of Electro-Motive was finalized on April 4, 2005, after which EMD stood for Electro-Motive Diesel. Included in the transaction were most aspects of Electro-Motive's business, including the locomotive sector, as well as marine and stationary engines. The La Grange and London facilities both were part of the transaction, estimated by *Railway Age* to be worth $500 million. So, after three-quarters of century, Electro-Motive was no longer a division of GM. For better or for worse, an era had ended.

On August 22, 2010, Norfolk Southern SD60M No. 6777 leads an eastbound special move, symbol 048, on the former Erie Railroad main line in the Canisteo Valley near Rathbone, New York. It consists of passenger cars for the James E. Straits carnival show. The locomotive was built for Conrail in 1993; NS and CSX bought and divided Conrail in 1998–1999. *Brian Solomon*

CHAPTER FIVE

THE CATERPILLAR ERA

After 75 years under the wing of America's largest automobile manufacturer, Electro-Motive was spun off. General Motors' sale of its Electro-Motive Division to the investment consortium of Berkshire Partners and Greenbriar Equity Group was sealed on April 4, 2005, and the company was renamed Electro-Motive Diesel (a clever way of retaining the EMD initials by which the builder has long been known).

Industry pundits viewed the sale as a transitional phase for the one-time giant locomotive builder. Although EMD had retained robust sales in the early 2000s, it faced tough competition from General Electric and needed an influx of talent and investment to engineer effective technology to meet the scheduled tightening of engine emissions standards. The economic recession that began in 2008 resulted in a bottoming out of locomotive sales. The locomotive-building business has traditionally followed cyclical trends, but 2008 ushered in one of the quietest times for new locomotive construction since EMD entered the business in the 1930s.

Five years after GM spun off EMD, Caterpillar purchased the locomotive builder, making it a subsidiary of Progress Rail, which the manufacturing giant had bought in 2007. Among Progress Rail's businesses was the manufacture of Genset locomotives using Cat model C18 engines. These employ low-emissions diesel

Opposite: On May 25, 2005, Union Pacific SD70ACe No. 8320 works with a General Electric unit at Lees Summit, Missouri. In the early 2000s, UP bought 1,000 SD70Ms numbered 4000–4999. Beginning in 2005, it began buying large blocks of EMD's AC-traction SD70ACes, numbering them sequentially after its 1990s-era SD90MACs (also designated SD9043MAC or SD9043AC), beginning with 8309. This locomotive was from the first order of UP SD70ACes. *Chris Guss*

341

Genset power packs used in multiple engines rather than the conventional choice of a single large diesel engine. Each onboard Genset is a complete, self-contained diesel engine-generator combination. Whereas a large engine must run all the time, individual Gensets are switched on only as needed to meet power demands. In addition, Progress Rail was involved in repowering old locomotives.

At the time of the Caterpillar acquisition, EMD offered five models: two for the North American market and three for overseas operations. Its DC-current SD70M-2 and AC-current SD70ACe AC were engineered for North American heavy-haul freight services. The SD70ACS is a specialized adaptation of the SD70ACe platform for operation in Saudi Arabia, while the JT42CWRM is better known as the "Class 66," reflecting the classification originally used in the United Kingdom, where locomotives were first used. This is now a standard model intended for European freight services.

A joint venture with the Chinese firm Dalian Locomotive Works resulted in supplying component kits for model JT56ACe locomotives for service on Chinese railways. These locomotives are significant for their application of EMD's 265H two-cycle, 6,000-horsepower diesel, developed in the 1990s for EMD's SD90MAC-H. Ironically, by the time the Chinese locomotives were under construction, EMD's 6,000-horsepower locomotive design was virtually extinct in North America.

In addition to the construction of new locomotives, EMD's other activities have included locomotive repowering using engines designed to comply with more stringent emissions requirements while significantly lowering both fuel and oil consumption. Its 710ECO Repower project was designed to fit 8- and 12-cylinder 710 diesels engines into locomotive models equipped with older, less efficient EMD diesels. The first of these ECO rebuilds were delivered to Kansas City Southern in 2009, smartly dressed in KCS's recently readopted yellow, red, and black "Southern Belle" livery, originally introduced on EMD E-units in the 1930s for service on the *Southern Belle* passenger train. Among EMD's other ECO projects was the remanufacturing of Union Pacific SD60Ms as low-emission SD59M locomotives.

In 2013, EMD advertised two ECO repowered models. The GP22ECO is a four-motor 2,150-horsepower locomotive using an 8-710G3A-T2 low-emissions diesel, while the SD32ECO is a six-motor, 3,150-horsepower locomotive

In August 2010, Alaska Railroad SD70MAC No. 4322 leads an Anchorage-to-Seward passenger train across the Snow River Bridge near Primrose, Alaska. ARR's routine assignment of SD70MACs to passenger service is an unusual application for the model designed for heavy freight work. ARR's SD70MACs feature head-end power, which may be used either for passenger-train electrical supply or to power temperature-controlled freight cars. Alaska's first SD70MACs were delivered at the end of 1999. *Andy Fayerweather*

EMD's model JT42CWRM diesel was originally developed for service in the United Kingdom, where the type was designated as "Class 66." It has become a standard model across Europe and has been authorized for use in more than 10 different countries. It features a dual-cab arrangement typical of European locomotives and is powered by EMD's 12N-710G3B-T2 diesel. This model has been a preferred locomotive for new European private operators, serving customers through open-access arrangements. On March 22, 2013, a Cross Rail Class 66 leads a freight at Antwerpen Noorderdokken, Belgium. *Brian Solomon*

Kansas City Southern placed several orders for EMD SD70ACes. The first of the models for KCS were built in late 2005. No. 4035, pictured here, has a September 2007 build date. *Chris Guss*

powered by a 12-710G3A-T2 engine. Both engines use an 18:1 compression ratio with a maximum 904 rpm.

Among the changes at EMD under Caterpillar has been the relocation of its primary manufacturing from London, Ontario (where EMD had shifted the bulk of its North American production 20 years earlier), to a new facility that opened in Muncie, Indiana, in 2011. Cost savings were cited as a primary reason for the move. The London facility was closed in 2012. In addition, EMD has production partners in other countries, including Mexico.

In recent decades, EMD had focused on high-horsepower freight locomotives for the North American market, having discontinued its F59PHI passenger diesel in 2001. In 2013, after a lapse of a dozen years, EMD introduced a modern passenger locomotive to its catalog. Designed for North American passenger services, the F125 Spirit-series high-speed locomotive will comply with EPA Tier 4 emissions requirements while delivering 4,700 horsepower. Furthermore, it is lighter than all of its contemporary competitors, thus keeping axle weights to a minimum to reduce stress to track and other infrastructure. Designed in

partnership with Vossloh Rail Vehicles, a component of the German transport giant, the F125 blends European concepts with North American technology. It employs a monocoque body in a modern, semi-streamlined, low-profile shape. It is only 14 feet 7 inches tall. Top design speed is 125 miles per hour, and the locomotive's power plant is a CAT C175-20 Diesel, a turbocharged four-cycle, 20-cylinder design.

In May 2013, Southern California Regional Rail Authority ordered up to 20 of them for Los Angeles–area Metrolink suburban services.

One of EMD's most common North American models in the last decade has been its SD70ACe. This looks nearly identical to its DC-traction SD70M-2 counterpart but is the descendent of the SD70MAC developed in the early 1990s for Burlington Northern. EMD's 2013 specifications for the SD70ACe included a 16-710G3C-T3 diesel designed to comply with EPA Tier 3 emissions standards while delivering 4,300 horsepower. Using EMD's modern three-phase traction system, the SD70ACe is rated for 189,000 pounds starting tractive effort, with 155,000 pounds continuous tractive effort and 105,000 pounds of dynamic braking.

This trailing view of Norfolk Southern's Lackawanna heritage-painted SD70ACe demonstrates the enormous radiator vents used by modern EMD locomotives. Improved cooling aids in lowering harmful exhaust emissions. *Patrick Yough*

BIBLIOGRAPHY

Books

Armstrong, John H. *The Railroad— What It Is, What It Does.* Omaha, Nebraska: Simmons-Boardman Books, Inc., 1982.

Bruce, Alfred W. *The Steam Locomotive in America.* New York: W. W. Norton & Company, Inc., 1952.

Bush, Donald J. *The Streamlined Decade.* New York: W. W. Norton & Company, Inc., 1975.

Churella, Albert, J. *From Steam to Diesel.* Princeton, New Jersey: Princeton University Press, 1998.

Cockle, George R. *Centennials in Action.* Muncie, Indiana: Overland Books, 1980.

Cook, Richard J. *Super Power Steam Locomotives.* San Marino, California: Golden West Books, 1966.

Dean, Murray W., and David D. Hanna. *Canadian Pacific Diesel Locomotives.* Toronto: Railfare Enterprises, Ltd., 1981.

Edison, William D. with H. L. Vail Jr. and C. M. Smith. *New York Central Diesel Locomotives.* Lynchburg, Virginia: TLC Publishing, 1995.

Farrington, S. Kip Jr. *Railroads at War.* New York: Coward-McCann, 1944.
——. *Railroading the Modern Way.* New York: Coward-McCann, 1951.

Garmany, John B. *Southern Pacific Dieselization.* Edmonds, Washington: Pacific Fast Mail, 1985.

Hidy, Ralph W., and Muriel E. Hidy, Roy V. Scott, and Don L. Hofsommer. *The Great Northern Railway.* Minneapolis, Minnesota: The University of Minnesota Press, 2004.

Hollingsworth, Brian, and Arthur Cook. *Modern Locomotives.* London: Salamander Books Ltd., 1983.

Hollingsworth, Brian. *Modern Trains.* London: Salamander Books LTD., 1985.

Hungerford, Edward. *Men of Erie.* New York: Random House, 1949

Jennison, Brian, and Victor Neves. *Southern Pacific Oregon Division.* Mukilteo, Washington: Hundman Publishing Company, 1997.

Jones, Robert C. *The Central Vermont Railway, Vol. VII.* Shelburne, Vermont: New England Press, 1995.

Keilty, Edmund. *Interurbans Without Wires.* Glendale, California: Interurban Press, 1979.

Kiefer, P. W. *A Practical Evaluation of Railroad Motive Power.* New York: Steam Locomotive Research Institute, 1948.

Kirkland, John, F. *Dawn of the Diesel Age.* Glendale, California: Interurban Press, 1983.

Kirkland, John, F. *The Diesel Builders, Vols. I, II, and III.* Glendale, California: Interurban Press, 1983.

Klein, Maury. *Union Pacific, Vols. I and II.* New York: Doubleday, 1989.

Liljestrand, Robert A., and David R. Sweetland. *Equipment of the Boston & Maine, Vol I.*

Lloyd, Gordon, Jr., and Louis A. Marre. *Conrail Motive Power Review, Vol. 1.* Glendale, California: Interurban Press, 1992.

Marre, Louis A. *Diesel Locomotives: The First 50 Years.* Waukesha, Wisconsin: Kalmbach Publishing Company, 1995.

Marre, Louis A., and Jerry A. Pinkepank. *The Contemporary Diesel Spotter's Guide.* Milwaukee, Wisconsin: Kalmbach Publishing Company, 1985.

Marre, Louis A. and Paul K. Withers. *The Contemporary Diesel Spotter's Guide, Year 2000 Edition.* Halifax, Pennsylvania: Diesel Era, 2000.

McDonald, Charles W. *Diesel Locomotive Rosters.* Milwaukee, Wisconsin: Kalmbach Publishing Company, 1982

McMillan, Joe. *Santa Fe's Diesel Fleet.* Burlingame, California: Chatham Publishing Company, 1975.

Middleton, William D. *When the Steam Railroads Electrified.* Milwaukee, Wisconsin: Kalmbach Publishing Company, 1974.

Mulhearn, Daniel J., and John R. Taibi. *General Motors' F-Units.* New York: Quadrant Press, 1982.

Pinkepank, Jerry A. *The Diesel Spotter's Guide.* Milwaukee, Wisconsin: Kalmbach Publishing Company, 1967.
——. *The Second Diesel Spotter's Guide.* Milwaukee, Wisconsin: Kalmbach Publishing Company, 1973.

Ransome-Wallis, P. *The Concise Encyclopedia of World Railway Locomotives.* London: Hutchinson & Company, 1959.

Reck, Franklin M. *On Time.* Electro-Motive Division of General Motors, 1948.
——. *The Dilworth Story.* New York: McGraw Hill, 1954.

Saunders, Richard Jr. *The Railroad Mergers and the Coming of Conrail.* Westport, Connecticut: Greenwood Press, 1978.
——. *Merging Lines: American Railroads 1900-1970.* DeKalb, Illinois: Northern Illinois University Press, 2001.

Schneider, Paul D. *GM's Geeps: The General Purpose Diesel.* Waukesha, Wisconsin: Kalmbach Publishing Company, 2001.

Schrenk, Lorenz P., and Robert L. Frey. *Northern Pacific Diesel Era 1945-1970.* San Marino, California: Golden West Books, 1988.

Solomon, Brian, and Mike Schafer. *New York Central Railroad.* Osceola, Wisconsin: MBI Publishing Company, 1999.

Solomon, Brian. *The American Steam Locomotive.* Osceola, Wisconsin: MBI Publishing Company, 1998.
——. *Southern Pacific Railroad.* Osceola, Wisconsin: MBI Publishing Company, 1999.
——. *The American Diesel Locomotive.* Osceola, Wisconsin: MBI Publishing Company, 2000.
——. *Locomotive.* Osceola, Wisconsin: MBI Publishing Company, 2001.
——. *Amtrak.* Osceola, Wisconsin: MBI Publishing Company, 2005.
——. *Burlington Northern Santa Fe Railway.* Osceola, Wisconsin: MBI Publishing Company, 2005.
——. *CSX.* Osceola, Wisconsin: MBI Publishing Company, 2005.
——. *EMD F-Unit Locomotives.* North Branch, Minnesota: Specialty Press, 2005.

Staff, Virgil. *D-Day on the Western Pacific.* Glendale, California: Interurban Press, 1982.

Strapac, Joseph A. *Southern Pacific Motive Power Annuals 1967-1968, 1970, 1971, 1972.* Burlingame, California: Chatham Publishing Company, 1968 to 1972.

Strapac, Joseph A. *Southern Pacific Review 1981*. Huntington Beach, California: Pacific Coast Chapter of the Railway and Locomotive Historical Society, 1982.

——. *Southern Pacific Review 1952-1982*. Huntington Beach, California: Pacific Coast Chapter of the Railway and Locomotive Historical Society, 1983.

——. *Southern Pacific Review 1953-1985*. Huntington Beach, California: Pacific Coast Chapter of the Railway and Locomotive Historical Society, 1986.

——. *Southern Pacific Historic Diesels Vol 3-10*. Huntington Beach, California, and Bellflower, California: Pacific Coast Chapter of the Railway and Locomotive Historical Society, 2003.

Staufer, Alvin F. *Pennsy Power II*. Medina, Ohio: Alvin F. Staufer Books, 1968.

——. *The Revolutionary Diesel: EMC's FT*. Halifax, Pennsylvania: Diesel Era, 1994.

Staufer, Alvin F., and Edward L. May. *New York Central's Later Power 1910-1968*. Medina, Ohio: Alvin F. Staufer Books, 1981.

——. *C&O Power*. Carrollton, Ohio: Alvin F. Staufer Books, 1965.

Waters, L. L. *Steel Trails to Santa Fe*. Lawrence, Kansas: University of Kansas Press, 1950.

Westing, Frederick. *Erie Power*. Medina, Ohio: Alvin F. Staufer Books, 1970.

Withers, Paul K. *Conrail Motive Power Review 1986-1991*. Halifax, Pennsylvania: Diesel Era, 1992.

Woodland, Dale W. *Reading Diesels, Vol. I*. Laury's Station, Pennsylvania: Garrigues House Publishers, 1991.

Periodicals

CTC Board—Railroads Illustrated
Diesel Era
Diesel Railway Traction, supplement to *Railway Gazette*
Extra 2200 South
Jane's World Railways.
Locomotive & Railway Preservation
Official Guide to the Railways
Passenger Train Journal
Passenger Train Annual, Nos. 3 & 4
RailNews
Railroad History, formerly *Railway and Locomotive Historical Society Bulletin*
Railway Age
Railway Mechanical Engineer
Shoreliner
Southern Pacific Bulletin
The Railway Gazette
Trains Magazine
Vintage Rails

Manuals, Timetables, Brochures

Amtrak. 1986. *Operating Instructions F40PH/P30CH Diesel-Electric Locomotives*. Washington, D.C.: Amtrak.

Central Vermont Railway. 1965. *Timetable 65, Northern and Southern Division*. Burlington, Vermont: Central Vermont Railway.

General Motors. 1945. *Electro-Motive Division Operating Manual No. 2300*. La Grange, Illinois: General Motors' Electro-Motive Division.

General Motors. 1948. *Electro-Motive Division Model F3 Operating Manual No. 2308B*. La Grange, Illinois: General Motors' Electro-Motive Division.

General Motors. 1948. *Electro-Motive Division Model 567B Engine Maintenance Manual*. La Grange, Illinois: General Motors' Electro-Motive Division.

General Motors. 1950. *Electro-Motive Division, Diesel Locomotive Operating Manual No. 2312 for Model GP7 with Vapor Car Steam Generator*. 2d ed. La Grange, Illinois: General Motors' Electro-Motive Division.

General Motors. 1951. *Electro-Motive Division Model F7 Operating Manual No. 2310*. La Grange, Illinois: General Motors' Electro-Motive Division.

General Motors Locomotives. 1952. *On the Road Trouble-Shooting. TS-4 GP7*. La Grange, Illinois: General Motors' Electro-Motive Division.

General Motors Locomotives, Electro-Motive Division. 1952. *Training Manual for General Motors Diesel Locomotives*. La Grange, Illinois: General Motors' Electro-Motive Division.

General Motors. 1954. *Electro-Motive Division Model F9 Operating Manual No. 2315*. La Grange, Illinois: General Motors' Electro-Motive Division.

General Motors. 1957. *Electro-Motive Division, Diesel Locomotive Operating Manual No. 2318 for Model GP9*. 3d ed. La Grange, Illinois: General Motors' Electro-Motive Division.

General Motors. 1977. *Electro-Motive Division SD45 Operator's Manual*. La Grange, Illinois: General Motors' Electro-Motive Division.

General Motors. 1970. *Electro-Motive Division Replacement Parts Catalog No. 301. Diesel Engines*. La Grange, Illinois: General Motors' Electro-Motive Division.

General Motors. 1970. *Electro-Motive Division Replacement Parts Catalog No. 301. Diesel Engines*. La Grange, Illinois: General Motors' Electro-Motive Division.

General Motors. 1977. *Electro-Motive Division GP40X Operator's Manual*. La Grange, Illinois: General Motors' Electro-Motive Division.

General Motors. 1978. *Electro-Motive Division F40PH Operator's Manual*. La Grange, Illinois: General Motors' Electro-Motive Division.

General Motors. 1988. *Electro-Motive Division F40PH-2C Operator's Manual*. La Grange, Illinois: General Motors' Electro-Motive Division.

General Motors. 1994. *Electro-Motive Division SD70M Operator's Manual*. La Grange, Ill., 1994.

General Motors. 1996. *Electro-Motive Division SD80MAC Locomotive Operation Manual*. La Grange, Illinois: General Motors' Electro-Motive Division.

Seaboard Coast Line Railroad Company. 1972. *Instructions and Information Pertaining to Diesel Electric Engines*. Jacksonville, Florida: Seaboard Coast Line Railroad Company.

INDEX

EMD Locomotives